Praise for *The Jewel*

"Yoga is the science of the self. It is a practical science ~~that val~~ dates the knowledge that the self of the individual is the self of the universe. When you are one with the Source of existence, you are one with infinite abundance and with the unlimited potential of all manifestation. This jewel of a book will show you how to tap into your inner intelligence, the ultimate and supreme genius that mirrors the wisdom of the cosmos. Cultivate wealth consciousness, and affluence and prosperity will effortlessly flow toward you in all their manifestations."

— **Deepak Chopra,** bestselling author of
The Seven Spiritual Laws of Success and *You Are the Universe*

"*The Jewel of Abundance* will inspire, challenge, and motivate readers to discover and express their innate potential to experience excellence in all aspects of life. Having known Ellen Grace O'Brian for almost four decades, I am pleased to affirm her good character and total commitment to living the principles she so clearly explains."

— **Roy Eugene Davis,** founder and director of
Center for Spiritual Awareness and author of
Paramahansa Yogananda as I Knew Him

"*The Jewel of Abundance* lays out a well-defined perspective on prosperity, wealth, and abundance. It presents a balanced view that takes into account common human needs and shows us simple ways to find happiness and satisfaction that lie beyond the accumulation of material objects. Ellen Grace O'Brian carefully and simply presents ancient wisdom so that one can easily begin to make the necessary changes to one's lifestyle. One does not have to be a saint to follow the path of righteousness; one simply has to learn the ways of dharma, kama, and artha and apply them to one's daily life. *The*

Jewel of Abundance is a very valuable book containing gems of wisdom. It can help the world change its course from the present crisis of materialism to a sustainable lifestyle."

— **Ela Gandhi,** peace activist and founder of the
Gandhi Development Trust

"A perennial issue for professional yoga teachers and therapists is the perceived tension between the need for reasonable material prosperity and the desire for spiritual growth. Hence, *The Jewel of Abundance* is a timely, practical, and indeed inspiring guide for reconciling these conflicts based on the classic teachings of the purusharthas — the four aims of human life — and many other timeless lessons from the yoga tradition. As Yogacharya Ellen Grace O'Brian says, 'Prosperity provides the means to fulfill our divine potential; it's the vehicle for the divine dream to manifest.' She writes paragraphs that are jewels in their own right. Thus my advice is to read as I did — slowly, to allow the time required to savor and reflect on her wisdom. Do her suggested practices. You will find yourself refreshed and renewed in both your work and your spirit."

— **John Kepner,** MA (Econ), MBA, C-IAYT,
executive director of the International Association of
Yoga Therapists

"Wealth (artha) is a difficult and yet necessary topic for all to contemplate, as we live in a world of greed, competition, and selfishness motivated by scarcity and desires. Ellen Grace O'Brian has dived to the depths of the soul to transform our fears into courage and our sense of lack into our joy of abundance. She not only enlightens the reader about what true abundance is but also reassures the reader that it is reachable step-by-step. *The Jewel of Abundance* is accessible to a vast audience with transparent, graceful, and wise words."

— **Swami Sitaramananda,** acharya of
International Sivananda Yoga Vedanta Centers

"To live well is to thrive physically, emotionally, intellectually, and spiritually. But how? Most self-help books focus on one of these factors, often at the expense of the other three. Ellen Grace O'Brian's *The Jewel of Abundance* recognizes the interdependence of all four. That's because this is not a self-help book, but a *Self*-help book: a manual for liberating the soul that optimizes body, heart, mind, and spirit as well. Please don't read this book. Practice it."

— **Rabbi Rami Shapiro,** author of
Perennial Wisdom for the Spiritually Independent

"Many of us aspire to purpose, and perhaps even enlightenment, in our lifetimes, but few realize that the path leads through prosperity and pleasure as equally important steps on the journey. Ellen Grace O'Brian's clear and compelling words bring unique perspective to wisdom from ancient teachings, in language that is even more powerful today."

— **Scott Kriens,** chairman and former CEO of
Juniper Networks and cofounder of 1440 Multiversity

"Gaining true prosperity rests upon understanding our karmas and fulfilling our dharma, or soul's purpose. Then we can achieve the outer success we need while continuing to progress along our spiritual path. In *The Jewel of Abundance*, Ellen Grace O'Brian provides us with the yogic keys to this process of realizing our inner abundance and letting it manifest in the world around us."

— **Dr. David Frawley (Vamadeva Shastri),** author of
Yoga and Ayurveda and *Shiva: The Lord of Yoga*

"Happiness, beauty, and abundance, symbolized by the goddess Lakshmi in yogic thought, arise along with Lord Vishnu, who represents wisdom, self-control, and detachment. Ellen Grace O'Brian reminds us that our outer life must be a mirror of our inner life in order for us to achieve our full potential in all that we do."

— **Yogini Shambhavi,** author of *Yogini: Unfolding the Goddess Within* and *Yogic Secrets of the Dark Goddess*

"*The Jewel of Abundance* by Yogacharya Ellen Grace O'Brian is an excellent template to truly understand the meaning of artha as a tool to fulfill your dharma and continue to strive toward moksha. Perfect health is the foundation for right action, contentment, and nonsensorial happiness. O'Brian offers wonderful yogic tools to help you attract abundance and make a difference in your own unique way. Read, practice, and enjoy the gifts of human potential."

— **Dr. Suhas Kshirsagar,** BAMS, MD (Ayurveda), author of *The Art and Science of Vedic Counseling* and *Change Your Schedule, Change Your Life*

"This epiphany-provoking, majestically written book, rich with life lessons and ancient wisdom, is a must-read. Every word rings with truth — it is a gem to be treasured. I stand in awe of Yogacharya O'Brian's honesty and brilliance as a spiritual teacher and writer. The majesty of her prose powerfully yet gently guides humanity along an awakened journey toward thriving both materially and spiritually, despite crisis and loss or deep-seated patterns of depravity and lack. This book imparts truth, courage, inspiration, and hope. I recommend it to Vedic, yoga, and Ayurveda students worldwide."

— **Acharya Shunya Mathur,** founder and preceptor of Vedika Global and author of *Ayurveda Lifestyle Wisdom*

"You are holding in your hands definitive proof that spirituality and prosperity are aligned. Even better, it's an easy-to-read guidebook for letting go of limiting beliefs and the behaviors that are likely blocking access to happiness and abundance — what we might call 'spiritual clutter.' In this book, Ellen Grace O'Brian gives us the tools and instructions to set ourselves free and to thrive in this fast-paced, unpredictable world. *The Jewel of Abundance* shows us how simple and attainable wealth is, in every form. And the best news is, as with every great coming-home story, she reminds us that we were born with everything we need to succeed already!"

— **Andrew Mellen,** speaker, professional organizer, and author of *Unstuff Your Life!*

the Jewel *of* Abundance

Also by Ellen Grace O'Brian

Living the Eternal Way:
Spiritual Meaning and Practice for Daily Life

A Single Blade of Grass: Finding the Sacred in Everyday Life

Living for the Sake of the Soul

The Moon Reminded Me

the Jewel *of* Abundance

Finding Prosperity through the
Ancient Wisdom of Yoga

Ellen Grace O'Brian

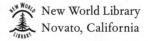 New World Library
Novato, California

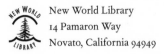

New World Library
14 Pamaron Way
Novato, California 94949

The material in this book is intended for education. It is not meant to take the place of diagnosis and treatment by a qualified medical practitioner or therapist. No expressed or implied guarantee of the effects of the use of the recommendations can be given or liability taken. Names and identifying details of the author's students and other individuals men-tioned in the text have been changed to protect the privacy of those involved.

Text design by Megan Colman. Typography by Tona Pearce Myers.

Library of Congress Cataloging-in-Publication Data
Names: O'Brian, Ellen Grace, author.
Title: The jewel of abundance : finding prosperity through the ancient wisdom of yoga /
    Ellen Grace O'Brian.
Description: Novato, California : New World Library, 2018. | Includes bibliographical
    references and index.
Identifiers: LCCN 2018022838 (print) | LCCN 2018040329 (ebook) | ISBN 9781608685578
    (ebook) | ISBN 9781608685561 (alk. paper)
Subjects: LCSH: Yoga, Kriya. | Well-being. | Wealth.
Classification: LCC BL1238.56.K74 (ebook) | LCC BL1238.56.K74 O27 2018
    (print) | DDC 294.5/436--dc23
LC record available at https://lccn.loc.gov/2018022838

First printing, November 2018
ISBN 978-1-60868-556-1
Ebook ISBN 978-1-60868-557-8
Printed in the USA on 30% postconsumer-waste recycled paper

New World Library is proud to be a Gold Certified Environmentally Responsi-ble Publisher. Publisher certification awarded by Green Press Initiative. www.greenpressinitiative.org

10   9   8   7   6   5   4   3   2   1

Dedicated to Roy Eugene Davis,

who taught me the real nature of abundance

Contents

Part I. Higher Purpose:
Set the Foundation Upon Your Heart

Part II. Insight:
Road Map for Abundant Living

Part III. A Skillful Way:
How to Realize Fulfillment

Part IV. Clarity:
Overcome Obstacles and Thrive

Part V. Generosity:
Live the Prosperous Life

Foreword

*G*radually, bit by bit, India's vast and venerable storehouse of knowledge has filtered into the West, informing disciplines from philosophy to psychology to medicine, and transforming how we understand religion and express our spirituality. Each new translation of a sacred or philosophical text, each new guru, each new scholarly article, each new pilgrim to swamis and yoga masters in India, and of course each new interpretive book, like this one, adds to the wealth of Indic resources for novice seekers and veteran yogis alike. The ongoing transmission of Vedic knowledge, now more than two hundred years in the making, penetrates our culture more widely and deeply every day. But while large numbers of Westerners are now familiar with concepts like karma and mind-body technologies like meditation and postural yoga, much of the Vedic treasure trove remains untapped or underappreciated. The four *purusharthas* — the proper aims of life or objects of pursuit — are among those neglected precepts. With this wise and practical book, Ellen Grace O'Brian admirably fills the gap.

Two of the purusharthas, *dharma* and *moksha*, are actually quite well known among yogis, meditators, and students of Eastern philosophy. This is because the purveyors of yogic knowledge have discussed those concepts at length in speech and writing and also because no precise equivalents exist in Western philosophical and religious systems. As a result, with varying degrees of depth and seriousness, seekers have delved into the understanding of dharma, a complex term that boils down to action that supports individual spiritual development and the well-being of the larger community; and of moksha, the liberation of the soul in yogic union with the divine. The other two purusharthas, *kama* (pleasure) and *artha* (prosperity, the focus of this book), have received far less attention.

The Indian teachers who journeyed West did not exactly neglect the human drive for material comfort and worldly enjoyment. They did not discourage anyone from enjoying life's safe, simple pleasures, and as leaders of organizations, they were fully aware of the positive uses of money; they had to pay bills, after all, and raise money to finance their work. More important, their success in reaching Western seekers depended on their ability to adapt and articulate age-old wisdom to the people who came to them for guidance. Paramahansa Yogananda and Maharishi Mahesh Yogi (to cite the twentieth century's best-known gurus in the West) emphasized that the yogic teachings they espoused had value not only for the rare ascetics but for people with jobs and families. They taught that material comfort is compatible with spiritual development and can actually support it by freeing one's time and energy for spiritual pursuits. They also taught that the reverse is true: Yogic methods that expand consciousness and open the heart can enhance the kind of thinking, acting, and relating that supports material success.

Yogacharya O'Brian is in that lineage, both literally (Yogananda was the guru of her guru, Roy Eugene Davis) and because her perspective accords with the inner/outer, spiritual/material complementarity advocated by the yogic missionaries. Her interpretation of artha, the aim of life addressed in this book, is consistent with that of the gurus who directed their teachings to householders.

This book is commendable for many reasons, among them its unfailingly practical orientation and its lucid explanation of yogic concepts that are often rendered in obtuse prose. Also, O'Brian understands that the purusharthas are connected, intertwined, and mutually reinforcing. As with the legs of a table, when you move one, the others also move. Hence, when pursued correctly, growth in one of the four aims of life enhances growth in the others. In the case of artha, properly obtained prosperity enhances pleasure, the fulfillment of dharma, and progress toward moksha — and, similarly, growth in any of the other three can enhance one's chances of becoming more prosperous.

Equally admirable is the author's treatment of prosperity as something more than financial success and material comfort. In her view, spiritual abundance is part and parcel of the proper definition of artha. She recognizes that abundance acquired in the absence of spiritual growth is relatively empty and unfulfilling — and, she contends, ambitious seekers of wealth are advised not to ignore their inner lives, for doing so can actually be detrimental to their material goals.

If you think this sounds as though Yogacharya O'Brian is echoing the many voices that have, for years, urged Americans to find a balance between work and home, or career advancement and personal happiness, you are only partially correct. Her yogic perspective extends beyond ordinary happiness and mental health, pointing the reader to the highest levels of human development and encouraging action that serves the larger society as well as personal goals — not in addition to material success but as integral to the very definition of prosperity.

By presenting this elevated vision of life balance and human aspiration, *The Jewel of Abundance* is a useful antidote to the hypermaterialism that poisons modern life. And for those who seek the fulfillment of both their souls and their material desires, the book is a wellspring of inspiration and intelligent guidance.

— **Philip Goldberg,** author of *The Life of Yogananda: The Story of the Yogi Who Became the First Modern Guru* and *American Veda: From Emerson and the Beatles to Yoga and Meditation, How Indian Spirituality Changed the West*

Introduction

Thrive for the Sake
of Your Soul

We are born to thrive. If we look, we can see this — everything in nature, including us, is geared toward the growth and fulfillment of its purpose. The sapling Red Delicious apple tree in the garden stretches toward the sun, and given the right conditions, it blossoms and bears sweet fruit. How we delight to witness that same impetus of blossoming growth in a baby! We applaud as she first lifts her head, then rocks on all fours and crawls forth to pursue adventure and taste the world. What next? She stands up, speaks, falls down, gets up, and runs off to school with the innate imperative to thrive that is her birthright.

The inclination to thrive, prosper, and fulfill our potential is the natural impulse of our divine capacity as spiritual beings. The same energy that gives birth to stars in the cosmos inspires music, literature, architecture, medicine, dance, technology — any and all forms of creative expression and manifestation. That energy is unlimited; it pervades all of nature, relentlessly encouraging all of life to realize its full potential: *Thrive!* it implores. It whispers in our dreams and stirs our imagination with its evolutionary call: *Prosper!* Live your *full* life; do what you came here to do. Follow the impulse to prosper and become all that you truly are in your fullness.

1

As a child, do you remember being asked, "What do you want to be when you grow up?" Even as a young girl in the 1950s and 1960s, when career options were more restricted for women, I thought about what I might do when I got older. I dreamed of who I might become. But like many young people even today, I didn't have a context for my dreams. I was not aware of a structure other than cultural expectations that could illumine the path ahead. Over the years, I've heard many spiritual seekers share a similar story. They often say something like, "Wouldn't it be great if life came with an instruction manual?"

That seemingly missing instruction manual can be found in ancient Vedic how-to-live teachings for seekers of all ages. One of the most important instructions we find there is what is called *purushartha* — the four universal goals of human life. This sublime and practical guidance is one of the precious jewels of *Sanatana Dharma*. Also known as the Eternal Way, Sanatana Dharma is the traditional name for the Vedic philosophical principles and spiritual practices that became known as Hinduism. Based on our individual connection to cosmic order, this comprehensive approach to spiritually conscious living is for all people and for all time.

The literal meaning of the Sanskrit term *purushartha* is "for the purpose of the soul."[1] That's it! What we do in life — our dreams, our aims, our goals, and our accomplishments — are to serve the soul, to support our spiritual destiny.

Pursuit of the four aims of life contributes to living with balance, integrity, and joy. When rightly understood and used as a guidepost, the four goals help us develop on all levels. We become both spiritually aware and worldly wise.

The first goal is *dharma*, which encompasses realizing our higher purpose and fulfilling our destiny in this lifetime. The word *dharma* is rich with meaning: the way of righteousness, purpose, duty, support, law, or a goal of life. Dharma is the fundamental law of life, the underlying cosmic order. Literally, it means "what holds together." Consider this "holding together" as the connection between divine order and our individual lives and destiny. Our lives are intertwined with the cosmic order. An intelligent, enlivening power is nurturing our universe and we can learn to cooperate with it.[2] Each of us has a purpose, a place, a duty, and a divine destiny.

The overarching dharma or universal purpose of life is to awaken to our essential spiritual nature. Waking up spiritually is Self-realization and God-realization — realizing the truth of our being and having knowledge and direct insight into Ultimate Reality. When we wake up, we can live in harmony with divine order, actualize our innate potential, and make a positive contribution to life. Beyond all else we are inspired to do, it is this highest priority that promises lasting fulfillment. Dharma is our north star. But dharma does not shine alone — its brilliance is set off by the three other life goals that surround it.

The second goal, *artha*, or prosperity, is the primary focus of this book. The aim of artha is to prosper in every way — to develop the consciousness and the skills to attract whatever is needed to fulfill our dharma or higher purpose. In this context, prosperity is understood as a spiritual goal — not for its own sake, but for the sake of the soul. It provides the means to live fully and freely. When prosperity is equated with material wealth attained for its own sake, the word *prosperity* loses its deep meaning. True prosperity is experienced in a spiritual context. Because this truth is frequently missed, the words *prosperity* and *wealth* are often narrowly defined or understood at the level of material accomplishment alone. But as you work through the teachings of this book with me, you'll see that these words can rightly be applied and understood in the highest way as spiritual goals. And that makes all the difference.

The third goal is *kama*, which is pleasure or enjoyment. This, too, is for the sake of the soul. Our inclination to seek pleasure springs from the simple joy of being alive and is linked to our higher quest for *ananda*, the soul's bliss. It doesn't take that long to realize that playing with pleasure is playing with fire; pleasure and pain are linked. To effectively embrace pleasure as one of life's essential goals without getting burned by it, we need to understand it. And we can. This requires discerning what enhances our joy and what depletes it. Ultimately, this life aim points us in the direction of the soul's bliss, where our search for unending joy can be realized. Life is meant to be lived fully and enjoyed.

The fourth goal is *moksha*. Moksha is the absolute freedom that blossoms from enlightenment. It is the liberation of consciousness from the errors of perception that cause identification with our small, personal self. It is the realization of our true, divine Self that makes it possible to live spontaneously, freely, and joyfully in the world. The first three aims are oriented toward this one. *Live with purpose. Prosper. Enjoy life. Set your sights on freedom.* Living with higher purpose, doing what is ours to do, thriving, enjoying life — all are meant to point us in the direction of ultimate fulfillment and freedom. Jesus highlighted this so well with the question, "What does it profit us to gain the entire world if we lose our soul?" Or, as Paramahansa Yogananda encouraged, "Why not live in the highest way?"[3]

Artha and kama, the goals to thrive and enjoy life, are supported, clarified, and constrained by dharma — purpose and duty — and moksha — the liberation of consciousness. Seen in this way, we live both a full and a balanced life. Too much spiritual striving, as if fulfillment is found at the end, neglects the aim of kama — to live joyfully now. Without the illumination of higher purpose, unbounded pursuit of either pleasure or wealth ultimately leads to a life of distraction and pain.

These four universal life goals offer a context for our life, the guiding light we yearn for. Our desire for a meaningful life is even greater than our desire for happiness. It's universal. No matter what our culture, ethnicity, gender, religion, spiritual path, or the particular time we live in — we are here to awaken and fulfill our potential. It's the soul's journey from the darkness of ignorance to the light of Self-realization, from confusion about who we are and what our purpose is to clarity and self-actualization.

Once we recognize the primary dharmic goal to awaken, we can see that our life is perfectly arranged to support us in doing just that. Not only that, we discover lasting fulfillment along the way as conscious partners in a world awakening to its potential. From the dark ages to the technological advances of today, we are ready for the greatest evolutionary jump the world has ever known — the awakening of our hearts and our minds to the unity of all life. Awakening, prospering, and fulfilling our potential is inextricably tied to the well-being of all. What we do matters. We are powerful agents, not only of personal prosperity, but of essential social change and planetary healing, so that all may prosper.

How do we do it? We wake up. We realize who we are as spiritual beings in a spiritual universe, joyously and inescapably connected in the one divine Ultimate Reality expressing itself as all that is. We grow up. We free ourselves from the shackles of blame and welcome responsibility for our life. We mature beyond the adolescent egocentric level of consciousness that fosters greed, the disease at the root of both personal and planetary malaise. And we show up. We discover how to prosper — how to realize our potential and bring forth our profound offering to life.

Let's begin.

PART I

Higher Purpose

∞

Set the Foundation Upon Your Heart

One

Artha: The Prosperity Imperative

A jewel fell into the core of the heart
Unlike any God gave to the seas or the sky.

— RUMI

D o you have a dream? A vision of possibility that calls to you
and returns again and again? A divine inspiration that is
yours to bring forth? As spiritual beings, we all have nudges
from the infinite, glimpses of life's greater potentials. This is life's
prosperity imperative. Those nudges are life's invitation to be the
growing edge of divine love, to rise up and contribute to the evolutionary thrust for planetary awakening. Each person's call is unique
— perhaps it's the desire to be a good parent and raise a healthy
family, to start a nonprofit to save the bees or the whales, to write a
book, or to build sustainable housing. The inspirations and potentials are as infinite as their Source. The common factor is the imperative to prosper, to thrive in a way that fulfills our potential by
actualizing the divine qualities within us. The prosperity imperative
is the call of becoming, of expressing our true Self in its fullness.

Divine qualities wait within us in seed form until they can blossom forth. Like any seed in nature, these spiritual potentials wait until conditions are right. Every divine idea requires a means of expression. What is needed to bring it into manifestation? How will it happen? What is the instrument for life's prosperity imperative? That instrument is artha, or wealth. In the context of purushartha, the four goals for a fulfilled life, artha is the wealth that goes hand in hand with the call to awaken. Its shining role is to support life's inherent, irrepressible demand to fulfill our potential and contribute to the happiness and well-being of others.

Dharma is the expression of one's inherent nature. It is a thing being what it is — a river flows, an ocean breaks into waves, a door opens and closes, a fruit tree blossoms and bears fruit. For humans, being as we truly are is to realize our essential spiritual nature and *express it*. Expressing, bringing forth possibility, contributing, revealing the divine, glorifying its presence — however we want to say it, that prospering activity arises from the creative power of the soul, which draws to itself whatever is needed to fulfill its purpose. That is artha. Prosperity provides the means to fulfill our divine potential; it's the vehicle for the divine dream to manifest.

It's no accident that artha sits on the right hand of dharma — higher purpose and the means to fulfill it are inseparable. Yet, time and again, we try to separate them by imagining enlightenment exists on an otherworldly plane where wealth cannot enter. It's the age-old split between Spirit and matter, or heaven and earth, a split that is now ready to be healed in this age of conscious evolution. Not only is the time ripe for healing this error in our thinking, it is necessary. If we are going to fulfill our potential, it's time to understand, befriend, and put wealth to good use. If we are going to stop plundering the earth and going to war over resources with our myopic, small self–centered actions, we need a higher vision — one that puts wealth into its proper service role. It's time to lift wealth into its higher potential on a personal and global scale.

We can turn to the riches of the Hindu tradition for a profound and beautiful image that portrays this higher vision. Sri Lakshmi, traditionally revered as the goddess of wealth, is one of the most popular images of Divine Mother. She is often portrayed either seated or standing on an eight-petaled lotus with golden coins flowing forth from her outstretched palm. When we see that divine image of Lakshmi with abundant material wealth flowing forth, we should also notice the open lotus blossom in her other hand, symbolizing the purity of awakened consciousness. In one hand, wealth. In the other, enlightenment. It is also helpful to know that Sri Lakshmi, the goddess of wealth, is the consort of Lord Vishnu. Vishnu is the divine One, the nurturer and preserver of all life, the protector of dharma and universal order. Lakshmi's role is to aid in the restoration of dharma. In this image of the goddess who symbolizes wealth, beauty, and the significance of dharma, we can see prosperity and spirituality hand in hand. That is the vision for our time. It's an outrageous vision, one that demands we heal the so-called split between Spirit and matter that has been around for thousands of years. Yet it is obvious that we're on the brink of that necessity and that possibility. Where do we begin?

Befriending Wealth

Dharma is the foundation of this world; and there is nothing of greater value than dharma. But undoubtedly dharma requires money. Always, dharma is a factor in wealth; but wealth is to be grasped for securing the ends of dharma....And money cannot be had by begging, or by cowardice, much less by concentrating on dharma alone.

— MAHABHARATA[1]

Susan told me her story of going to India to seek the guidance of a holy man. She had been on the "spiritual, but not religious," path for many years, dabbling in yoga and metaphysics. Once her kids were grown and on their own, she enjoyed having more free time to study, attend classes, and go on meditation retreats. She was happy; everything in her life seemed to flow with grace and ease. That is, until her husband unexpectedly suffered a heart attack and died. She was suddenly unmoored — understandably shocked and grieving. She was at a loss. How would she live? A radical inspiration came to her. A friend suggested she travel to a remote village in India and meet with a holy man who could guide her. *Why not?* she thought. *What do I have to lose?*

She made the long journey from her home in the United States and was granted a coveted private audience with the guru. What happened next changed her view about spirituality. The guru asked her, "What do you want?" Having been on the path for a while, she responded with what she considered the right answer, the sure cure for anyone's pain and problems: "I want enlightenment!"

The guru paused, smiled gently, and replied, "No, you want money."

The holy man told her to take care of her finances! She was at first taken aback, then embarrassed to feel the sting of what she knew was true. When her husband died, he left her with more debts than savings, and she had no source of income. Next, she felt relief, then inspiration, as she realized that her practical needs could be an integral part of her spiritual journey.

Susan and the hundreds of similar students I've worked with over the years inspired this book about artha, the life goal of wealth. The beginnings of my own journey on the path of yoga inspired it, too. Like many others I have known, I came to the spiritual path looking for a way to end my sorrow. I thought that meditation and spiritual practice would transport me to a "higher consciousness" where I would transcend my worldly difficulties. I could stop worrying about work, paying the bills, or harmony in my relationship by learning how to rise above mundane concerns. I would do something more important. I would become "spiritual" — an out-of-this-world idea of enlightenment.

I discovered that the spiritual path and practice of yoga does take us out of the world as we once perceived it, then sends us back into the world with a profoundly different view. The transformed viewpoint includes understanding that the spiritual life is not otherworldly at all. It's about being awake in the world, not "rising above it." By engaging in the world fully, we learn how to live skillfully — meeting our difficulties with wisdom and compassion, and thriving without falling asleep or losing our balance. Enlightenment is not about "becoming spiritual." It's discovering the truth that we are already spiritual and we can find freedom from sorrow right where we are. While we are at it, we can thrive and help others thrive along the way.

In the context of spiritual awakening, learning how to prosper is a path of transformation. Not just a utility, and not an option, prospering is our necessity, our way of awakening. The great nineteenth-century yoga master Lahiri Mahasaya, whose life was widely introduced to the West through Paramahansa Yogananda's seminal book *Autobiography of a Yogi*, remarked that the world is an auspicious place for *sadhana*, or spiritual practice.[2] The conditions in our life right now are exactly what we need to help us wake up, grow up, and show up — to learn how to live with higher purpose and to develop skillful means. Our learning curve is our vehicle for awakening. As we engage, we grow and awaken. As we thrive, we transform. It's a revolutionary approach to wealth, one that challenges the old paradigm that wealth is separate from spirituality and only for a select few. It's a universal life goal. It's life's imperative, and it's available to everyone. Prospering is so much more than we think, and its importance and potential are so much more than we realize.

The Ancient Question

The universal question found in sacred texts throughout time is one that resounds in every awakening heart: Does material prosperity enhance and support, or distract and destroy, our spiritual life? It's a question well worth asking. Both the ancient and present-day answer is: *It depends.*

There is a tension, an inner conflict, that arises alongside our innate tendency to thrive, as timeless as the impulse itself. This tension is reflected in the abundance of spiritual or religious teachings that either praise wealth as a demonstration of goodness or warn us of its evil nature. Many sources do both at the same time. Plenty of religious dogma touts the dangers of money, all the while praising those who give generously. Even the Vedic texts that shine a bright light on the value of wealth and the necessity to acquire and use it also point out its shadow side. One verse says, "Not to know the importance of wealth is to remain in darkness; to have knowledge of the primacy of wealth is to have the light of understanding."[3] Then another warns, "The wise look upon wealth as productive only of pain, and neither aspire for it, nor do they grieve at the loss of it."[4] It's confounding. What is the right relationship between prosperity and spirituality? Is there one?

We don't have to look far to see how wealth in general, and money in particular, has garnered a bad name. We live in an out-of-balance world, where massive, incomprehensible wealth is concentrated in a few hands while millions go without the most basic human needs for food, clean water, and shelter. Corporate greed, which could be defined as choosing unbridled economic expansion over the health and well-being of people and the planet, is only too familiar. The United States is measured as the "wealthiest" nation in the world, yet we are not the happiest.

We stand in awe of self-made multimillionaires who invent the latest technological breakthrough in their garage. We applaud the entrepreneurial spirit that successfully prospers. We are inspired by the talent and wealth of sports heroes, movie stars, best-selling authors, and TED-Talking CEOs. At the same time, we honor those, like Mother Teresa and Cesar Chavez, who choose lives of self-denial in order to serve others. As much as we admire wealth, we are inclined to see the latter as the path of genuine spirituality, further widening and reinforcing the gap between wealth and the spiritual life.

The question of wealth and spirituality is one we must answer. As we do, we can affirm and demonstrate the evolutionary potential of humanity. The unprecedented humanitarian and environmental crises we face today pose a critical path for awakening. It's time to change our consciousness about scarcity and wealth, time to open the floodgates of compassion and generosity. Time to foster a new distribution system, one that provides enough for all to thrive.

What Does Thriving Require?

Some say wealth, and the power it brings, corrupts the human heart. Yet wealth is the necessary means for accomplishing good works, for turning possibilities into actualities. Like the spiritual path itself, our relationship with wealth is a razor's edge. Approached selfishly, without necessary insight, prosperity becomes an avenue of difficulty, taking us further away from the goal of liberation and leaving suffering in its wake. Approached consciously, and in the right way, prosperity becomes an avenue of freedom, a way to get beyond the limiting confines of our ego-based self, even as we sow seeds of happiness for others.

What does thriving require of us? What does it take to prosper and be successful in harmony with spiritual principles? It requires these five attributes, which correlate to the five parts of this book:

HIGHER PURPOSE: We realize the essential connection between prosperity and purpose — why it's important to thrive and commit ourselves to it.

INSIGHT: We know who we really are — the unfailing Source of our innate abundance, unconditional happiness, and divine destiny.

A SKILLFUL WAY: We discern how to live a prosperous, spiritually awakened life through contemplation, meditation, and joyful self-discipline.

CLARITY: We use spiritual principles to overcome obstacles and optimize success.

GENEROSITY: We discover how radical prosperity, generosity, and spiritual generativity can foster lasting fulfillment and positive change for generations to come.

Take heart. You are holding in your hands an artha manual — a time-tested guide to wealth with a spiritual perspective, wealth with the wisdom of the ages illuminating the way.

Two

True Wealth

*The jewel of abundance comes to those who are
established in nonstealing.*

— YOGA SUTRAS

What is *true* wealth, wealth that is real? In contemporary society, the definition of wealth usually defaults to material prosperity measured in economic terms — factors like money, socioeconomic status, investments, ownership, and inheritance. The wealthy are those who have money and the power that accompanies it. However, on a deeper level, most of us know that material wealth is incomplete or insufficient by itself. Financial wealth provides an easier or more comfortable life in certain respects, but it cannot buy health, lasting happiness, or love. Who can be truly wealthy without those life essentials? No one.

The great yoga master Paramahansa Yogananda defined wealth more broadly when he said, "Prosperity doesn't always mean having what you want, but having what is needed when it is needed."[1] The measure of our wealth is our ability to be in the prosperous flow of resources that allow us to readily and abundantly do what we need to do, have what we need to have, and experience what we need to experience. True wealth is access to resources on all levels — physical, mental, emotional, and spiritual. It is the expression of a harmonious relationship with Spirit, nature, and all of life. Those who know how to work with the spiritual laws of prosperity discover that lasting, sustainable wealth is not only possible, it is the natural, easeful expression of an awakened life.

The Basic Law of Wealth

Prosperity comes to us when we are established in nonstealing. This is the succinct guidance for thriving found in the Yoga Sutras, the primary text for yoga philosophy and practice compiled somewhere around the first to second century CE by the sage Patanjali. Throughout the centuries, gurus and scholars, both ancient and modern, have translated the Sanskrit aphorisms of Patanjali's Yoga Sutras and added their commentaries. For this text, I have drawn from several different translations and added my own versions as well. You can find references for sources in the endnotes. Although most translations of the sutras are similar, they differ slightly in ways that reflect a particular teaching emphasis or writing style.

For example, sutra 2:37, quoted at the beginning of this chapter, is also translated, "When a man becomes established in abstention from theft, all wealth comes to him."[2] In the two versions, prosperity is described in different ways — as "jewels" or as "wealth" — but it comes down to the same principle. That principle is nonstealing, the basic law of wealth. What are we to make of this? Not many of us seriously consider ourselves thieves. Bank robbing, shoplifting, or even fraudulent financial deals are not the norm. Why then is abstention from theft the pivotal point of prosperity? It takes deeper consideration of its basis, as well as contemplation of the subtle nuances of what can be considered theft, to discover its essential tie to our abundance.

The heart of the spiritual principle of nonstealing is Self-sufficiency. It rests on realizing who we are as spiritual beings — fully cognizant of our essential wholeness. Nonstealing practice proceeds from awareness of our innate fullness as expressions of the one, omnipresent Ultimate Reality. As spiritual beings, we are inseparable from the Source. Its wholeness is our wholeness. Its sufficiency is our sufficiency, and its wealth is our wealth. Aware of our own wholeness and our ability to attract necessary resources, we have no compulsion to steal or take what is not rightfully ours. This awareness illumines our relationship with others and with the world. It expresses itself in all levels of interaction, from the subtle realms of thought and feeling to the gross material expression of things.

Rather than offering the restrictive imperative "thou shalt not steal," yoga points to the change in consciousness that accompanies true wealth. It offers the profound and practical key: *Change your mind and consciousness from lack to abundance, and wealth will naturally follow*. You will not have to seek it out. It will come to you. This is the promise of being established in nonstealing.

Uprooting the Weeds of Theft

Stealing appears in various shades of greed and envy that spring from the egocentric drive to overcome a sense of insufficiency. When stealing occurs — taking what is not ours by right of consciousness, what we did not earn, or have no right to acquire — it always has this sense of lack at its root. From the spiritual perspective, to know true wealth is to uproot this erroneous perception of insufficiency and discover how to live from the innate fullness of our awakened consciousness. Two fundamental strategies can help us make necessary adjustments for prosperous living. The first is to identify and implement changes at the mental and behavioral levels. To do this, we become aware of any forms of stealing that we engage in and consider why we do it. Once we are aware of our behavior and the motive or need behind it, we can make changes that are more consistent with our commitment to thrive. The second strategy is at the spiritual level of awareness. It requires strengthening our knowledge and experience of our essential nature. Once we become more proficient at anchoring our awareness in the wholeness of the Self, we are naturally released from the mistaken idea that we need to deal with life in an underhanded way.

The first step in practicing any of yoga's ethical guidelines is to refrain from injurious habits or ways of doing things that are contraindicated to living an awakened life. We start at the most obvious physical level. For nonstealing, we stop taking things that do not belong to us — we don't steal. Outright theft is easy to spot, but then we must look at its subtler permutations. If we find money someone drops in the grocery store parking lot, do we keep it or take it into the store in case someone returns for it? Have we borrowed things without returning them? Taken advantage of the services that others have provided without giving anything in return? Cheated on taxes by intentionally not reporting accurately?

A traditional tale from the East can help us see deeper into the heart of this practice of nonstealing. Once a guru gathered his students around him and pointed out how, though they were doing useful work, their ashram was falling into disrepair. Their buildings needed renovation and even their meals were becoming sparse. They would need to do something for this good cause. He suggested they go into town on market day when the square was teeming with vendors and shoppers, wait until no one was watching, and steal some money or food.

The monks were at first reticent, since this was contrary to their vows and ethics, but thinking that he knew best, they decided to follow their guru's instructions. They rationalized that this would support their good work, and after all, no one had to know. They all headed into town, except one monk who stayed behind. "What's the matter," the guru asked him. "Don't you want to follow my instructions?" "I can't," replied the monk. "Why not?" the guru wanted to know. The monk explained, "I cannot follow your instructions because, wherever I go, there is no place where no one is watching. Even when I am alone, my Self is watching." He was, of course, the disciple who "got it."[3]

It is not possible to cheat or steal from anyone without compromising our own self. When we look deeper, we see how this compromise begins in our mind. It arises from a faulty idea of insufficiency. That belief turns out to be the real problem, the block in the flow of infinite supply.

The Transformational Power of Truth

Stealing can also take the form of appropriating another's ideas or creative efforts, such as plagiarism or illegally downloading music or movies without payment. Or it might be accepting acknowledgment when we don't deserve it, when an idea, inspiration, or work belongs to someone else. It can even show up as living beyond our means — using credit to acquire what we cannot rightfully afford or borrowing and not paying others back what we owe them. Taking more than we need, refusing to consider the impact of our consumption on future generations, and not sharing what we have are all considered forms of theft.

Stealing also springs up in the subtle form of envy — wanting what belongs to someone else. We notice this when someone else succeeds and we feel jealous instead of celebrating their good fortune. Desiring another person's committed partner is also a subtle form of theft. We begin by identifying these and the myriad other methods the wily ego looks for as an unethical way (usually a quick fix) to fill the tank of perceived emptiness.

Why do we do these things? When we have not yet discovered and claimed our own abundance, taking from others seems the only way to get what we want or need. We're operating at a material level of consciousness. We don't see the spiritual perspective, a higher vision showing us that any form of stealing is a custom-made affirmation of lack. Every time we step outside the circle of our integrity and act in ways that are inconsistent with our highest good and innate fullness, we demonstrate our belief in insufficiency. In the long run, our misguided schemes to get what we want have the opposite effect.

Aided by our commitment to thrive and our practice of inquiry, we can become aware of these errant beliefs and behaviors. Identifying them as impediments to thriving gives us the inspiration and motivation to change. Once we see the deep root of the error in our thinking and behavior, the light of what is true comes forth. Insight into truth is always transformational. It changes our consciousness, and that contributes to becoming *established* in nonstealing. It prepares us for the next step, which is realization of our true Self. With these insights born of self-examination and contemplation, we begin to see how we have shortchanged ourselves, how we have ignored our own fullness and left ourselves wanting.

Doing the Inner Work

I was privileged to witness Ken make the transformational ascent to prosperity through the practice of nonstealing. He was already a successful yoga teacher with his own studio and a modest following of students. He was doing the meaningful work he had always dreamed of and paying the bills as well. Yet, with all his progress and prosperity, there was a wisp of lack. The initial passion he had for his vision of serving others by offering practices for greater health and well-being was waning as students would come and go, and his reach hit a plateau. No matter what he did, whether it was more advertising or newcomer discounts, he ended up with the same number of students. His work was not growing, and he was stymied. At the same time, he was watching some of his colleagues and their studios grow to overflow. As a longtime student of yoga philosophy, he knew where to look to unlock his prosperity, but at first it was puzzling and difficult to see.

When he did a "nonstealing inventory," everything was in order — he was paying his bills gratefully and on time, serving others fairly, was truthful in his communications, doing what he loved to do with integrity, and generously sharing his gifts, talents, and prosperity. What was it? There was one thing. He had been aware of it for a while but dismissed it as unimportant. There it was — jealousy. He would notice it lingering around the edges of his awareness, showing up as envy. As content as he was with all the good things he was experiencing, when others in his field were visibly growing and thriving, attracting more students, and showing up as presenters at prestigious conferences, he felt jealous. He thought, *Why them? It should be me.* He wanted that momentum for his work, and he desired the recognition they had.

With his foundation of spiritual practice, he knew he could look deeper into this recurring experience and find the root belief that was "stealing" his own greater prosperity by declaring time and again that he was unsuccessful. He needed clear insight into this jealousy. What was holding him back? Why was his once-thriving practice stuck in a rut? What was causing him to think that others were somehow better than him, that he would always fall short of fully succeeding?

When he inwardly asked to know what was underlying his jealousy, he discovered a persistent belief that there was not enough to go around. Like in a race, if someone else got there first, it meant he could never win. He knew that was not true. Dismantling this deeply ingrained belief through insight was like removing a logjam. He knew that everyone, including himself, has their own gifts and contribution to make. Through his willingness to sit with his feelings of jealousy and inquire into them, he freed himself from his old restrictive thoughts about thriving. Instead of staying stuck in a recurring reactive mode that affirmed his lack, he was now free to proactively embrace his own fullness.

Out of this change in consciousness, he discovered two things he could do. He chose to celebrate the success of others and to connect their success to his own. The news of someone else's success gave him an opportunity to affirm the prosperity imperative at work in his life as well. He remembered the prosperity principle that thriving is not a zero-sum game. When we work in consciousness at the spiritual level, we realize there is no limit to prosperity. Getting back in touch with his own limitless potential gave him new zeal for his work. It wasn't long before his inner shift from "less than" to "infinitely inspired and resourceful" began to attract more students to work with him. When his consciousness shifted from lack to abundance, it showed — he was radiant and enthused about his work. Ken started to grow again, and so did his business.

His inner work also made him aware of what else he wanted to accomplish. Instead of being jealous of colleagues who were reaching more students through their publications and presentations, he was now inspired to take his place on the larger stage of life by sharing his model and method. As he prepared his materials and *himself* to reach more people, he held on to the most important question: *How can I serve in the highest way?*

The last time I saw Ken, he was thriving. He was receiving more invitations to speak than he could accommodate and more recognition than he knew how to take in. His classes were full to overflowing, and he was considering a larger venue. He had reached the next stage of his inner work — learning how to receive and stay open to life's abundant flow of resources.

Foundation for True Wealth

This core teaching on true wealth through nonstealing is one of yoga's *yamas*, the five spiritually based ethical guidelines for fulfilled living found in Patanjali's Yoga Sutras. Those guidelines are nonharming (*ahimsa*), truthfulness (*satya*), nonstealing (*asteya*), right use of vital force (*brahmacharya*), and nonattachment (*aparigraha*). The ethical restraints of the five yamas are paired with five *niyamas*, the observances that support spiritual awakening, which include purity (*shaucha*), contentment (*santosha*), self-discipline (*tapas*), study of the nature of consciousness, also called Self-inquiry or self-study (*svadhyaya*), and surrender of the illusional sense of separate existence or self-surrender (*Ishwara pranidhana*). The yamas and niyamas are the first two limbs of yoga's eight limbs of practice. I explore these limbs in more detail in chapters 10 and 13.

The sutra on nonstealing offering the key to true wealth (2:37) is situated in the middle of the five yamas. It's useful to consider yoga disciplines as sequential and contiguous — one preparing the way for the next. In this case, nonstealing is preceded by both nonharming and truthfulness. These two prior restraints set the foundation for our wealth to be dharmic, in harmony with the natural order of life. They ensure that our pursuit of prosperity is ethically sound and spiritually informed with the awareness of our connection to all. Nonstealing is then followed by the right use of vital force and nonattachment, further guidance that supports, directs, and inspires our experience of wealth to be deeper than the material level alone.

Our greatest wealth is our awakened consciousness, realization of the unbounded truth of our essential Self and, through it, our interconnection to all life. Ignorance of that is our greatest error and our greatest poverty.

Yama means "self-restraint" and refers to the five methods for changing our thoughts and behavior. Their purpose, as restraints, is to restrain ego-based thinking and behavior arising from the misguided sense of a separate self. Ultimately, practice of the restraints aids in transforming the ego from a petty tyrant always looking after the interests of its own insecure, small self into a transparent, luminous vehicle for the higher true Self.

The restraint of nonharming is considered the foundation for all the other yamas and niyamas and the litmus test for every ethical choice we make. The scriptures refer to it as *"ahimsa paramo dharma"* — the highest dharma, the greatest of all guides to spiritually conscious living. It shines universally as the golden rule, the one scripture that finds its way into many traditions. The harm, or good, that we do returns to us because we are not separate from others.

Following nonharming is its lifelong companion, truthfulness. The two are inseparable. Truthfulness is the call to know the true Self and live with complete integrity as the spiritual beings we are. Both restraints point to the Oneness of life and the creative power that becomes available to us when we awaken to higher truth and learn to cooperate with its laws. Flourishing through nonstealing naturally arises on this foundation.

Experiencing the Jewel of Abundance

What exactly is the jewel of abundance? Another version of Patanjali's sutra 2:37 reads: "When one is established in refrainment from stealing, all jewels manifest." In this passage, the Sanskrit word *ratna* is translated as jewels, pearls, gems, or (occasionally) more generally as wealth.[4] "Manifesting jewels" is a metaphor that signifies one who is spiritually awake — Self-aware, content, and Self-reliant — and naturally attracts the very best in life. In this case, "jewels" means the wealth that is the best of everything, the finest or most valued. It refers not only to material things but to relationships and even inspired ideas. A person established in nonstealing exudes a graceful sufficiency and magnetism that draws others and resources to her or him. The "jewel of abundance" is both the power of our awakened consciousness, which has become free from the ego's drive to acquire more and more, and all the good things in life that such freedom attracts. Finding that freedom is the result of insight, spiritual practice, and the supportive presence of grace.

Each of the five restraints is built upon a spiritual principle or spiritual law. To fully realize the inherent benefits of each spiritual law requires spiritual practices that span the spectrum of the physical, mental, emotional, and spiritual components of our being. Each restraint also promises what we can expect from a change in consciousness once we fully realize that virtue or divine quality. The principles, practices, and promises light the path to thriving, prospering, and succeeding in the highest way.

The principle behind nonstealing is the law of abundance. The universe is imbued with unbounded creative energy and power. As Roy

Eugene Davis, my spiritual teacher, notes, "Whether your lifestyle is simple and your needs are few, or your lifestyle is expansive and more resources are needed to accomplish your purposes — whatever is needed the universe can easily supply. The universe is whole and self-sufficient. Its energy is constant: energy manifests as material things and material things are transformed into energy."[5] That divine energy and power flows unimpeded into expression in our lives when we learn how to cooperate with it. Then the jewels of all good things come to us on their own.

The restraint of nonstealing in all its permutations leads us into a direct encounter with the unbounded divine Self. The stream that is no longer constrained finds its way to the ocean. At this point, what was once restraint of erroneous belief becomes an opening to realization, being established in life's prosperous flow. Here, nonstealing is effortlessly transmuted into generosity. We become a nourishing presence — transformed from someone who takes into someone who gives.

When I embarked on the spiritual path of Kriya Yoga, the classical yoga tradition brought to the West in 1920 by Paramahansa Yogananda, I had no idea that it would provide a pathway to thriving, to experiencing true wealth beyond measure, which it has. With the guidance of Roy Eugene Davis, a direct disciple of Yogananda, I learned that life is one Ultimate Reality, which is both beyond and within all that exists — from the transcendental field to the expanse of billions of galaxies to the vastness of the earth with its multitude of teeming lifeforms right down to the still point in the heart of every being radiating as the divine Self. The nature of that Ultimate Reality, referred to as God, or Brahman, is expansive. The word *Brahman* itself means "to expand, greater than the greatest."[6] To discover that is to discover our own expansive nature, always the source of true wealth.

Three

Imagine Enlightenment

Go, seek the jewel that's rarely found!

— RUMI

How many people do you know who would say they are seeking enlightenment? I would guess none. Those who are close enough to it know better than to say they seek it, and those who are further away tend to see it as a goal only for a select few. Perhaps we can name many who would say they are seeking spiritual awakening. That sounds somehow more attainable. But what about enlightenment? Can we imagine it? Imagine it for ourselves? How about a world where people are spiritually awake? That is really what enlightenment is — being spiritually awake, realizing what is, having true knowledge of higher realities. Knowing our Self and knowing the world for what it is — one omnipresent Ultimate Reality, one Supreme Consciousness, beyond, within, through, and as everyone and everything. One.

Realizing Oneness — nothing less than *wholeness* — is our greatest prosperity. It is the source of true fulfillment that opens the inner door to infinite resources and the highest happiness. Yet in our search for abundance, enlightenment is often the last thing we genuinely look for. Perhaps that is understandable for many reasons, not the least of which is that we can't see how being enlightened will put food on the table or pay the rent or college tuition. Even if it did, it is not something most of us have considered attainable, anyway. So off we go, looking for wealth, happiness, and security in things and circumstances that can only be temporary. However, we are wired for enlightenment, and there is a juncture in life when the search for it begins. As emanations of Supreme Consciousness, we are already enlightened at the core of our being. Because we are, we naturally yearn to realize that truth of our being. A time comes when we start looking for something we've all had hints of, something that money can't buy, something that won't come and go, something that won't disappoint. Something that's been with us all along.

The Brihadaranyaka Upanishad tells a story of coming to this juncture.[1] Sage Yajnavalkya is ready to retire to the forest, ready to simplify his life and focus on spiritual knowledge. He informs his wife, Maitreyi, of his plan, assuring her that he will leave his wealth for her and his other wife, Katyayani, so they will have no worries for their well-being. When I read this ancient text, I feel how crucial this moment is. I imagine Maitreyi facing him, standing tall, with her hands on her hips, looking him straight in the eye with a soul-piercing gaze many husbands would recognize. Her reply is strong; it resonates through the ages. She says: "If I were to have the wealth of all the earth, would that make me immortal?" "No," he says. "It would just make you rich. Like any other rich person, you would have plenty of things but you wouldn't be immortal. You would live, and you would die, like a rich person." "Well, then," she says, "what good would it ultimately do me? Tell me what you know about the way to immortality, the way to ultimate freedom." Seeing through the temporary nature of material things, she wants to know about spiritual enlightenment. She asks, *How do I get that?*

A beautiful, inspired teaching follows Maitreyi's question. Yajna-valkya tells her that the root of all we truly love and desire is, in fact, the joyous, boundless, divine Self. What we are really looking for is, indeed, within us. Even wealth. He says: "A wife loves her husband not for his own sake, dear, but because the Self lives in him. A husband loves his wife not for her own sake, dear, but because the Self lives in her.... Wealth is loved not for its own sake, but because the Self lives in it.... The universe is loved not for its own sake, but because the Self lives in it."[2]

The answer to her question: *It's right here.*

Yes, And

Rather than seeing our search for the abundant life as an either/ or situation, a choice between material wealth or worship, job or joy, family or freedom, the four universal goals of life suggest we bring them all together. Work in the world, experience it fully, love it, serve it, and see it for what it is — and all the while, remember God, remember the One. Work in the world, but don't leave your soul behind. Seek enlightenment, but don't leave your family for it or leave your work out of it.

We always want to leave something behind, leave something out, but enlightenment is about restoring our innate *wholeness* — and wholeness naturally offers an all-embracing, all-inclusive vision of life. I remember having tea with a Zen teacher when one of her students brought up this topic. He was struggling with how to inte-grate his spiritual yearnings and practice with his chaotic family life, and he offered the example that the Buddha left his family behind when he embarked on his spiritual journey. "What about that?" he asked. A mother with children of her own, I will never forget the Zen teacher's soft, compassionate, yet radically clear response. She said, "The Buddha was not yet enlightened when he did that."

One of the greatest gifts of awakening to our prosperous nature is realizing we can have it all. This is not the foolhardy, immature vision of a child in a candy shop. We know where that one goes. It's a mature vision, moderated by the constraints of the big picture — live purposefully, insightfully, skillfully, with clarity and generosity. That is the way to thrive. It's a big vision, and one of the ways we open to it is to imagine what that means for us. What does it look like?

Imagine

Imagine being spiritually enlightened. Don't allow yourself to be confined by mundane circumstances, subjective (mental and emotional) conditions, or mental processes. Imagine that you are always established in conscious awareness of your pure essence – which is a unit of the pure essence of ultimate Reality.

— Roy Eugene Davis[3]

We often spend time envisioning the fulfillment of important but more mundane goals in life. We envision a successful conclusion to a project, dream about finding more fulfilling work or greater harmony in our relationships — which are all significant to prosperous living. But the most essential goal is the liberation of consciousness — the ultimate realization that brings complete freedom. Released from the error of narrowing our potential by ascribing it to external factors, or even from our own subjective conditioning, we are free to fully prosper. Why not use the powerful tool of imagination to move our awareness, thoughts, and feelings in the direction of what we know is the greatest goal of all?

In the same way that we use our creative ability of imagination to call forth positive changes in our outer life, we can use it to cultivate spiritual advancement. We can use the power of the mind to imagine ourselves as fully enlightened now, elicit the feelings we imagine would be associated with liberation of consciousness, and become more familiar with Self- and God-realization as our innate potential and certain destiny.

Imagining ourselves enlightened is not likely to suddenly transform us into fully awakened sages, yet it is a useful method to raise our consciousness, purify the mental field, and prepare the way for our ultimate success in life. It's a good antidote to the stubborn, erroneous story that enlightenment is not for us. As meditation teacher Sally Kempton writes: "We can't imagine how someone like ourselves, with all our foibles, aversions, and desires, could ever enter such an exalted state. The truth is, we can — and we should. Enlightenment, according to the yogic traditions, is one of the four legitimate goals of human existence, and despite centuries of propaganda to the contrary, it's something that can be sought — and practiced — in the context of a so-called normal life."[4]

Ask

The most formidable obstacle we face on the path of enlightenment is the belief that it's not possible for us. This misguided idea is due to many factors, a few of which include: mistakenly identifying our essential nature with the limited mind and body; accepting the prevailing cultural myth that enlightenment is rare and only for a special few; and having a sense of unworthiness, believing we are somehow fundamentally flawed or lack what is needed. Envisioning, imagining, and cultivating the perception of enlightenment can loosen the grip of these incorrect ideas.

It can be a useful practice to imagine enlightenment, and to do this not only as a passing fantasy, but to use what we discover about our innate potential to help us during difficult times. In the opening chapters of the Bhagavad Gita, when the warrior Arjuna is challenged by Lord Krishna to stand up, fight, and engage fully in the battle of his life, he is incapacitated by self-doubt. He wonders what to do; he wonders what an *enlightened* person would do.

Arjuna asks Krishna to describe someone who is established in wisdom and, specifically, what that looks like in everyday life. Arjuna asks how an awakened person sits, speaks, and moves around. Considered metaphysically, this scene represents the inner dialogue between the embodied soul (Arjuna) and the higher true Self (Lord Krishna); in it, Arjuna engages his creative imagination. He is asking *himself: What would it be like for me to be enlightened?* This is the question we all can and should ask ourselves.

Lord Krishna responds that one who is established in wisdom is content.[5] With awareness resting in the divine Self, the enlightened person remains unmoved by fleeting desires, passion, loss or gain, fear or anger, pain or pleasure. Able to withdraw attention and awareness away from the pull of the objects of the senses, or the sway of subjective phenomena, the awakened one anchors attention within. This person is not tossed about by the winds of worry, the gales of grief, or the fires of fear.

One established in the Self is not swayed by circumstances.

Does this sound "out of this world"? Is an enlightened person inert, cold, and unfeeling, sitting in meditation all day, withdrawn from life? According to Krishna, of course not. What is unmoving is the mind. Unlike our fragmented, ordinary waking state where the mind restlessly moves at the whim of sensory stimulation or subconscious prompting, the awakened mind is like a calm lake where the light of the moon is clearly reflected without distortion. When our mind is clear and calm like that, inspiration flows unimpeded from the soul. Then we are free to consider our choices in the conscious light of wisdom rather than being motivated by the subconscious shadows of reaction.

A person who is free from reactivity is free to *respond* — free to enjoy, free to engage, free to serve, free to love, and free to be happy without any external cause. We find this description in the Mahabharata: "Those who have attained that state are assailed no more by the duality of opposites. Feeling equality and friendship for all, they are engaged in obtaining the good of all beings."[6] Imagine what our relationships could be like with that kind of freedom. What if we didn't need to "get something" from others — love, attention, affirmation, security, or happiness? What if we knew we already had it to give? What if we could be fully present with others, yet free of any "buttons" that could be pushed?

To use your imagination to envision your life as a fully enlightened being, take instruction from Arjuna: *Ask.* In a calm and quiet time, when you will not be interrupted and can let your thoughts soar, inquire about this. Ask yourself: *What would I be like if I were living as a fully enlightened being right now? What would that look like? How would I feel? What would I be doing? What would remain the same and what would be different?*

Beyond contemplating and imagining, allow the felt sense of enlightened living to emerge from within you. Feel it in your body. Remember that as an individualized expression of Spirit you are already enlightened at the core of your being. "Becoming enlightened" is a matter of removing obstacles to the full expression of your true Self and allowing your innate radiance to emerge. Let the feeling of being enlightened remain in your heart and in the background of your awareness. Let it be a reference point for conscious living.

When opportunities for discernment arise, ask: *What is my response to this as an enlightened soul?* Live into it.

Occupy the Subtle Body

In addition to using the tools of contemplation and imagination to cultivate enlightened awareness, we can also direct our attention to the higher centers of consciousness in the subtle body — the vortices of energy known as *chakras*. The higher chakras — the heart, throat, third eye, and crown chakra — are associated with the virtuous attitudes and behaviors that are natural to awakened consciousness. Lifting our awareness to these centers helps to activate and elicit thoughts, feelings, and behaviors associated with enlightenment. It encourages vital force to flow upward and contributes to being more awake, aware, and open to inspiration.

We can practice moving our attention to each of these centers at the conclusion of meditation. Begin with the heart, then move awareness progressively to the throat, the third eye, and finally, the crown chakra. Notice if there is a felt sense of energy at any of the centers — a warmth, tingling, or feeling of slight pressure. Investigate, be open and curious. If you feel drawn to one particular center, let your focus remain there. Allow your awareness to expand through this energetic portal into your boundless Self. Observe how you feel, the quality of your awareness, and your mental state.

We can "occupy" these higher centers through intention and remembrance throughout the day. Decide you will do it, and then allow your awareness to move there as you recall your intention. Whether you're sitting, standing, walking, or lying down, consciously straighten your spine, feel that vital force is flowing more freely, and then let your attention be anchored in one of the higher centers. You can use your breath to contribute to the felt sense of it as well. Simply imagine that as you breathe, energy is moving along with the breath through that chakra center. As you feel the breath in your heart, throat, third eye, or crown, you'll naturally experience your mood lift and your awareness expand. Try it.

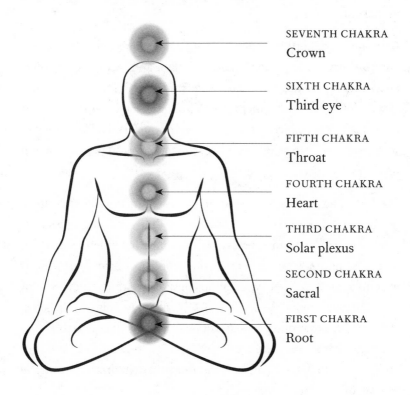

SEVENTH CHAKRA
Crown

SIXTH CHAKRA
Third eye

FIFTH CHAKRA
Throat

FOURTH CHAKRA
Heart

THIRD CHAKRA
Solar plexus

SECOND CHAKRA
Sacral

FIRST CHAKRA
Root

Enlightened Individuals, Awakened World

We now have the opportunity to live the most meaningful lives any generation of humankind has ever lived.

— LYNNE TWIST[7]

Imagining and opening to our own enlightenment, and that of others, can contribute to planetary healing and awakening. How else will our world evolve into a planet of peace and prosperity if not through the global awakening of people everywhere? Along with imagining what it would be like to be fully spiritually awake ourselves, let's also engage in possibility thinking for our world. It's a way to begin opening to our full potential, as individuals and as a global community.

Our mind, as a portion of universal mind, is connected to the Source and to every other person. What we think and feel not only influences our experience of life and what we can bring forth, it also exerts an influence upon others. Spending our time in worry and fear adds that to the collective consciousness of our planet. Why do that, when we can change our minds and make a positive contribution instead?

We live in an awakening world, in a time of individual and global awakening to the great truth that life is One, and that one life is God. As life is God in expression, it is whole, complete, abundant, and lacks nothing. Awakening to this wholeness brings the experience of radical prosperity, or sufficiency, and with it, a new way of living. There is enough for all in God's economy. It is time for us to shed the idea that one person's good is another's loss and to rise to the truth that all can, and must, prosper. It is time to free ourselves and our world — our children and our grandchildren — from the specter of scarcity.

Many times, students have asked me: If there is no lack in God, why do we see it in our world? We see it because we have collectively believed in it. We have structured our lives and our world by that belief. The lack that we perceive in our world is not a problem with the Source; it is a spiritual development problem. Humanity is right now like a toddler with a power tool or a computer. The power is there, the potential is there, but we don't yet fully understand it and know how to put it to good use.

We are awakening to our potential to create a prospering world that works for everyone — evolving from an egocentric model of life to a spiritually based one. As long as we remain in the egocentric system, and are unaware of wholeness, there will be lack, fear, and scarcity arising from the collective consciousness. That unawakened consciousness cannot see that we are connected to one another, to the earth and nature, and to God.

Humanity has lived for centuries with a consciousness of scarcity — the limited thinking that has fomented fear, greed, sexism, racism, xenophobia, militarism, war, and injustice of every kind. It's time for this to change, and we are ready. There is no turning back the tide of spiritual evolution. To cooperate with this transformation, this evolutionary jump for humanity, we must not allow ourselves to get sidetracked, fooled, set up, or put down by fear-based messages — no matter where they come from. The worst ones are those in our own minds, and those we can readily change.

Go to the Mountaintop

Fear arises when I narrow my vision and lose faith in something greater than what I can see with my eyes or understand with my intellect. I fall into material consciousness, become frightened by the scarcity specter, and lose touch with my enlightened vision for my life and the life of our world. When that happens, I know I need to "go to the mountaintop." It's time to lift my consciousness to a higher plane, a higher level, one that is beyond thought, where I can get a new perspective on life — a spiritual view.

Here's what I do: I pray and I meditate. I release my worries; I let them go. The process I use is to think of a prayer word, one like *peace*, and let it float on my breath. I mentally chant *peace* with each inhalation and exhalation. I observe my breath and attend to the word until my attention is concentrated and my restless, worrisome thoughts are stilled. Then I let go of the word and *experience* the soul's peace beyond mind. When that peace pervades my mind and I sit in the stillness, I am restored to wholeness. I abide in that perfect love, which is wholeness, and my fears are removed — "perfect love casts out fear" (1 John 4:18, ESV). Then I am ready to walk in faith, to carry the vision of an awakened world with me. I don't have to pick up those worries again, I don't have to take on that fear — it doesn't belong to me and I don't belong to it. I can change my mind. I remember I am a spiritual being and that infinite, divine Spirit is my source and my supply.

Now Is the Time

Whenever dharma declines and the purpose of life is forgotten,
I manifest myself on earth. I am born in every age to protect the good,
to destroy evil, and to reestablish dharma.

— Bhagavad Gita[8]

The scriptures of many traditions offer the promise of an awakened world, and many indicate the return or appearance of an enlightened being to bring it forth. In the Vedic tradition, this divine descent of fully illumined consciousness into physical form is known as an *avatar*. While such an appearance is possible, what is more likely, and more essential in our era, is for this illumined consciousness to be awakened in every heart to shine forth and uplift humanity. The avatars or awakened masters who have appeared on earth throughout time have uttered the same cry to humanity: *Wake up! Wake up to the truth of your being. The kingdom is within you. You are That.* Now it is time for this message, which is widely available in our age, to be realized. When it is, there will be a global awakening of consciousness. The spiritual truth that once surfaced solely through an avatar, the illumined consciousness of a single individual like a lone voice crying in the wilderness, will radiantly resound through the hearts and minds of awakened souls the world over. This is a shift from a single avatar to many awakened souls who become the *avatar influence*.

The avatar influence — the innate response to the indwelling Spirit to fully incarnate and make itself known though the illumined consciousness of many receptive souls — is the great hope and potential of this time. Revered Buddhist teacher and peace activist Thich Nhat Hanh spoke of the timely need for this global awakening in his 2015 address to the United Nations:

> There's a revolution that needs to happen and it starts from inside each one of us. We need to wake up and fall in love with Earth. We've been *Homo sapiens* for a long time. Now it's time to become homo conscious. Our love and admiration for the Earth has the power to unite us and remove all boundaries, separation and discrimination. Centuries of individualism and competition have brought about tremendous destruction and alienation. We need to reestablish true communication — true communion — with ourselves, with the Earth, and with one another as children of the same mother. We need more than new technology to protect the planet. We need real community and cooperation.[9]

In this time of profound global stress, what is most needed is the shift in consciousness that enlightenment brings. To see others as they are — the same divine Self — and to see the earth with all its life forms, and the universe itself, as it is — Supreme Consciousness in expression — is the vision of an awakened world. Established in that wisdom, humanity will unlock its potential and do what needs to be done to cooperate with life's evolutionary promise. Can you imagine? What will it look like? How will it be to live in such a time? When you think of future generations, is there anything you want more? Anything that matters more?

Four

Be Willing to Thrive

Don't ask yourself what the world needs.
Ask yourself what makes you come alive, and go do that,
because what the world needs is people who have come alive.

— Howard Thurman

True prosperity is less about *having* than it is about *being* and its process, *becoming*. It's the spiritual journey of becoming in fullness that which we are in potential. Awakened to our previously dormant inner power and promise, we actualize it, live with higher purpose, and become wealthy in all ways.

In between discovering the truth of our being and actualizing it, there is a courageous leap for us to take. That leap is *willingness*. Willingness bridges the gap between what we say we want, what we are open to have, and what that requires us to become. If we were fully ready to receive our heart's desire, we would already have it. To be ready to receive, we have to grow. We must grow and keep growing, ever expanding our consciousness — this is the way of unbounded Spirit.

To live abundantly, to thrive and prosper, is to vow to grow. This is not growth measured by accumulation of things or status. To vow to grow is the willingness to *be* more — more awake and more aware — to experience more joy, clarity, aliveness, freedom, and creativity. It's a life-changing, transformational commitment to flourish. To open ourselves to infinite possibility is the willingness to step into the unknown, rising to meet our divine capacity.

Our willingness to become — to fully express our potential — springs from and mirrors the initial impulse of the divine Self moving into manifestation. According to Vedic seers, in the beginning, omnipresent Supreme Consciousness was unmanifest. The Upanishads describe this consciousness as meditating — conscious and still with all dormant powers resting in harmonious balance — absorbed in absolute Oneness. An urge, a willingness, arose within to express itself — for the One to become many: "I am One, let Me become many!"[1]

Out of the divine intention to become many, by expressing its creative energy, the universe and everything within it comes into being and is infused with Supreme Consciousness. On the individual scale, within each of us is that same inherent primal urge to become, to allow our divine potential to be realized: *Let me be in fullness what I might become! Let my potential expand and be expressed!*

Yoga philosophy offers us some helpful insights about that leap of willingness — not only where the willingness impulse comes from, but how we can cooperate with it.

Where Possible Meets Practical

The first chapter of Patanjali's Yoga Sutras is called "Samadhi Pada." *Pada* means chapter or part and *samadhi* is the Sanskrit term for meditative absorption and means "to hold together completely." Samadhi is total absorption of our attention and awareness in the object of meditation, which facilitates union with it. It refers to "a state beyond expression and above all thought. Here speech and mind cannot reach. It is a state of utter calmness in which consciousness is unwavering."[2] This is the superconscious state — a higher state of consciousness where our attention and awareness have moved beyond involvement with thought activity to consciously rest in the object of our meditation.

Samadhi is becoming one with what we are focused on — complete absorption into it, which brings direct experience of it. When what we are contemplating is Absolute Reality, samadhi is the direct experience of the divine Self, that which we are. This is yoga — conscious union with the true Self. This meditative absorption and ineffable experience of the Self is the goal of yoga. It is identified as the eighth, or final limb, of yoga practice. Because it is a revelation of the Self that is always present, samadhi is not reliant on, or restricted to, any method. However, the scientific approach of yoga's eight limbs of practice systematically prepares the mind for the experience. See chapter 10 for more about the eight limbs, meditation, and samadhi.

Patanjali explains that our attention and awareness can flow in two different directions. Knowing this, and choosing one direction or the other, makes all the difference between a conscious life and sleepwalking through the world in the ordinary, distracted waking state. One direction for our attention is outward toward thought activity, all the movements and changes in the mind, and the objects of sense perception — everything we think about and perceive. The other direction is for our attention to flow inward, toward the stillness of the divine Self. This is the way of meditation and mindful living.

When our attention is captivated by thoughts, we identify with them. When this happens, our awareness, which is innately expansive, becomes confined. In contrast, when our attention is freed from engaging in thought activity and flows toward the divine Self, it expands. When thought activity becomes calm and quiet, or recedes to the background of awareness, the true Self is revealed. It's as if we open a door in consciousness that allows the inner light of the divine Self to shine through and illumine the mind. That numinous Self is always present, but it can be obscured by mental restlessness. Samadhi, the quieting of the mind, opens that door. What we are, the divine Self, is then revealed. Then we know. We know the truth of what we are, and we open an access route to inner guidance, inspiration, and resources. Swami Bodhananda Saraswati, a contemporary teacher of Vedanta, writes, "Yoga is the ability to draw from your own inner resources.... When your mind is abiding in samadhi, when you are able to draw from that source, then you are in yoga.... Samadhi is the atman [the divine Self], the source of infinite potentiality, the field of infinitude."[3]

The possibility of consciously accessing the soul's wisdom becomes predictable through yoga's step-by-step approach to superconscious meditation and conscious living with higher awareness and purpose. Since the source of what we are looking for is within us, it's a matter of getting ready by arranging conditions to allow our innate potential to shine forth and be expressed.

Get Ready

...where and when God finds you ready, God must act and overflow into you, just as when the air is clean and pure, and sun must overflow into it and cannot refrain from doing that.
— MEISTER ECKHART[4]

How to get ready for superconscious living is the next thing that Patanjali offers us in his Yoga Sutras. In the second chapter, he introduces Kriya Yoga, which is a universally applicable, practical method for Self-realization and superconscious living. Kriya may sound exotic, but it simply means "action." Kriya Yoga refers to those actions we take that support the goal of yoga — spiritually conscious living, the Oneness-realization that is samadhi.

In essence, Patanjali is like a salesman who informs us that we already have what we are trying to buy. While the purpose of Kriya Yoga is to foster our ability to experience samadhi, the method is simply to remove any obstruction to experiencing that which is natural to us. Superconsciousness is the ground of our being, our essence. Kriya Yoga is not about doing anything to become spiritual. It's an affirmation that we already are. Through yoga, we remove anything that gets in the way of knowing and experiencing it. We get ready to expand our consciousness, ready to grow and prosper.

Align with the Prospering Power

The three strategies or practices that Patanjali offers as the way to remove obstructions and cultivate superconsciousness are self-discipline, self-study, and self-surrender. Self-discipline is practiced every day through intentionally joyful living, by staying focused on higher purpose and true fulfillment. It's all the choices we make to live in harmony with the soul, to align our thoughts, speech, and action with the spiritual truth of our being. Self-study is investigation of higher realities and inquiry into the nature of consciousness, which includes contemplation and superconscious meditation. Self-surrender is letting go of the illusional sense of a separate self, releasing the erroneous idea that we are separate from the Source of life and its ongoing support. The first two strategies — self-discipline and self-study — will be explored in later chapters. Here, let's begin with surrender.

Surrender is the key to willingness.

With surrender, we realize that omnipresent, unlimited, Absolute Reality is all that is. It is the source, substance, and boundless supply of all creation. Its fundamental nature is expansive, infinite, and eternal — without beginning or end. Think of it this way: Absolute Reality, commonly called God, does not withhold. Its very nature is to give: It continually pours itself forth as goodness and blessing. Here's what that means to us — never, at any time, is goodness ever withheld from us, any more than the ocean holds back from a wave.

The question for us becomes, if Absolute Reality does not withhold its creative power, how do we sign up to receive? How do we enter that prospering stream of divine grace and blessing? We're already in that stream. It's a matter of flowing with it by cooperating with its power. As writer Anne Lamott notes, "The Gulf Stream will flow through a straw provided the straw is aligned to the Gulf Stream, and not at cross purposes with it."[5] Our alignment with that prospering power is willingness to thrive.

The Willingness Diagnostic

Imagine someone knocking on your door, and when you open it, they ask, "Would you like to thrive, to prosper, and be successful in all ways?" We'd like to think we'd say, "Yes, of course!" But many of us are a little suspicious of that question. Our first thought is not, "Yes, I am ready to prosper!" The first thought is, "What will it cost me?" Our inner dialogue with the divine Self is not that different. Sure, we might consider that the divine prospering power is omnipresent and ready to infuse our life, but what will it cost? What will it require of us?

Let's face it, becoming willing to fully thrive, to pull out all the limiting stops held in place by the small self, is a leap into the unknown.

Many questions arise when we arrive at the threshold of willingness. Those ever-branching quandaries arise from two main arteries of doubt or two big questions: (1) What if what God (or Spirit, or Higher Power) wants for my life is not what I want? And (2) what if I try and fail?

Question 1: What If What God Wants Is Not What I Want?

I remember this one. The very mention of spiritual surrender had me fearing my next destination would be the convent, my next outfit a full black habit complete with a pair of Birkenstocks. And I'm not even Catholic. This misunderstanding obviously had to be cleared up before I could progress on the divine path that was right for me. Whatever fears we have about where Spirit might send us if we become willing to follow divine direction are rooted in what yoga calls the primal error — *avidya* — ignorance, or wrong knowledge of the Self. We fear what God might ask of us if we surrender because we have not yet discovered that God is already our life.

This question is like the wave asking, "What if the ocean doesn't want what I want?" The answer to our question lies in knowledge of the true Self, knowledge that reveals what surrender is.

The practice of surrender is introduced in the sutras as "surrender to Ishwara." The phrase used is *Ishwara pranidhana* — which means surrender to God, the Lord, or Creator. *Ishwara* is an interesting term. It is translated as "God," yet it does not refer to any particular form of deity that we might identify as someone's idea of God. Instead, Ishwara is more of a generic term, referring to that divine intelligence and power that brings forth creation, permeates it, regulates and sustains it — the Creator or Lord. In other words, surrender to the One that is the Source of all that is. Surrender to your Higher Power, your Higher True Self.

Sutra 2:45 offers the promise of surrender this way: "From surrender to Ishwara, comes the perfection of samadhi." Or, "Self-realization is perfected by surrender to the divine." The crux of this practice is simply letting go of the false belief that we are separate, that we are egoic, autonomous individuals — on our own, without a basis of support, without a foundation for our existence.

Yes, we are individuals. Yes, we operate through an ego-identity. Yes, we are autonomous. And yet, all of that is only possible because we are individualized expressions of a higher Absolute Reality. Remember the wave and the ocean. We are always rooted in the divine Source. Surrender is coming to recognize that and count on it as our unfailing Source of support. With surrender comes the culmination of all practice; we are restored to our original, innate wholeness. No longer at odds with our Self, we can live from our center of wholeness. We can lead with the experience of fullness, rather than any perception of lack motivating our action.

Question 2: What If I Try and Fail?

This perennial question, too, represents a misunderstanding of who we are and what it means to prosper. It arises from the ego's need to apparently control outcomes. We don't mind signing up if we know what we're signing up for. We'd like to see the outcome before we begin, even though life doesn't work that way. This is confusing prosperity with a result, accomplishment, or destination.

Prospering is a process. Whatever we are inspired to do is our path of becoming, a way of allowing our divine powers and qualities to be developed and revealed. Even though we can, and do, discover many outer signs of prosperity along the way, the real journey is an inner one. By releasing our attachment to an outcome, we become free to prosper beyond expectation.

The Bhagavad Gita (2:40) offers this inspiration in response to our question about the possibility of failure on the spiritual path: "On this path effort never goes to waste, and there is no failure. Even a little effort toward spiritual awareness will protect you from the greatest fear."[6]

Surrender, Surrender, Surrender

What will surrender cost? Everything. And nothing. The cost of surrender is relinquishing the false sense of a separate self. It requires giving up the wrong idea of who we think we are.

Over the years, many students have asked me: *How* do I surrender? It's easier if we know that surrender is letting go *into* infinite support. The strategies of Kriya Yoga help us discern that. Meditation gives us the experience of being something more than mind, something beyond ego. Study of sacred texts gives us a map that explains the role of surrender, while contemplation born of inner inquiry facilitates insight into who we really are. We realize we are that Supreme Consciousness which illumines the mind. Surrender is then understood as letting go into our higher true Self.

A simple way of approaching surrender is to look for where we struggle and how we make life a burden. From the perspective of the divine Self, life is never a struggle or a burden. Letting that go is releasing the ego's grip. It's a backdoor approach into the house of plenty.

Surrender of the sense of separation does not mean extinction of the individual. It means that the activity of the divine can now flow freely through that individual without the inner conflict of will. Surrender is letting go of our resistance to take the step, speak the word, open our heart — do what we need to do to honor the inspiration of the soul that rises again and again. Surrender is a commitment we make to no longer dampen down our soul fire. It's our commitment to thrive.

Surrender is the "yes" we say to our Self.

What Yes Can Look Like

The Center for Spiritual Enlightenment in San Jose, California, is a beautiful place, an oasis of peace in the heart of the city. Flowering gardens with walking paths, flowing fountains, and sitting areas for silent meditation surround the temple, meditation hall, and three 1920s Spanish-style buildings that house our Meru Institute for Kriya Yoga studies, youth education, retreat house, and offices. We've been there for decades now, so it's not uncommon for newcomers to think we've always been there, to think we started there. That's not how it happened.

When I began teaching Kriya Yoga in the 1980s, yoga was not as well known as it is today — especially yoga philosophy and meditation. Starting a center where people from any, or no, faith background could learn about meditation, yoga, and Self- and God-realization seemed like an idea whose time had come. We began offering services and programs in a small rented chapel right on a main street in town. The initial response from the community was positive and encouraging, but it didn't take long before opposition showed up. A few people didn't approve of a yoga center with its wisdom from the East, and they let us know. That caught me by surprise. I had to ask myself: If this is what I've come to do, will I have to face opposition? Are there going to be people who don't like me? People who criticize and disagree with me? Then the real question: Am I willing to say yes, to stand up for what I believe? Am I willing to prosper? Am I willing to thrive?

After the initial yes and the beginnings of the center, I drifted off into "maybe." I didn't realize it at the time, but it is easy to see now. When our lease was up on the chapel on the main street, we moved to a building underground! It was a retail and office center with an underground level that required steps or an elevator to reach. After that, we moved to a local Oddfellows temple, which was a brick building with no windows. The step up from there was to a lovely office complex with nine separate buildings. We picked the farthest one in the back with no signage and dared people to find us. Because it was a divine idea, they did.

After a while, it became clear that I had work to do. Was I really willing to thrive? I had a teaching to offer. Was I willing to put myself out there again where people could easily find me? Where people could oppose or criticize me? By this time, a small community of students had begun attending programs, studying, and practicing together. I asked the community and I asked our board of directors: Are we willing? Are we willing to stand up and stand out? Are we willing to thrive, to prosper, and to grow? Beyond that, are we willing to be instruments for this message in the world? To help others find the way of spiritual awakening? Many said yes. Those who said no left to find another place. Those who said yes began the proverbial building fund drive. In a relatively short period of time, we raised $10,000, which was matched by another ten. With $20,000, off we went to look for property in Silicon Valley, one of the most expensive places to live in the entire country.

With our less-than-modest nest egg, we looked at several properties seriously beyond our budget that were not spacious enough to house our growing community, let alone all those we imagined would come once we became visible. We learned that property owned by a church in the Rose Garden area of San Jose, one of the city's most beautiful historic neighborhoods, was for sale — for $2 million. It was sorely in need of repair, but it had everything we needed, including a temple. When we walked through the property, I remember seeing it with eyes far into the future, beyond roof and foundation repair. I thought, "This place is perfect!" The board, understandably, saw the price tag and the repairs needed. They weren't so sure. But they did recognize it as an opportunity for spiritual service and growth.

We had a meeting. I asked them a bold question. I said, "If it wasn't for the asking price and the additional expense that will be needed to repair it, if it wasn't about that money, is this our place?" Is this the place where souls could be served — where our mission to contribute to individual and planetary awakening could thrive? They said, unanimously, yes. They were willing. They were willing to enter the prospering stream of possibility. Everything hinges on that yes of willingness. Once we arrive there, we have opened ourselves to the prospering power of the universe. We didn't know how it was going to happen. We had no idea. We prayed, we committed ourselves, and we opened to the possibility. We were willing. When we shared our vision for how people could be served there, support came forth — including a $2-million anonymous donation that completely paid for the property.

Stop Struggling and Start Living

When I first started teaching and offering programs in the community, the first flyer that went out said, "Stop Struggling and Start Living!" It was an invitation that I, myself, would need to live into. That is the way of the abundant life. We grow, we learn, we are prospered beyond measure as we surrender, again and again, to the divine prospering influence within us.

The first, and last, word of advice on establishing our spiritual foundation is surrender. Let go of the mistaken idea that you are now, ever were, or ever can be, separate from the Source. You are whole, inextricably connected to the Source of all that is. Recognizing this truth and, further, realizing it, changes our approach to life and our fundamental experience of it. We don't stop bringing forth our very best energy and effort, but we do stop struggling. We no longer make our life a burden, but allow it to be a prospering joy.

PART II

Insight
~

Road Map for Abundant Living

Five

Bring Forth
Your Divine Potential

Now the eternal way of yoga begins.

— Yoga Sutras

*I*t is natural to think that bringing forth our potential is something that will occur in the future after we have done whatever is required. Almost by definition, the phrase "bringing forth" implies starting in one place and expressing oneself more fully over time — like a seed that opens and becomes a tree. There's a before and an after, a now and a then. The seed, first all potential, only later becomes seedling, sapling, branch, bud, flower, and fruit. Many things happen to support that little seed's expression of its full potential over the seasons of time. Yet that tree in its *fullness* exists within the seed from the beginning — otherwise it could not come into manifestation as it does. Not only is the tree contained in the seed, but the seed is contained in the tree. Yoga, from the outset, directs us to recognize that all that we are to become in our fullness exists *now*, in this *now* moment.

"Now" is where the Yoga Sutras begin. It's the first word of the treatise, which gives it profound emphasis. Out of 196 terse aphorisms, not a single word is wasted, yet the sentence that starts it off sounds like a mere introduction. Sutra 1:1: "Now the ancient way of yoga begins." We might easily pass by this first sutra, thinking it means only, "Now we're going to study yoga." While this sutra does announce the subject, as many of the classics of Indian philosophy traditionally do, it would be a mistake to stop there. It also teaches.

When does the way of yoga begin? When we get to our yoga class, unroll our mat, and find our balance in tree pose? When we ring the bell at the altar? When we sit to meditate? When we feed the hungry? When? Yoga is the direct, conscious realization of the Self. *It is always now.* Self-realization is not the result of any action, nor is it the accumulation of information, the dawning of intellectual knowledge, or even intuitive insight. It is a spiritual experience that occurs beyond mind — beyond the limits of thought where time dwells. It is only and ever now, free of the constraints of time and the causality that time indicates. Yoga occurs in the eternal present.

Spiritual realization cannot be a past or future event. It is not an event. Events have a cause, a beginning, and an end. Yoga is samadhi — Oneness-realization of Supreme Consciousness without beginning or end, without any cause. It is forever what it is. Think about it this way: There is never a moment when a wave becomes the ocean — not at the swell, the crest, or the dissolution. Now the ocean at the swell, now the ocean at the crest, now the ocean as it settles back in — it is always that which it is. We are ever that which we are.

Yoga is the conscious, now, realization of what we are. *Now* is always our yoga moment. Now is where yoga ever abides. Not later, not when, not if, simply *now.* When our awareness, once constrained by time-bound thought, slips into the expanse of the boundless Self, we enter the conscious now of yoga, the now of Oneness. We return to our Self in wholeness and consciously meet the fullness of our divine potential now.

When we look through the lens of yoga's ancient wisdom, fulfillment of our potential is seen the same way. True fulfillment is always found now. How could it be a future event? We might arguably say, "Yes, but": "Yes, but it *can't* be now. Right now, I can't pay my bills. I'm stuck in an unhappy relationship and an unfulfilling job. Surely, bringing forth my divine potential looks like more than this!" If that's what you are thinking, you are right. Bringing forth our innate fullness is more than outer conditions, regardless of how they look — whether restricted or opulent. Many people spend their lives chasing after the future fulfillment they hope will arrive "someday" — which is an ever-changing, ever-receding destination. The awakened ones ask, "How would we ever find lasting fulfillment if we don't have it within ourselves to begin with?" As a wave arises with the fullness of the ocean, our life of fullness arises from fullness itself. From the invocation to the Isa Upanishad: "All this is full. All that is full." From fullness, only fullness comes.

Then, and Therefore

The Sanskrit word for "now," *atha*, also means "then" and "therefore." Here we are with this exquisite word bringing us right into *now* — the only and always present moment — and we discover it has brought along a couple of its friends, namely, "then" and "therefore." Somehow, I think of my mother's face when I was a teenager — as she watched the entourage of scruffy-looking companions trailing through the front door in my wake. Where did *they* come from? *Now, then, and therefore.* This puzzling combination announces the auspiciousness of the now moment. Like the tree in the seed, the tiny word *atha* proclaims that everything has brought us to this moment of realization. Everything is contained within this moment, and everything flows from it. Everything in our life has led us to this moment of opening to realization. Everything that we have learned, experienced, celebrated, or regretted is part of the great trajectory of now arising in the very moment we encounter the way of Self-realization. It's an auspicious moment, and the indications are — we are ready for it.

When I came to the path of yoga and learned I had always held the key to thriving that I was searching for, I wondered why I hadn't discovered that sooner. So much suffering could have been avoided, had I only known. I was, like most other seekers, the proverbial fish in water looking for the ocean — swimming in a sea of prosperity, asking "Yes, but where can I find it?"

And Always

Besides directing us to the ever-present now experience of spiritual awakening, the first sutra points us to that which has always existed — that which has come before. Patanjali was a compiler of Vedic wisdom, not an originator. The teaching being offered is in accordance with an established tradition — the ancient wisdom that has always existed. The way is timeless because spiritual truth is timeless. It is not new, not something that changes or comes and goes. It is eternal. It is not something that anyone can invent, claim, or copyright. It is the sacred inheritance of all. How beautiful to encounter this ancient, ever-new doorway into the infinite allness of the true Self and discover our own divine potential waiting to welcome us home.

Yoga is both the goal and the way. It is the destination as well as the journey. All the way to Oneness is Oneness. All the way to now is now. All the way to lasting fulfillment is fulfillment. To bring forth our divine potential is to realize it here and now; it exists *now*. As the mystic saint Catherine of Siena proclaimed, "All the way to heaven is heaven!"

Go Straight to the Goal

Once we know we are innately whole, that our divine potential is not something we need to work to acquire, the question naturally arises: Why practice? Why meditate or study? What is the point of spiritual practice when we already have what we are looking for? The word in the yoga tradition that is commonly translated as "spiritual practice" points to the answer. That word is *sadhana*. Translated literally, it means "to go straight to the goal." Yoga is both the goal — the goal of Self-realization and ultimate freedom — and the way of living it. Spiritual practice is not something we do to become spiritual. It is how we live as the spiritual beings we are — expressing our divine potential through our thoughts, speech, and actions.

Spiritual practice is the way we cooperate with the powers of nature and the presence of divine grace. Life continually conspires to prosper us with the uplifting elements of nature and its divine, freely given favor, known as grace. With its origins in the expressive aspect of Ultimate Reality, grace is built into life. Our lives are grace-filled already. It arises within us, through us, and around us. Every moment is permeated with grace. Even though grace is unconditional and freely given, it seems it does not act alone.

The winning combination for a prosperous life is grace met by effort.

Although we are inherently full, that fullness does not overflow into expression without our participation. Fortuitous rain may fall on the field, but if it has not been plowed and planted, our crop will not be forthcoming. Sayings of Lord Shiva in the Mahabharata point this out: "[Those] who do not make an effort, providence does not help

[them] either. Therefore, all acts are dependent upon human effort and providence together."[1]

Whatever it is we dream to do, the way we bring forth our divine potential is to begin. We take the first step and invite divine grace to meet us.

Step Out

No great idea can have a place in the heart
unless one steps out of his little corner.

— SWAMI VIVEKANANDA[2]

Nothing contributes more to unfolding our divine potential than "stepping out of our little corner," reaching out beyond our personal needs alone, and opening to abundance for uplifting others. This is how we enter the stream of divine grace in its fullest expression. We open ourselves to be divine instruments of healing and blessing. When we do, grace overflows as supply, meeting every real need on time and in abundance. The immutable spiritual law is: *Individual prosperity cannot be separated from the good of all.* Spiritual law always rests on wholeness.

It is not uncommon to think, "Once I take care of myself and my family, then I'll find a way to contribute to others." It's true that it's a mistake to get so involved with serving the world that we neglect our family and those entrusted to our care. Yet without realizing that all life is one interconnected whole, we can spend our entire lifetime trying to provide solely for our personal needs and wants and those of our dear ones. It is endless.

The step we take into serving life comes through the activity of grace itself. Life is always aiming to support us, to bring about the actualization of our innate potential. At some point, we wake up beyond our little corner of self-concern — our heart opens, and compassion begins to flow like a river.

My daughter, who was our first born, broke open my heart. The love I felt for her was beyond anything I had ever experienced — tenderness, caring, and grave responsibility for this young life. Even though I was a very young and inexperienced mother, certain things are both soulful and instinctual. I wanted her to live. I wanted her to be healthy, happy, and free from suffering. I was so grateful that, when she was hungry, I could feed her. When she was sick, I could take her to a doctor.

This is what happened to my heart: I took what I was experiencing here, with this tiny, beautiful little girl, and extended it there — across the nation and across the world.

I felt every mother and every child on the earth in my heart. I knew other mothers loved their children just like I did mine, and I felt what it would be like if you could not provide for them. What if I had no food for this child? What if she was suffering and I could not help her? The feeling was so clear that I knew I needed to act on it. I took a simple step and volunteered for UNICEF, the United Nations organization for supporting children worldwide. It gave me a way that I could take my heart *here* and apply it *there*.

Serving others became for me the first step toward truly prospering, which has only become richer and more soul-satisfying over the years. Many of the important life and professional skills I learned during my time serving through UNICEF were what I needed for my next step, when I turned to the vocation of teaching Kriya Yoga. The initial impetus of my heart to serve parents and children over the years has blossomed, at our meditation center, into our youth spiritual education program as well as into an educational non-profit organization to teach skills of nonviolence and mindfulness to at-risk children in schools and mothers in prison. It's amazing what can flow from the inspiration of our hearts, our willingness to act, and the presence of grace.

Sometimes people don't open themselves to being instruments for greater good because they haven't understood how life itself will provide what is needed to accomplish the necessary good. They don't know how resourceful life is and how resourceful they are. Here is the secret: *We can't find out until we step out.*

Here, There, and Everywhere

The ideal for a conscious person is to be so in the flow of life that he understands that everything about him is given from the source and that his responsibility is to give himself to the purposes of the source.... In all that you do think in terms of serving life.

— Roy Eugene Davis[3]

As expressions of the infinite Source, we have within us the creative power of imagination for tapping into higher potential and aligning ourselves with the greater good. Not *how to use* this dynamic creative power for our good, but *how to be used* by it, to be an instrument for the good of all. When we are willing to be creative instruments for the good of all, the bonds of self-interest that hold us back are loosed, and the imagination soars. When we help others prosper, we prosper.

There are infinite ways to serve and to prosper — each according to our talents, dreams, and duties. For some the avenue is public — such as through organizational or community service. For others, it may be familial — by raising a child, tending an organic garden, or caring for aging parents. Either way, as we serve we are naturally learning and teaching love, wisdom, and compassion. What has broken your heart open and awakened your passion? What do you care most deeply about? What have you learned and experienced that makes all the difference? What is the inspiration that won't leave you alone? That is where we begin. We begin with what is most alive in us.

We simply begin by inwardly dedicating our life to serving others. By expanding our awareness and our compassion, we step beyond the limiting boundaries of self.

We enter the prospering stream of divine grace and experience the expansion of our imagination and creative abilities. This flows into and through our lives as resources — as inspiration, peace, well-being, love, and the connectedness that brings forth whatever is needed.

All we have to do is take this heart *here* and apply it to what is over *there*.

Six

Realize Your
Essentially Abundant Nature

[Humanity] naturally feels great necessity for Sat, Existence;
Chit, Consciousness; and Ananda, Bliss. These three are the real
necessities of the human heart and have nothing to do with anything
outside [the] Self. They are essential properties of [our] own nature.

— SRI YUKTESWAR

*O*ur essential nature is that which we are — what is inherently true and unchanging about us. With discernment and direct experience of the true Self, we perceive the difference between our physical and mental characteristics and our spiritual nature. This practice is svadhyaya or Self-inquiry. We observe our body, personality, thoughts, and emotions and notice that they all change over time. The very fact that we can observe these functions gives us insight about our true Self. Who is seeing? What is observing? The Seer, the Witness, is the unchanging essential Self.

Often what we think we are, invest in as important, and give so much time and energy to is not our true Self, but simply its temporary expression in this lifetime. One meditation teacher aptly compared all the time we spend on external things to time spent decorating our hotel room! Living a spiritually conscious life helps us establish the right priorities. To live in the soul is to live in the awareness of our true nature, allowing its radiance to illumine body and mind.

The characteristics of our true nature are pure existence-being, conscious awareness, and joy or bliss. These qualities — *Sat, chit,* and *ananda,* or existence, consciousness, and bliss — are the reflection of Supreme Consciousness in the soul. The soul is an individualized expression of Ultimate Reality (commonly called God), which is omnipresent (unchanging, immortal being, always and everywhere present); omniscient (supremely conscious, all-knowing); and omnipotent (infinitely creative, all-powerful, and blissful). Just as a drop of ocean water will be found to contain the same basic qualities as the ocean, so do the characteristics of God exist within the soul as our divine potential.

We naturally yearn to know and experience the fullness of our being — to realize our divine inheritance. We want to live, not just for a short time, but forever. There is an old saying that the strangest thing about human beings is that everyone dies — it's a natural occurrence so obviously pervasive in nature — yet no one thinks *they* will die. Perhaps it's our self-protective denial mechanism at work, but more likely, it is our innate sense of immortality. In the depths of our being, we know we are not limited to the physical body that is born and dies. We have all had "intimations of immortality" — in the depth of our soul, we know we are birthless, deathless, immortal spiritual beings.

We want knowledge, but not just a little. We want knowledge without limits. We have curious minds and unbounded imagination ready to soar into the unknown and discern its secrets. And we can. Paramahansa Yogananda wrote, "To discover any truth, we have only to turn our consciousness inward to the soul, whose omniscience is one with God."[1]

We want to avoid pain and suffering, know unconditional happiness, and experience lasting satisfaction. That irrepressible yearning for happiness motivating all that we do is our soul yearning to return to bliss — the pure joy of Self-knowledge.

These three longings of the soul — for infinite life, unbounded wisdom, and pure joy — are the desire to return to its truth, to break free of the bonds of the false self. Human beings naturally long for a freedom and joy we know is ours. We have tasted it and remember its sweetness. Our life journeys, whether feeble or grand, come down to our attempts to recover our divine inheritance. We want to reclaim it.

Start with Wholeness

An endless fountain of milk is within you:
Why are you seeking milk with a pail?
— RUMI[2]

The key to fulfilling these three deepest desires is Self-realization. There are many meaningful and important things we yearn to have or experience, such as a healthy, loving intimate relationship; inspiring work; an avenue for expressing our creative talents; and finding a way to implement positive social change. Even though our goals are important, must be addressed, and can be achieved — they are not the best starting point. Why not start with our greatest yearning and realize it?

The way of yoga is to start with wholeness, to begin with Self-knowing.

It's not recommended that we begin with "wanting" something, no matter how lofty or important it is. We start by working in consciousness; first and foremost, we engage in life from fullness. We begin with sufficiency — recognition that all the necessary potentials are within us to become what we need to be a match for our goal. For example, if we want a healthy, loving, relationship, the first thing we do is free ourselves of the *need* for love. Instead, we draw upon our inner fullness to be loving — *to be a match for love*. Ultimately, we will realize we are already divine Love itself.

Establishing abundance first is based on a fundamental metaphysical principle — we attract what we establish in mind and consciousness. Have you ever noticed that when you are in love, love is everywhere? It surrounds you, it lights up your life, and it meets you everywhere you go. Strangers on the street will smile and greet you; a heart-warming connection is palpable, undeniable. You are a love-magnet! The other side of that coin is when we want love so badly, when we *need* it, a healthy relationship will run from us! When we are miserable and just want someone to love us, when we need affirmation and appreciation — will someone give it to us? No. Not likely. Why not? We have become a love-repellent. People around us seem cold and uncaring; kindness and compassion are nowhere to be found. We might as well be a walking neon sign that declares "I need." That belief — "I need. I am without." — will demonstrate itself as sure as night follows day.

We might possibly attract a relationship with that consciousness, but most likely with another person who is also coming from need — not the recipe for a healthy match. Better to become who we are in the fullness of love by unfolding that divine potential within us, then attracting another who also realizes their wholeness. Not someone who is going to be our "better half," but someone who knows they are already whole. Freed from the limits of neediness, love can truly prosper the relationship. As Joseph Campbell wrote, "If you want the whole thing, the gods will give it to you. But you must be ready for it."[3]

If we are wise, once we understand that the origin of what we yearn for is within us, we will establish Self-realization as our highest priority. Meaningful thriving unfolds naturally from this awareness. We have an inner doorway into the infinite soul-mine of precious, prospering gems of radiant aliveness, wisdom, and fulfillment. All we need do is enter.

Find Your Within

If you get the inside right, the outside will fall into place.
Primary reality is within; secondary reality without.

— ECKHART TOLLE[4]

Sometimes we wonder how we can possibly give time to spiritual practice when our days are already full. If we are going to accomplish something in life, we need to put our time and energy into it. Usually, *all* our time and energy, right? The sages of all traditions, throughout time, have offered a different message: *Don't think so much about secondary things. If you put realization of the Truth at the center of your life, everything else will come to you with grace and ease.* One of my favorite verses from the Hebrew scriptures (Isaiah 40:31, KJV) reminds us, "They that wait upon the Lord shall renew their strength; they shall mount up with wings as eagles; they shall run, and not be weary; and they shall walk, and not faint." "Finding our within" is taking the time to shift our attention from the periphery of our awareness to the center, where our consciousness expands and we are inspired, energized, renewed, and revitalized.

Daily prayer and meditation help us return to the center, to live the life of the soul. Mahatma Gandhi said, "Silence is a great help to a seeker after truth. In the attitude of silence the soul finds the path in a clearer light and what is elusive and deceptive resolves itself into crystal clearness."[5] Prayer and meditation is our time to return to our Self. It's the best way to begin and end the day, but even better — it's the best way to live throughout the day. Again and again, we can redirect our attention from the noise of thoughts — from considerations of this or that — into our center, the divine Self. It's as easy as a conscious breath. As you breathe in, withdraw attention from externals and move your awareness into the chapel of your soul. Go in. Sit. Remember. It only takes a moment to reorient our attention. When we do, we open ourselves to the graceful flow of inspiration, strength, insight, and peace. It's there within us, awaiting our conscious recognition.

There's an App for That

In this age of technological gadgetry, programs for our computers and phones exist that will buzz gently or sound a bell at a determined interval to remind us to stop for a mindful moment, breathe, and return awareness to the deeper Self. While any of these might provide some assistance, the truth is, we already have the app. The app is our conscious awareness, and we can program it ourselves. Setting our "consciousness app" helps strengthen our experience of inner power, instead of thinking we need something external to wake us up. We don't.

Here's how to do it:

DECIDE. Set a clear intention that you will pause for moments of mindful reflection throughout your day.

PRACTICE. Pause right after you set the intention to feel what it is like. Take time to notice what it is like to be peacefully aware of your breath, of the sights and sounds around you. Soften your gaze. Let your awareness expand from your center. Feel your body relax and your mind become quiet.

PAY ATTENTION. You will naturally be inclined to turn your attention within many times during the day. It may occur as simply an arising of mindful awareness from within, or it may be prompted as a response to a sensory experience — the song of a bird, the sight of a child at play, or the beauty of a stream of car lights crossing a bridge at night. Notice how awareness touches the experience and expands, while the ordinary thinking mind connects with something and then contracts or narrows into commentary about it. In a mindful moment, the mental field is relatively quiet. Pay attention to this inclination for awareness to expand; that's your app letting you know it's time for a soul break.

Your consciousness app works best when you respond to it, when you pay attention and follow through by stopping to pause in the moment that it calls you to. It only takes a moment.

If you ignore the prompts, it stops reminding you. If you honor them, you will find your awareness expanding more often into the soul, even during activity. The practice of mindful moments increases our awareness of our essential nature over time, until our entire day becomes a rich tapestry of such moments of conscious awareness. We are living in the soul — a new peace dawns in our heart.

Let Your Mind Sink into Your Heart

We must each discover our way within. Meditation, prayer, walks in nature, dance, music, cooking — there are many ways to quiet the mind and inwardly walk through the soul's door.

Many creative people say that the key to their inspiration is found in nature. For some, it's as simple as a daily walk. Prolific author Stephen King advises aspiring writers about the importance of walking several miles every day. Daily nature breaks are valuable not just for the physical exercise and health benefits but to open our mind and imagination to the abundance that is so evident in nature.

Some days when I walk along the beach I see people running with their ear buds firmly in place listening to their devices, perhaps catching up on lectures or listening to books, music, or news. However, we also need space and time in our day for the mind and imagination to stretch out. We need open space for our thoughts to settle and for inspiration to arise. St. Augustine purportedly advised in Latin: *Solvitur ambulando.* "It is solved by walking."

At the next possible opportunity, take a walk or just sit outdoors with the intention of expanding your awareness. Take in the sights, sounds, smells, and textures of nature all around you. Let your thoughts become quiet. Notice the abundant energy of life in nature. Remember that this same abundance is inherent in your life and being.

When we do, we recognize and affirm that abundance is the natural experience of cosmic creation and the innate reality of our being; we practice mindful moments of remembering and experiencing wholeness. We practice inviting our narrow, ordinary thinking mind to "sink into the heart" — to expand our awareness beyond the confines of thought into the unbounded Self. These practices "seed" moments of remembrance when we need them most — those times when we forget the truth.

Waking Up to Abundance

The journey of spiritual awakening includes times of forgetting the truth of our being as well as times of remembering. As author and teacher Mark Nepo writes, "Just as we inhale and exhale constantly, our wakefulness ebbs and flows. The practice of being human is the practice of coming awake, staying awake and returning to wakefulness when we go to sleep."[6]

The process of remembering and forgetting — being anchored in the freedom and wisdom of our essential Self and then wrapped up in ego's cloak of fear and forgetfulness — is familiar to those of us who embark on the path of Self- and God-realization. Awakening is a transformational process. We discover we are not what we thought we were. We shed the old, erroneous identity of the false self — believing we are the body and the mind. That erroneous thought, called *avidya* in Sanskrit, is translated as "ignorance." We imagine ignorance to be something we do not yet know, but avidya is a qualitatively different kind of ignorance. It literally means "wrong knowledge." Our ignorance is not so much that we do not know. We know who we are. But we are wrong.

Once we encounter the truth about what we are, the journey of awakening begins. We hear the truth — an awakened spiritual teacher tells us, we read it in a book, or it arises spontaneously within.

We are not the body, mind, or personality we thought we were.

We are Spirit.

We are That.

When we meet the truth, we recognize it — like a long-lost relative we have always known. It resonates in our mind and stirs the soul. We can see through the dark veil that has shrouded our consciousness through the years. That veil is rent by the sword of truth, and the light of the Self shines through. It was that way for me when I met my spiritual teacher. I didn't know I was looking for truth, but of course I was. In 1979, I unsuspectingly went to a lecture by Roy Eugene Davis in a nearby town. He taught us to meditate and spoke about the direct path of spiritual awakening to our true Self — realizing the spiritual being we are, have always been, and ever will be. I felt as if my heart were awakening from a long slumber of living on the surface of my life. I remembered the depths — now I knew how to return, how to be restored to my original wholeness.

Then I forgot.

Overcoming the primary error, the misperception of identity that is the root of our suffering, must move from recognition to realization. We hear the truth, we recognize it, and then we must validate it in our experience. It has to become real for us, not just an intellectual understanding or even an intuitive perception. Fortunately for us, life is rigged in our favor. Awakening is both natural and destined to occur. We are certain to awaken at some point because it is simply the unfolding of the truth of our being. It is already there. Nothing external is needed, nothing is missing, nothing need be created. What we are is revealed, remembered, and then realized. We live into the truth of our being.

The Remembrance Sutras

The teachings of classical yoga are offered in sutra form. The Sanskrit word *sutra* means "thread." It is derived from the verb root *siv*, which means "to sew."[7] A sutra is a terse aphorism, a condensed statement that carries the depth of the philosophy being taught. Originally mnemonic aids that a student could chant and readily commit to memory, the concentrated sutra form captures not only the meaning of the philosophical principle but sparks memory of the teacher's commentary — a thread that connects to a great tapestry of knowledge.

What better way than sutra form to describe our spiritual journey of awakening, with its minicycles of forgetting and remembering?

Here is a simple four-sutra series I compiled as a condensed version of Vedic wisdom that we can easily relate to, remember, and use to consciously connect us to that vast ocean of divine inspiration:

It is.
We are It.
We forget.
We remember.[8]

IT IS: One Ultimate Reality alone exists. It is the source and substance of all that is.

WE ARE IT: Since there is only one omnipresent Ultimate Reality, we cannot be other than that. As an extension of this single reality, we have the inherent ability to experience it directly — to awaken and remember our essential nature.

WE FORGET: Identification with the mind and the body veils our perception of the spiritual reality of our being, causing us to temporarily forget the truth of what we are.

WE REMEMBER: Revelation of the divine truth of our nature is unavoidable; spiritual awakening is the purpose of life and the certain destiny of every person. The way of remembrance is yoga, a combination of self-discipline and divine grace.

A New Day Dawns

Years ago, I took a walk near the ocean and had an insight that transformed my way of thinking. Today I'm certain that because of that insight — that moment of divine remembrance — and the resultant change in my consciousness, the course of my life changed for the better.

I set out on that walk because my mind was troubled. I was "stuck" — my mind churning through old hurts, perceived slights, and unmet desires. I wanted something to go my way that was not forthcoming. All I could think about was what I did not have. My thoughts kept returning to what I could do to get what I wanted, building a case for how I was "right," and feeling upset about how things were. Fortunately for me, things were about to change.

That spot on the Pacific Coast has a breathtaking panoramic view. I walked down a long pier to where it seemed I could see forever. As I stood there fuming and looking out at the great expanse of ocean, I happened to glance down at the pier under my feet. It might have rained recently, or perhaps a wave had earlier reached the top of the pier and left some water behind. Whatever the source, right next to where I was standing was a little puddle of water. In the kind of inspired leap of insight that's infused with divine grace, I thought, *That's it! Here I am, fixated on a tiny puddle, when the entire ocean stands before me. Is it possible that I am so focused on the thing that I want that I cannot even see the abundance that life would offer me if only I would let go?* In that moment, I let go. No longer willing to cling to a sad little shred of "could-be, if-only," I remembered the expansive truth of my being and let go into Oneness instead.

As it often turns out, what I thought I wanted was not the highest good for me. Once I let go, I could see the error in my thinking. I began to notice new possibilities. I opened my mind to the abundant goodness life was already offering me.

Whenever we put ourselves in a box of limitation, we *feel* it. It hurts — the mind thrashes like a fish out of water. We struggle, trying to find our way back to our center, back to the ocean of freedom and power within us. We try to figure out what to do, how we can regain our happiness and peace of mind. The harder we try to find a solution, the more one escapes us. We need to return to the Self. When we do, a solution will emerge. A sleepless night spent tossing and turning — then, the sun rises, the fog clears, and we can see the way things are.

A new day dawns. Nothing lacking — the radiant, abundant reality of Spirit pervades the universe. It brings forth out of itself whatever is needed to fulfill its purposes. We are one with the Source. We are abundant.

Seven

The Streams of Happiness and the Ocean of Bliss

*Your soul, being a reflection of the ever-joyous Spirit,
is, in essence, happiness itself.*

— PARAMAHANSA YOGANANDA

*H*appiness has many hues. We experience it in various ways, such as satisfaction, pleasure, delight, contentment, joy, and bliss. What is it, really? Where does it come from? What is the source of happiness?

When Paramahansa Yogananda came from India to America in 1920, his first formal speech delivered at an International Congress of Religious Liberals was titled "The Science of Religion." The title sounds like it was a treatise on comparative religions, but it was not. That speech, which is available today as a little book of the same title, is a systematic, reasoned argument that explores what we truly want and how we can find it.[1] His conclusion: We all want happiness. He was right.

If we look deeply, we can see that our basic drive is to avoid suffering and to experience happiness. What most people do not realize, Yogananda reasoned, is that this universal search for happiness — common to all people at all times — is actually our search for God. It is our search to realize our true Self, our quest for a spiritually awakened, fulfilled life. How did Yogananda make that leap in logic? He made that leap like this. Ask yourself: *Do I want to be happy?* Then ask: *Do I want happiness today and suffering tomorrow?* Likely your response to the second question is no. No, we do not want happiness that is taken away in a moment's time. The happiness we want is happiness that is unconditional — happiness that does not change, that cannot be affected by circumstances or taken away from us.

What we are looking for, Yogananda concluded, is not the temporary happiness we experience as pleasure — not the result of anything external, the satisfaction of any desire or change in circumstances — but the higher, unconditional happiness that is bliss. The bliss that we seek is a divine quality inherent to the soul. Its origin is the presence of God — the blissful divine Self — within us. When this is truly understood, we can see that what we are all seeking is nothing less than God or Spirit.

To recognize this fundamental longing of the soul to realize its own joy is to peer into the mystical heart of the world's religions. We are all on the soul's journey in search of the highest happiness. Spiritually conscious people recognize that even though we have different approaches to the divine — different rituals, names, forms, and ideas of it — we are worshiping one Ultimate Reality. This awareness was clear to the *rishis* and *rishikas*, the awakened men and women of ancient India, whose revelation is recorded in the Rig Veda: "Truth is one, the sages call it by different names."[2]

Beyond intellectual knowledge or debate about the Source of happiness, Yogananda pointed to yoga's scientific approach to *realization* of the divine Self. We can discover, and validate, the truth ourselves. Yoga's invitation is for us to see that, not only do we seek and worship the same Ultimate Reality, our longing to realize it is the universal longing of every soul. Without recognizing the nature of that yearning and how it is satisfied, we are apt to wander through the world searching in vain for it and fighting over what we think it is. Words attributed to the Buddha sum it up:

> *For greater than all the joys*
> *Of heaven and of earth,*
> *Greater still than dominion*
> *Over all the worlds,*
> *Is the joy of reaching the stream.*[3]

To discover bliss is to discover our essential Self, which is the Self of all. The happiness we're looking for can be found within, but first we must learn how to find it, recognize it in its many derivative forms, and stay in contact with it.

Finding the Streams of Happiness

We can easily verify that the search for happiness is a fundamental motivation underlying all that we do. From the moment we get up in the morning, we are on a quest to avoid suffering and gather as much happiness as possible — from mundane desires to satisfy hunger or thirst to our search for comforts and pleasures, and even to our higher aspirations for connection and meaning. All have one thing in common: Like a trained hound on a hunt, they are aimed at happiness.

Simply inquiring into the nature of happiness will instigate positive changes. Observe yourself. Inquire: *What makes me happy?* Explore what happiness is for you. At the end of the day, take a quick happiness assessment. Ask: *Did I experience happiness today?* If yes, what was it? If no, why not? What do you think was the obstacle?

See if you can perceive the drive to find happiness behind your desires throughout the day. Notice what you want. Ask if behind that drive is a desire for happiness, some form of satisfaction, or avoidance of pain or suffering. Then ask if getting what you want can bring the happiness you seek.

Often the satisfaction of a desire will momentarily quiet the mind. That inner calm allows our innate joy to arise. The thing we acquired or the situation we found did not *create* the happiness. It was ours to begin with, just obscured by our restless desire to possess that thing. If we are not aware of how that works, we say, *Yes, satisfying this desire does make me happy!* The next question is: If we associate our happiness with what we acquire or achieve, how long will it last?

This process of inquiry is not to say that we shouldn't have desires or experience the happiness that arises when they are fulfilled. Rather, it's a simple but powerful tool to help us discern the distinction between fleeting pleasures and the innate joy of the soul. When we become skillful at this process of inquiry and readily discern the source of happiness, we are freer to make choices that serve us well.

There Is Pleasure

The Buddha said, "There is pleasure and there is bliss. Forgo the first to possess the second."[4] Does this mean that to experience bliss we must avoid pleasure? Heavens, no! Even the Buddha's experiments with pleasureless asceticism led him to the middle way of moderation.

Life is, fortunately, permeated with pleasure. Pleasure is unavoidable and experienced in ways great and small. When we are thirsty and we have a drink of water, we experience pleasure. When we work diligently toward a goal and it is accomplished, we experience pleasure. What is helpful is to understand the difference between pleasure and bliss. Thankfully, it is simple to make that distinction. Pleasure comes to us as the result of satisfying desires. The satisfaction of desires is always limited and potentially problematic. The satisfaction of desire generally leads to more desire. If we are not attentive, we can bind ourselves to certain desires. Bliss, however, is innate. It is unconditional; it is not the result of anything. No desire needs to be satisfied to experience it. It is a divine quality of the soul that is revealed when the mental field is calm and we are aware. We are not required to give up pleasure to know bliss. We are advised, however, to know which is which — and not lose the joy we already have while we look everywhere else for happiness.

The most transitory happiness we experience is physical. When a desire related to the senses is fulfilled, we experience relief and happiness but soon find that particular form of pleasure to be short-lived. After our bellies are filled, we are hungry again.

The happiness we experience when we set goals and reach them, or succeed in life, stays with us longer. Even more enduring than that is the happiness we experience when we serve life by selflessly helping others. Being of service to others brings a deep and long-lasting sense of inner peace and happiness.

Beyond all of those, however, is the highest happiness. The highest happiness is the bliss we experience through Self-knowing, through realizing our true nature. When we experience our essential nature, we discover our innate wholeness. That experience is free from desire. Nothing needs to be added or attained for us to be happy. We are inherently blissful.

Waking Up to Joy

Spiritual realization puts us in touch with the soul's bliss. As we experience it more frequently, it's enjoyable for us and uplifts those around us. To be a divine instrument uplifting others with joy is one of the simplest, most accessible, and profound ways to live prosperously.

Bliss is unconditional and available to us anytime we connect with it. How do we do that? Here are three steps we can take:

1. Get to know innate joy by experiencing it regularly after meditation.
2. Affirm that your joy is there.
3. Let go of beliefs that interfere with your ability to access joy.

Experience Innate Joy Regularly

*Learn to carry all the conditions of happiness within yourself
by meditating and attuning your consciousness to the ever-existing,
ever-conscious, ever-new Joy, which is God.*

— Paramahansa Yogananda[5]

An excellent time to touch our innate happiness and invite it to arise more fully is right after meditation. When we meditate superconsciously, thoughts settle and awareness expands into the unbounded divine Self. We abide there — conscious, serene, and observant. Thoughts may arise, but they can be easily ignored as we continue to experience a more expansive consciousness. In the moments immediately following meditation, take some time to cultivate awareness of the unshakable happiness or bliss that is the joy of Self-knowing. Do this by observing your natural state when you are relaxed, relatively thought-free, and aware of your higher true Self. *Notice how you feel.* There will be a pervasive sense of peace, wholeness, and contentment.

When the mind is restless, the body is also restless, and desires are stirred. We feel the need to do or have something — the urge to get moving! But right after superconscious meditation, when the mental field is still calm, it's possible to experience the calm and perfect joy of Self-knowing, of Self-remembrance. With this awareness, peace pervades the body and mind. We feel complete, no rush to go anywhere or do anything. Be aware of that. When you are, make a mental note of it — inwardly record what it is like. Remind yourself that this wholeness, this innate happiness, is always there.

When cultivating awareness of joy becomes a regular practice, joy will arise later in the day on its own. Like rays of the sun breaking through the clouds, you'll find joy shining through your heart and your mind, radiating through your smile.

Affirm Your Joy

The question often arises: If happiness is innate, why are so many people unhappy? Why are we continually seeking happiness, and why does it elude us? The key lies in understanding the role of the ego. Ego is one of the functions of the mind. It plays an important role by allowing us to express our individuality and interact with others. However, the downside is that ego constructs a false self that attempts to usurp the rightful role of the true Self. Although the ego is just a function of the mind that is made conscious through the presence of the Self, it will attempt to claim that consciousness as its own. Ego says, "I know" and "I do," falsely claiming to be the true Self.

Ego goes about building a separate (false or illusional) self by establishing a persona based on likes and dislikes. Because the ego is a mental construct founded on the false assumption that we are separate from the Source, that viewpoint will always convey a pervasive sense of "something missing." Mistakenly "cut off" from our own completeness by this ruse of the ego, we continually search for it. Engaging in the ongoing search for happiness and fulfillment allows the ego to maintain the illusion that there is something missing. Here is something to consider: *Underlying our persistent search for happiness is the ego's unrelenting dedication to unhappiness.*

The moment we are truly fulfilled, the moment we awaken to our wholeness, the ego is out of a job. No more searching for that external something that will make us okay, no more quest for what's missing. When we realize nothing is missing, when we know we are inherently enough, the ego's racket is over. The first old belief to let go of is the one that says we need something or someone to make us whole. We are already whole. We can give up the endless search for lasting happiness and claim it instead. We can affirm it: *I am a joyful soul! Joy permeates my heart, my mind, and my body. I overflow with joy this moment and every moment.*

Release Joyless Beliefs

Beyond the ego's tenacious commitment to suffering, other beliefs can interfere with our ability to experience happiness, such as those inherited from family or culture. I have known people who discovered they had unconsciously adopted a family pattern of unhappiness, fear, or insecurity. As children, surrounded by others who were unhappy, they decided this was the way to be. Not only that, they decided that being happy would be disloyal to the family system. It sounds so odd to think we might inwardly agree not to be happy, yet many do this. Thankfully, it's easy enough to undo by becoming aware of it and declaring our own freedom to be happy. Because we are all connected, our willingness to be happy can positively impact our family as well.

Another common belief that blocks happiness is the idea that it's selfish to be happy when so many people around us, or in the world, are suffering. This, too, can be easily remedied by becoming aware that our happiness doesn't take away from the happiness of others — it contributes to it. Being happy doesn't mean we lack awareness of suffering. Boldly embracing our inherent happiness in the face of suffering enables us to be more skillful in doing something about it.

If we allow ourselves to be brought down by conditions, how can we constructively participate in changing them? Just as anger and fear can be contagious, so can happiness. Let your innate joy blossom and share the sweet fragrance of it with those around you. The Buddhist monk and peace activist Thich Nhat Hanh, who has known great suffering in life, suggests smiling as a spiritual practice. We can smile gently, even in the face of sorrow. This, he says, is a practice of declaring that we are greater than our sorrows. Practice smiling the smile of the Buddha and dwelling in the joyful realization of your true Self.

The Ocean of Bliss

This joy that I have, the world didn't give it to me.
The world didn't give it and the world can't take it away.
— Shirley Caesar, "This Joy I Have"

When the renowned mythologist Joseph Campbell offered his now-famous injunction to "follow your bliss," it was frequently misunderstood as a call to personal pleasure, first and foremost. Joseph Campbell, however, was well-versed in Vedic wisdom and understood that the life journey of following our bliss is not the way of pleasure-seeking but the way of soul-seeking — the hero's journey of following the soul's ananda, bliss, or joy.

While pleasure may certainly be a part of what we discover along the way, it's seen for what it is: temporary. In contrast to the fickle nature of pleasure, the soul's joy, the inherent bliss of the Self, is not temporary. It's not conditional, changeable, or fleeting. It's the revelation of the wholeness or fullness of our essential nature. Prosperity is its natural expression. When we realize that at the core of our being there is nothing lacking, we're freed from the ever-turning wheel of desire for more and more. Once we see that our highest happiness does not come from the fulfillment of desire, we're free to enjoy life as it is. Our bliss is the experience of Self-revelation, the perfect joy of Self-knowledge.

Staying Connected to Bliss

What's the true meaning of following our bliss? In order to follow something like a trail in the woods, or even to follow another person's lead, we have to pay attention to two things: where we are in the moment, and where (or how) the way is unfolding before us. We must notice, stay present and connected to our Self, and respond to what is occurring. Like a meditation on the breath, we must always begin with the deeper connection to our Self. We cannot use our awareness to follow the breath if we are distracted by our attention flitting about, moving from one thought to another. We must detach our awareness from restless thoughts and anchor it on the breath — feel the breath in the body, notice what is arising in the body and mind, and keep returning to the point of focus. Following our bliss works exactly like that. It's a matter of staying connected to our essential Self, then thinking, speaking, and acting in ways that enhance and support that connection.

Our ability to follow our bliss by being mindfully aware of our essential wholeness determines the kind of life we live. Especially as we prosper, this is crucial. It's our top strategy to avoid getting lost — it's how we avoid losing our Self.

The Hindu epic the Mahabharata contains a profound teaching about our ability to keep, or lose, our inherent bliss. In the story, Yudhishthira, the eldest of the righteous Pandava brothers, allows himself to be enticed into a game of dice. He gambles, risks, and loses everything, including the entire kingdom that he and his brother princes are entitled to. He plays round after round, losing more each time, thinking that with just the next roll of the dice, he will win. Watching the scene unfold, we wonder: *How could he be so foolish as to gamble away everything that is truly of value? Where are his priorities?* Yet, the story portrays epic truths about the human condition. When we view it in that light, we have to ask ourselves how it is that we often gamble and lose what is most important to us.

The Gamble

When we're willing to look at our lives, we see that we gamble all the time. Sometimes we imagine we can ignore the promptings of the soul without suffering as a result, such as thinking we can put all of our life force into outer pursuits while our spiritual life waits, or expecting that our health will continue to flourish when we don't follow a healthy lifestyle, or imagining that spending time with those nearest and dearest to us can wait while we relentlessly pursue our career. Where are our priorities? Are we able to see when we're gambling with our very life or are we too caught up in the frenzy like Yudhishthira, thinking somehow we can afford the risk?

First, Yudhishthira loses all his material possessions, then he begins to wager his relationships — offering his army, his servants, his brothers, and finally, even his wife, Draupadi. The crux of the teaching is brought home by Draupadi when she is dragged before the winners to be surrendered to the ego-driven Kauravas. She asks, "Tell me, which did Yudhishthira lose first — himself or me?" She is aware that only by losing conscious awareness of himself could he have gambled away his relationship with her. She represents Shakti, our divine life force. Only by losing conscious contact with our divine Self do we lose our bliss, our creative energy, our Shakti, our joy. Imagine: How many failed marriages, business deals gone awry, or creative projects lost could be traced to that fateful loss of the Self?

Returning to Fullness

Nothing — no circumstance; no person, event, or obstacle — can take our bliss from us. Our bliss only "leaves" us when we lose awareness of our true Self. There are times when something happens and we lose track of the bliss trail — someone does something that angers or hurts us, we make a mistake, difficult circumstances arise, or we unconsciously fall into a mood. We can use that occasion as an opportunity for spiritual practice. Inquire. Instead of becoming too involved in the challenge or struggle, we can look at how we allow ourselves to lose our bliss, how we gamble or give it away. We can take it back by returning to the fullness of our divine Self, remembering that the joy we have is abundantly, inherently ours. No one gives it to us. No one can take it away.

Eight

Embrace Your Divine Destiny

You must return with the bliss and integrate it.
— Joseph Campbell

We wake up. We discover who we are as spiritual beings and realize that unconditional happiness — bliss — is inherent to our soul. The happiness we have been seeking all our life is at hand. Then what? Then we take the next step on our soul journey of prosperity and live it. Living it is the way we grow up.

Integrating our bliss is how we mature, how we ripen as human beings, prosper, and realize our potential.

What we do, how we engage fully in life, is the pathway for our prosperity to be realized. Although we are inherently prosperous, prosperity is not a static state. It is a divine destiny, waiting for us to step forth into it. That step, even though it is toward our Self, can seem like the most terrifying step we have ever taken. We are about to cross the chasm between who we thought we were with our doubts and self-imposed limitations and discover what becomes possible when we open ourselves to divine grace and power. Arriving at that chasm stretching between the small self and the great Self is a moment of profound grace. What does this moment hold? Love and fear, Self-knowing and doubt, courage and resistance. Which will we choose?

Like many steps we take along the spiritual path of awakening, we are following in the footsteps of those who have made this journey before. We are following a universal pattern of the soul's unfolding, though, paradoxically, we can only do that in our unique way. Sri Aurobindo, in his commentary on the Bhagavad Gita, wrote:

> The supreme, the faultless largest law of action is to find out the truth of your own highest and inmost existence and live in it and not to follow any outer standard. . . . Know then your self; know your true self to be God and one with the self of all others; know your soul to be a portion of God.[1]

Traveling west, we can hear it from Ralph Waldo Emerson, too:

> Trust thyself: every heart vibrates to that iron string. Accept the place the divine providence has found for you. . . . Great [souls] have always done so, and confided themselves child-like to the genius of their age, betraying their perception that the absolutely trustworthy was seated at their heart, working through their hands, predominating in all their being.[2]

The Precipice of Potential

On the soul journey of living our bliss and fulfilling our divine potential, we find a kindred soul with the warrior Arjuna in the Bhagavad Gita. The scripture opens with Arjuna in a funk. He's poised on the edge of that chasm of Self-actualization and about to step into fulfilling his potential when he loses heart. The paralysis of doubt sets in.

A consummate warrior, he has trained all his life for the battle he is about to face. He has what he needs. That is, all except one thing — Self-confidence, trust in his divine destiny. When he surveys the battlefield before him, he recognizes his own relatives — uncles, teachers, cousins. These "relatives" represent his own lower tendencies, attachments, and self-imposed limitations that will have to be overcome if he is going to prosper. Looking at what it's going to take, Arjuna stops short. In a familiar moment of self-doubt, he throws down his bow and declares, "I won't fight." How many of us have stood on that precipice of potential and declared, "I won't"? *I won't write that thesis; I won't make that call; I won't speak my truth; I won't apply; I won't submit my work; I won't fight for what is mine; I won't move on. I won't.*

Fortunately for Arjuna, and for us, that moment of resistance is not the end. It's a beginning. In his resistance — throwing down his bow and refusing to fight — he becomes silent, and the still small voice — the voice of the divine within him — begins to speak. This is represented by the words of Krishna, the divine Presence seated in the heart of all. The divine dialogue begins in this moment of crisis, when there is a conflict between what is known at the soul level and what is being rationalized by ego. When the mind becomes still, inner wisdom opens.

Be Still and Know

Like a galloping horse,
the mind can run far...
A man of knowledge
keeps it under control
with the reins of his breath
and with discrimination.

— LALLESHWARI[3]

Krishna reminds Arjuna of the truth of his being and the fact that he is here to express it. He gives him the spiritual insight he needs to take that critical step: *Soul is superior to mind, mind is superior to body.*

"Yoga," he says, "is evenness of mind."[4]

Arjuna has let his doubt-filled mind keep him from moving forward. One who is spiritually awake learns mastery over thoughts and feelings — they no longer get to run the show. Krishna introduces him to yoga as "evenness of mind," which becomes "skill in action" — the ability to withdraw attention from what is not useful, turn it toward that which serves our higher purpose, and move into action. Not to be mistaken for suppression or denial, it is using the reins of our discrimination to guide the steed of the mind. It's the skill we need to make the leap beyond self-doubt and fear. It takes mindful awareness — supported by meditation, discernment, and nonattachment.

Turn the Mind from Worry to Worship

One night I got a call from Alan, a young man I've known for many years who was about to begin his first job related to his life's work as a teacher. It was a dream job teaching language arts at a local high school. The new teaching credential on his wall was the culmination of years of study and internship as a teaching aide. He was ready for his solo flight, piloting his own classroom. Yet, on the eve of beginning this life work, he was talking himself into a fit of anxiety over every perceived shortcoming, everything that could possibly go wrong — literally making himself sick. He had already failed and the job had not even begun.

I could see he needed to master his attention, to turn his mind from "worry to worship" — instead of being caught in the whirl of worried thoughts, he could pause, lift his awareness, and recognize the divine power within, already at work in his life. I reminded him that a stream of divine grace had brought him to this time of opportunity and it was still carrying him. He had a choice: He could relax a bit and float on this stream or go to meet his prosperity thrashing about for his very life.

It's not that we are not willing, or even that we are not ready, at this critical juncture. It's a case of the small self attempting to hold fast to its territory of limitation. Just as we are about to take that step — say yes to that dream job, make the proposal, take the call — the ego digs in its little heels and creates a dust storm of worries and doubts in the mental field. All of a sudden, we are in the midst of a "what-if " storm. Just as Krishna instructed Arjuna, we, too, can discover the soul is greater than the mind.

We have the power to command the wind of worry: *Peace, be still!*

When we do, we begin to live with confidence in the infinite divine Self, to have faith in that which we are, and that which is ours to do.

Seven Marks of *Svadharma*

The two essential life streams — living with higher purpose (dharma) and prosperity (artha) — merge as we integrate our bliss by doing what is ours to do. This is *svadharma* — fulfilling our own natural duty, embracing our divine destiny. Svadharma is the unique expression of our spiritual purpose, which does not follow any outer standard but is guided by our obligation toward our own nature. We follow our dream to the place divine providence has prepared for us. Svardharma arises from our talents, dreams, obligations to our nature, relationship to family and society, and the divine evolutionary call of the place and time we live in.

In Western culture, identifying our life purpose often seems like a great mystery. When I teach about this juncture of purpose and prosperity, many students are not certain how to identify, or claim, what is theirs to do. Sometimes it is an abundance dilemma: There are so many interests, so many possibilities, how to choose one thing as "it"? Other times it's a sense of nothing seeming grand enough: There's working at a useful, but uninteresting, job; raising a family; serving in the community — all good, but nothing that feels like a life quest. Or it's a life unexamined. Or sometimes the pull of purpose is there but not the courage to name it or live it.

At the core, life purpose is about being who we are in fullness. It is not a job or a project — it's the art of living as the divine being we are. Whatever we do is simply a vehicle for that divine potential to express and serve.

What follows are seven marks of svadharma, seven ways to consider what is ours to do:

> It contributes to the welfare of all. Our specific purpose — svadharma — is a subset of dharma: cosmic order, divine evolutionary intent, and the fulfillment of higher purpose for all creation. We cannot have a genuine life purpose that does not serve Spirit.
>
> It supports our maturity — our soul unfoldment and development of our character. Through engaging in what is ours to do, we awaken spiritually and ripen into compassionate and wise human beings. It offers ample opportunities to fulfill our potential.
>
> Our purpose is in harmony with our inner disposition, inclinations, or makeup. What we are called to do, and to be, is in complete agreement with our innate potentials.
>
> It unfolds with grace. It is natural to us, like breathing. Even though it may feel difficult or challenging, or we need training to become skillful, it is a recognizable comfort zone.

LIVING OUR PURPOSE MAKES OUR HEART SING WITH JOY. It's soul-satisfying. It enhances our vitality, our felt sense of being fully alive.

WHAT WE DO IS NOT DRIVEN BY RESULTS OR ATTACHMENT TO THE OUTCOME. The joy is in the doing, the opportunity it offers to serve — for us to wake up, grow up, and show up. If there were no paycheck or product attached to it, if no one ever saw it, or appreciated it, we would do it anyway.

WE SEE AN OPPORTUNITY TO SERVE — IT IS REVEALED TO US AND ALLOWS US TO EXPRESS OUR POTENTIAL. We hear the song, recognize the possibility, or see what is missing and know it is ours to do. Those who don't own their life purpose often give suggestions to others about what they could or should do while their own life purpose languishes in the shadows. When we know what is ours to do, we get on with it, rather than pointing out to others the opportunities we see for them.

Inexplicable, Precious, Prosperous

Even without considering the seven marks of svadharma, most of us already know about our purpose, mysterious as it may be. Why? Because it is something that has been with us all along; it's not something we choose separate from being who we already are. It's a precious thread in the tapestry of our life — either in the foreground or the background. But it is there, nevertheless; it's always been there. If you talk with someone who has named their purpose, that is what they will tell you. It makes sense.

Expressing our unique nature and purpose doesn't just start at some point of revelation in adulthood; it's there in its nascent stage in our early years, too. I ask people: What is that thread of interest or inclination that has always been with you? What is it that you have cared about all your life? What captured your heart as a child? What qualities can you see in your young self that remain important today?

Several years ago, I was riding on a train from Los Angeles to San Jose, which had been chartered as a "peace train" in commemoration of the tenth anniversary of "Season for Nonviolence," the dynamic, grassroots movement cofounded by Dr. Arun Gandhi and the Association for Global New Thought to raise awareness of the power of nonviolence.[5] I was watching and listening to Dolores Huerta — the social justice activist, community organizer, advocate for the rights of farmworkers and of women, and cofounder with Cesar Chavez of the National Farm Workers Association. Dolores was talking informally with a small group that had gathered, eager to learn from her. Vibrant, clear, and focused, her energy seemed unstoppable and her enthusiasm for what can be done when people bring their energy together was contagious. At that time, she was seventy-seven years old — a font of overflowing vitality and inspiration. I remember thinking, *This is what it looks like when someone knows their purpose and is living it.*

At a private meeting with her later, I asked what motivated her work for justice. I wanted to know what fueled her seemingly tireless engagement. Like all of us, there are many threads in the tapestry of Dolores Huerta's life of purpose — including her talents, dreams, the time and place she was born, and her steadfast commitment to her spiritual life.

She told me how she began her work as a first-grade teacher in a classroom full of farmworker's children. They were eager to learn, but they came to school each day without shoes or breakfast, and she realized the inequality at the root of that situation would have to be addressed if those children, and others like them, were going to live better lives. She saw the opportunity, knew the possibility, and recognized what was hers to do.

The fire lit in her heart turned to activism for economic justice, which to this day includes work for a better future for all, and especially for women and children. Elsewhere, she said:

> What I would like to leave behind is for people to realize that they have power and they need to use it. Every one of us has power. We need to use it and not be afraid to use it. We need to share what we learn. We have to go beyond our own fears. If we don't come out of our own comfort zone, we can't do anything.[6]

In 2012, at the age of eighty-two still fully engaged in service, Dolores Huerta was awarded the highest civilian award in the United States by President Barack Obama — the prestigious Presidential Medal of Freedom. President Obama introduced the awards that evening by saying,

> This is the highest civilian honor this country can bestow, which is ironic because nobody sets out to win it....That wasn't in the plan.... What sets these men and women apart is the incredible impact they have had on so many people — not in short, blinding bursts, but steadily, over the course of a lifetime.[7]

It's the sure, steady, prosperous sign of living with higher purpose.

As much as we might like to imagine it, integrating our bliss and embracing our divine destiny does not culminate in taking our seat in the comfort zone in the game of life. It's not a place we arrive and sit back. Arjuna tried making his case for that: "No, I won't fight, I won't engage, I won't participate." Inaction is not the way. The way is skill in action.

It's taking our bliss with us into the world and lighting it up.

PART III

A Skillful Way

How to Realize Fulfillment

Nine

What We Really Want

Show us the path that says, "stand up, get going, do it!"
which resurrects us from the slumber of the drugged
and leads to the consummation of Heart's desire,
like all the stars and galaxies in tune, in time, straight on.

— NEIL DOUGLAS-KLOTZ

We are multifaceted beings, and as we awaken spiritually, the richness of our composite self becomes even more apparent. Prior to awakening, most of us experience the physical, mental, and emotional aspects of our being, but we rarely see into the subtle permutations of the mental field, nor understand how all the functions arise from, and connect to, the soul. If we are spiritually oriented but caught in the limited egoic perception of ordinary mind, we believe we "have a soul." As we start to wake up, we experience and know that we are not the body-mind that "has a soul" — we are, indeed, the soul itself. And that which we are, the inner light of Supreme Consciousness that we call soul, or the divine Self, illumines all the functions of the mind and body. With this revelation, we begin to have greater access to the subtle functions of mind, making a life of Self-referral possible. We can live a soul-guided life. But what does that look like? On any given day, how do we determine our priorities? How do we set ourselves on a prosperity course?

The body with its delights, pains, and hungers; the mind with its sensory pull, vortices of thought, and higher judicial courts of decision making; and the soul's peace, clarity, and joy are like streams rushing toward us all at once. Which stream do we travel? Where will each take us? Which do we pay attention to? If we aren't sufficiently aware, and don't have a sense of higher purpose and worthwhile goals shining a light on our path, we can easily get pulled downstream by the sheer force of the inner and outer demands for our time and attention.

A teaching story from the Sufi tradition reminds us of this possibility of our life force running away without discernment or direction. The wise fool Mullah Nasruddin is spotted riding a horse galloping at top speed, careening through the main street of town. His friend shouts to him as he goes by, "Mullah, where are you going?" "I don't know," Mullah yells back. "Ask the horse."

I've surely felt that way at times, and I know many others who do, such as the young parents I teach who are balancing spiritual practice, career development, child raising, and self-care (usually last on the list). They have the desire to meditate, study, attend retreats, and offer service, but they are juggling an overfull, demanding work schedule, weekend food shopping, midweek meal preparation, and their children's activities and school obligations, such as figuring out how they can make it to their third-grader's open-school night to meet the teacher. Some add the need to support an ill parent or close friend, along with challenges to their own health, relationships, or finances. Where are they going? How do they begin to sort it out?

Fortunately, yoga's spiritual practice for intentional living is doable at every stage of life — whether we are students, young adults, new parents, middle aged, or elders. Yoga is supportive of discerning what we really want and need at any given time by creating an atmosphere conducive to Self-referral through the balance of body-mind-spirit. We arrange conditions within and around us to encourage the prosperous flow of energy in our life.

What's Most Important

An ancient Vedic story in the Brihadaranyaka Upanishad illustrates how the various components of our being must work in harmony. In the story, several of these vital functions are overcome with pride and start arguing over which is the most essential. They can't agree because each one says, "I am the most important!" Speech says, "I'm the essential one." So do the eyes, ears, mind, vital force, and even the semen! Since they can't reach a conclusion, they go to Brahma, the Creator of the universe, with their question. Brahma says, "That one is most important whose departure has the most profound ill effect on the body."

Each of the vital functions, convinced they are the most important, vows to prove it to the others. Speech is first and announces it will depart for a year, thinking the others will be incapacitated without it. "You'll miss me!" When speech returns, the question is asked, "What was life like without speech?" "Well," the others report, "it was quiet. But other than that, everything continued as normal." "Okay, then," say the eyes, "watch this." The eyes depart for a year and return, but the reaction is the same: Other than not having sight, little changed. The same process continues with the other functions until it is finally the turn for vital force or energy. When energy starts to depart, it is immediately obvious that vital force supports all the other functions, and if it departs, the body will die. "Venerable sir," they cry, "do not go out. We shall not be able to live without you."[1]

We can live without sensory capacities, even for a time without food or water — but not so with vital force. This subtle vital force called *prana*, whose Sanskrit root means "to breathe forth," is the connecting link between the physical, mental, and spiritual dimensions of our being.

Prana acts as a courier for our awareness, allowing the mind, intellect, and intuition to investigate higher realities, leading up to the threshold of the highest realization. It allows us to breathe, sing, love, dance, create, worry, run, and imagine. All that we do depends on prana. It allows us to function, and it facilitates spiritual experience and perception. When the systems are out of balance, prana cannot flow efficiently. A body that is out of balance may be shouting the loudest, "I am most important!" While a worried mind insists, "I am the one you must listen to." What's happening? How do we discern? How do we find our way to our center?

Five Essential Layers

Yoga philosophy offers us several models for discerning, understanding, and working with the various components of the body and mind. One is the *panchakosha* model, meaning "five sheaths." It is a framework delineating five coverings surrounding the soul. The root derivation *kush* of the Sanskrit word *kosha* means "to enfold." To enfold describes more accurately the function of the *koshas*. They are coverings that enfold the Self, making physical expression, mental cognition, intellectual reasoning, intuitive ability, and Self-awareness possible.

The five koshas are:

> *Annamaya*: the physical sheath
> *Pranamaya*: the energy or vital force sheath
> *Manomaya*: the mental sheath

Vijnanamaya: the wisdom or intelligence sheath

Anandamaya: the bliss sheath

These five coverings of the soul are not physical or linearly arranged, as if they were bedcovers, stacked one upon the other. A
better analogy might be of Russian nesting dolls; each covering is
contained "inside" the others, but in truth, they are not actually separate — they overlap and interpenetrate one another like the color
spectrum in a rainbow. In this case, the physical body is the only visible covering, and the others are progressively subtler. These coverings, though not visible, are still tangible. We experience them. The
coverings exist from the periphery at the physical level to the most
interior at the spiritual level.

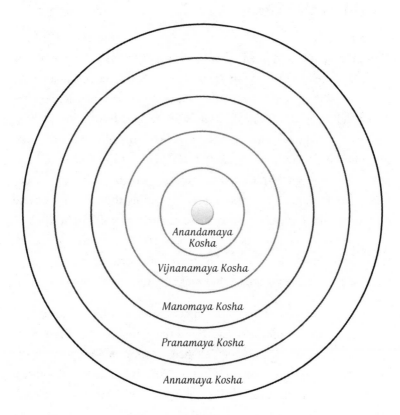

Each sheath name ends with *maya,* which is Sanskrit for "illusion," the cosmic principle of appearance. This refers to God's creative power. Maya indicates the insubstantial nature of what we are calling coverings, which are real but changeable. They are illusions of distinction shining forth from the One without distinction. There is only one Self, without division. There are no "parts" to our essential being, only wholeness. The apparent divisions refer to different functions, like different rooms in the house of the Self. Our task is to understand the *function* of the different sheaths and support their harmonious balance. That's what allows us to have a clear path of perception into the chamber of the soul.

Honor the Messenger: Nourish Your Energy

We can think of vital force as the "Queen" — the consort of the King, the divine Self. She is Shakti, the divine energy that has access to all the sheaths. The pranamaya kosha — the covering of vital force — is like a queen's attendant. It supports communication between the outer physical body and the inner sheaths of mind — connecting the physical with the subtle components of our being. Vital force is the divine messenger. It behooves us to nurture the messenger by paying attention to our energy — taking care to do those things that enhance and support it, and avoiding those behaviors and environments that weaken or deplete it. Perhaps you might think of your energy messenger as a sacred runner. To run the course between body, mind, and spirit, she must be fit. A runner who is out of shape cannot make it around the track.

We nourish our vital force by paying attention to what enhances and depletes it. Here are some of the things that enhance or uplift our energy: yogic breathing practices, silence, devotional practices, meditation, time in nature, and uplifting, joyful experiences with others. Things known to decrease energy are toxic environments, too much talking, worry, stress, or overextending ourselves. When we tune in to our energy level to observe how various environments, attitudes, and behaviors affect us, it is relatively easy to discern their influence. We feel it.

Ever notice how a conversation full of complaints (whether we are the speaker or the listener) leaves you drained? In contrast, a conversation that is about something positive — something that touches the heart of truth, even if difficult — leaves us with more energy, not less. When I'm checking in on my own vital force, I like to ask myself one question: *Am I living an energy-enhancing or an energy-depleting lifestyle right now?* If my answer is energy-depleting, then I have to ask how long I think I can do that before the body suffers as a result. How long can I navigate through my life without the benefit of deeper guidance that can only be reached when vital force can flow freely? Sometimes we think we don't have time to make necessary adjustments, even though we know they are needed. If that's the case, we can ask: *What's the cost of being out of balance?* Better yet: *What could I do right now that is a turn toward regaining my balance?*

It's up to us to be masters of our energy; no one else can do that for us.

Check for Flow

Next, we familiarize ourselves with the overall well-being of each "place" that vital force visits — the body and the various components of the mind. We can do that by paying attention to what our energetic access is like at any given time. If one of the "destinations" for vital force is out of balance, energy tends to get stopped there, and our full functionality is impaired. For example, when we don't take care of our physical body — when we have a poor diet or neglect needed exercise or rest — the body will send out distress signals. Our vital force and our attention will go there. It will be difficult to think — let alone reason or experience bliss. This same kind of imbalance can occur at any stop along the journey of our vital energy.

If the mental field is overcome with sensory desire, it will keep returning there, taking vital force along for the ride while discernment languishes by the wayside. If our faculty of discernment is out of balance, say with too much information or stimulus and not enough meditation to keep it clarified, energy will be playing the tennis game of doubt — traveling back and forth, back and forth, across the field of possibilities, while wisdom remains obscured.

Once we are familiar with the five sheaths and their functions, we can discern whether our energy is bogged down by imbalance at any juncture. We can then take remedial action to bring back balance and allow our vital force to flow freely once again.

Bring Back Balance

Several years ago, I suffered a torn rotator cuff in my left shoulder. Ouch! I was in constant pain, unable to lift my arm above my head or move it much beyond a sling position in front of my body. This is one of those injuries that comes with several options for healing — physical therapy, steroid injections, surgery, or healing on its own over time. My vital force was bogged down at the physical level.

I had an MRI to diagnose the exact nature and extent of the damage. Then I saw several specialists, whose recommendations fell into two main categories: have surgery or let it heal on its own. Even though I know the Self is always the true healer, I am not opposed to medical intervention to help it along.

Most of the experts urged surgery, though they admitted surgery doesn't always correct the problem or end the pain. However, if I let the injury try to heal on its own, I risked being left with a permanent inability to raise my arm. As you can imagine, my mental sheath was in high gear. What to do? I sat each day and watched my thoughts spin and my intellect zoom back and forth between those choices. One minute I was signing up for surgery, and the other I was declining it. I became weary as my energy messenger bogged down in pain, confusion, and doubt. The remedy? Encouragement, faith, and patience.

I knew that beyond the whirlwinds of pain and doubt was the clarity to be found at the deeper level of my wisdom sheath and the peace of my bliss sheath, situated as it is right next to the soul. I was encouraged by knowing those "destinations" were there; it bolstered my faith and my patience. It made all the difference. I sat. I breathed. I remembered that I had access to higher wisdom that would tell me what was right for me. When I reached that destination, I would know. *I would know because the energy would be connected through all the coverings.* Calm — the soul's peace — would pervade the body and mind. That is exactly what happened. At a certain point, I knew what to do. I knew it was best for me to let the body heal. It did, and without any lingering disability.

Travel the Subtle Pathway with Ease

Yoga's model of the five sheaths helps us discover the pathway from the outer, physical expression of our being to the innermost connection to the soul. Once we know this pathway, we can reliably "travel it." We can keep the various destinations along the way clear and balanced, allowing the path of vital force to be unobstructed. The soul's peaceful splendor and the higher mind's pearls of wisdom then arrive on time and in abundance, bringing the clarity we need to discern what is right for us, what we really want.

Radiant health, delight in life, abundant energy, discerning mind, compassionate heart, loving relationships, meaningful work — all are symptomatic of a prosperous life overflowing with vital force. Being in the flow of life's abundant blessings begins with our own energetic flow.

Ten

Meditate and Experience Wholeness

*The contemplative state may be compared to a bee buzzing around
a flower, about to alight on it and sip the nectar from it.
The state of meditation is reached when the bee is already seated
on the flower and has begun to taste the sweetness of the nectar.*

— SWAMI ADISWARANANDA

*T*here is a time-tested way into the sanctuary of the soul.
Through the step-by-step process of superconscious meditation, we can guide our attention and awareness to move
from the outer periphery of sensory perception and thought activity to rest in our essential, unbounded, spiritual nature — that
which is full, whole, and complete. The experience we have of our
essential nature is peace. This peace is the peace of the soul — the
nothing-is-lacking fullness of being. What does that mean to us in
practical terms? The short answer is fulfillment. The fulfillment that
changes everything.

How much time in any given day is spent thinking about what
we want or need? Without spiritual realization, we get caught up
in ego's error-driven ideas, thinking that to be fulfilled we need
to attain or accomplish something. Spiritual realization brings the

opposite perspective: First we experience and know our wholeness, then we freely participate in doing what is ours to do and having what we will have. None of that defines us. We are already whole and complete.

The idea of being fulfilled, just as we are, is compelling. A sigh of relief comes when we recognize we are already complete. Now we can free ourselves from the pernicious striving to be something or someone — constantly running on the treadmill toward an ever-receding horizon called "more." Yet the idea of fullness alone will not actually free us. Beyond grasping the concept, it's necessary to *experience* our wholeness. It's like the difference between reading the menu and eating the meal. Reading about, thinking about, even knowing about those delicious items on the menu will not give us a taste, satisfy our hunger, or nourish our body. Only eating the meal does that. So it is with spiritual knowledge. Information must be followed by realization through actual experience. And not just an occasional experience but regular, repeated experiences of super-consciousness.

When we meditate, our awareness expands beyond the confines of thought activity and we experience the Self, our essence, as whole. In this thought-free state, we know our wholeness to be true because we experience it. The key to true fulfillment in life is to know we are *already* full, whole, and complete. Then, whatever we choose to do, have, or be is an expression of that innate fullness.

Aham Brahmasmi: I Am That

Recognizing and remembering our own wholeness is the great antidote to various afflictive emotions and states of mind (such as fear, anger, or jealousy) that arise from ignorance of our essential Self. One of the great sayings of Vedanta, which is found in the

Brihadaranyaka Upanishad, is *"Aham Brahmasmi"*: "I am That," or "I am totality."[1]

If we identify with the personality or ego-self, we are prone to think we need something that will improve us. With spiritual awareness, we still engage in helpful activities that hone our skills, enrich our situation in life, and allow us to make a positive contribution to others — we just don't mistake what we have or do with what we are. We realize these things do not change the soul. Nothing improves or changes that. It's already complete. It is whole and unchanging. Knowing this frees us from restless striving, trying to be other than what we are, or attempting to fill a perceived lack that is not inherently true.

I once had a lovely conversation with a colleague about business and collaboration. We reflected on how true collaboration could be difficult if partners try to "get" something from one another. An underlying sense of scarcity, a belief that you do not have enough yourself, will undermine the potential for rich partnership. My friend said, "We are each already full, and from that fullness we can share with one another." A breath of fresh air! Her statement about fullness highlights the way to truly partner in any relationship. See yourself and others in the light of wholeness, lift up the divine potential of every encounter by knowing you are meeting soul to soul.

To live our fullness, we tune in to it. As our foundation, we can experience our fullness every morning in meditation as we start our day. Then, throughout the day, use discernment to remember that innate sufficiency. Always carry the jewel of abundance — awareness of your soul riches — with you. If you catch yourself thinking you need someone else's approval or wanting something in order to "improve" — come back to your divine Self. Say to yourself: *I am full. I am whole. I am totality.* Then decide what you want, need, or can contribute.

Superconscious Meditation

Meditate! The greatest thing is meditation. It is the nearest approach to
spiritual life – the mind meditating. It is the one moment in our daily
life that we are not at all material – the Soul thinking of itself, free
from all matter – this marvelous touch of the Soul.

— Swami Vivekananda[2]

Superconscious meditation is the most effective tool we have for enhanced well-being and spiritual realization. Although many different techniques may be used as preparation for superconscious meditation, the ultimate goal is always the same: conscious, direct experience of our essential Self. "Superconscious" refers to a heightened level of awareness. In this term, *super* means superior to, above, or beyond ordinary fragmented states of consciousness, which confine, blur, or restrict awareness. During superconscious meditation, our attention and awareness are intentionally directed toward, and ultimately flow unimpeded to, the unbounded, unchanging field of pure existence-being. When our awareness expands beyond the restrictive influences of thought, emotion, or mental modifications, we experience our spiritual nature. No longer confined or obscured by changes in the mental field, our awareness naturally abides in our essence, which is pure (unmodified), still (unchanging), and eternally conscious. Superconscious meditation is samadhi, the realization of Oneness — Self-realization.

Anyone who has sincerely tried meditation can attest that the greatest obstacle to samadhi is the ever-moving mind. Within moments of focusing on our breath, or a mantra, our attention runs off to mentally gather the soup ingredients for dinner, or it spins around rehashing yesterday's aggravating conversation with a coworker, lifting up whatever shiny thought thread can capture our interest. Ever so lovingly, and gently, we return our awareness to our focus and proceed to gather the energies of the mind to one point of attention. Back to the breath. Back to the present moment. There can be days when it seems that all we do is that — wander off and re-turn. It takes dedication, regular practice, faith, vigor, commitment over time, and the supportive influence of divine grace to experience the depths of meditation practice that is samadhi. Yet it is important to recognize that while it requires some training and perseverance, meditation is as natural as breathing itself. It can be easy and enjoy-able as long as we don't become overly goal oriented.

While we are training the mind to be still, we reap numerous bene-fits from our practice — our stress level is reduced, we become more peaceful, our ability to concentrate improves, and we notice more frequent bouts of contentment. Even with all the benefits, the sage Patanjali was not unaware of the obstacles we face in meditation. His guidebook contains many suggestions for overcoming them. Ulti-mately, he notes that, like anything else, our success is commensurate with the amount of energy we put forth. Sutra 1:21 notes, "Those who have an intense drive [to attain samadhi] get results quickly."[3]

We are naturally superconscious. Knowing superconsciousness as our *natural state* of pure awareness is the key to success in meditation. Meditation practice is not aimed at acquiring or attaining anything. It is consciously abiding in the fullness of what we are — *simply being present now.* Superconsciousness is the ground of our being. All other states of consciousness — the ordinary waking state, the dream state, and the deep sleep state — are superimpositions on this foundational essence. Superconsciousness is always present; it never changes. The changing states of consciousness we experience arise from the superconscious ground of our being, the same way waves arise from the ocean and then return. Our essence, like the vast ocean, is always present beneath any wave. Thought, sleep, fantasy, memory, or emotion are like ocean waves that rise and fall. Only our thoughts and emotions come and go. Our essential Self — the Witness — remains unmoved, unchanged, and always full.

Meditation is shifting our attention and identification from the wave-like activity of mind to the oceanic stillness of the Self. Superconsciousness is not a spiritual condition that we are trying to create; it's the natural revelation of our essential nature. This revelation happens by itself. When the mental field becomes calm and we are paying attention, we notice it. Our meditation practice is the way we arrange conditions for this to occur.

Step by Conscious Step

The eight limbs of spiritual practice outlined in the second chapter of Patanjali's Yoga Sutras give us a comprehensive method for training the mind to concentrate, improving our ability to discern, and letting go into the flow state of meditation.

1. Restraints (*Yamas*)
2. Observances (*Niyamas*)
3. Posture (*Asana*)
4. Regulation of the Breath (*Pranayama*)
5. Introversion by Withdrawing Senses (*Pratyahara*)
6. Concentration (*Dharana*)
7. Meditation (*Dhyana*)
8. Superconsciousness or Oneness Absorption (*Samadhi*)

The first two practices — the five restraints and the five observances, (introduced in chapter 2, page 25) — remind us that a focused, meditative mind is supported by an ethical, spiritually oriented life. These foundational steps indicate the necessity of cultivating ten virtues: the five yamas (nonharming, truthfulness, nonstealing, right use of vital force, and nonattachment) and the five niyamas (purity, contentment, self-discipline, study of the nature of consciousness, and self-surrender).

Following the first two steps that address the ethical and spiritual foundation for conscious living, the next six steps facilitate the meditative journey of interiorization — our awareness moves from body to vital force, mind, and then beyond.

We begin at the physical level of our being with attention to posture. In this context, the word *asana* means "seat," and the third practice in Patanjali's eight-limbed system of meditation training; it specifically refers to a seated posture that is most conducive for meditation. Sutra 2:46 notes that the posture should be steady (*sthira*) and pleasant, easy, or comfortable (*sukham*). The emphasis is on sitting still so that the mind can be absorbed in meditation. When the body is uncomfortable or restless, it influences the mind, which then becomes disturbed and unfit for meditation.

In the yogic system of Hatha Yoga, many yoga postures or asanas are used, along with pranayama (regulated breathing) and *mudras* (hand poses or gestures to seal, circulate, or channel subtle energy) to bring flexibility, overall well-being, lightness, and balance to the body in support of meditation practice and healthy living.

Next, we focus our attention deeper by enhancing the flow of vital force through conscious breathing (pranayama) and internalizing awareness (pratyahara) — reversing the ordinary outward flow of attention by turning it within. These first five steps in the eight-limbed practice are considered the external limbs.

The final three steps are the internal limbs, a subtle process using the mind in order to, ultimately, transcend it. These practices address the progressive focusing and stilling of our attention. They are concentration, meditation, and superconsciousness.

Ordinarily, we think of meditation as a spiritual tool, a practice we can learn and do. While it is that, the ancient yogic system has a higher goal in mind. Meditation is just one practice in an entire system that is designed for awakening our potential. It's part of a way of life, a spiritually conscious, thriving life.

All Will Be Well

Meditation can be difficult when we are at odds with our Self. When we are out of integrity with our deepest values, whenever we sit to meditate, that inner conflict will arise. That's not a bad thing; it helps us become more aware of what matters most to us and prompts us to make the changes we need to make. Meditation helps us get our life in order, and when we get our life in order, deeper meditation becomes possible. Without this conscious connection to the Self, how can we prosper? How can we live the soul-infused life?

We experience wholeness in meditation as inner peace and a felt sense of fullness or sufficiency. As the soul's peace pervades the mental field, we are free from restless drives to do, want, have, or be *more*. We are whole. We are complete. We are consciously still. In that moment, we do not need or want anything. All is well. Mystics throughout time have witnessed and proclaimed their experience of this, such as Julian of Norwich's famous, oft-quoted line, "All will be well and all will be well and every kind of thing will be well."[4] We, too, can know what the mystics have known.

By providing a scientific, proven method for directing our attention within, superconscious meditation helps us experience our essential nature, realize the truth of our being, and free ourselves from error-prone identification with thoughts and emotions.

The Purpose of Superconscious Meditation

The highest goal of superconscious meditation is Self- and God-realization. To realize the truth of our being, we must have a way to experience it for ourselves. Otherwise, no matter how much knowledge we have about our spiritual nature, at that level, we only know intellectually. We just know *about* it. We do not *know* "it." We cannot know the fullness of our essential Self through thought alone because any thought, no matter how grand, is limiting. Spirit is unbounded. It is unlimited, and thus beyond words and thoughts. Superconscious meditation gives us a systematic way to perceive that which is beyond the limits of mind.

What does Self-realization have to do with prosperity? Spiritual realization is a practical goal as well as a lofty one. Roy Eugene Davis writes:

> Meditation practice removes our awareness from limiting conditions, enabling us to acknowledge and experience ourselves as spiritual beings independent of relative circumstances. We become enabled to view ourselves in relationship to the universe from a higher perspective, to choose our thoughts and actions and to flow with the rhythms of life with natural ease. Meditators can learn to prosper: to thrive, to flourish, and to be successful in all aspects of their lives.[5]

With the skills of superconscious meditation, we learn to direct our attention at will, hone our power of discernment, and inwardly attune to higher guidance.

When you meditate each day, intend to meditate superconsciously. To experience the fullness of the divine Self beyond restless and confining mental activity, follow this process:

Sit until you experience stillness.

Observe the expansion of your conscious awareness beyond thoughts and recognize the freedom inherent to your essential Self.

Let your awareness soar into that freedom and realize fullness.

Remain in that experience of wholeness as you sit in the silence, looking and listening within.

After meditation, enter your day in fullness.

Remember you are whole.

Meditate for No Reason

If you continue this simple practice every day you will obtain
wonderful power. Before you attain it, it is something wonderful,
but after you attain it, it is nothing special.

— Shunryu Suzuki[6]

When I first sat to meditate, I felt like an inexperienced river-rafter careening through the rapids of my mind. Before trying to meditate, I was not aware of my restless thoughts. The mental deluge of chatter remained just below the threshold of my perception. Once I sat to meditate and tried to focus my attention on one thing, I became acutely aware of the torrent of thoughts. I was afraid I would never succeed as a meditator. My closed eyelids twitched; I couldn't sit still; and my thoughts raced from past to future in a nanosecond. I was the rafter tossed out of the boat, swirling in the current.

Fortunately, before I gave up in despair, I came across the words of Zen teacher Shunryu Suzuki, who said, "Just to sit."[7] Just to sit is enough. I thought, "Oh, I can do that!" I was clueless about the deep meaning of the Zen saying, but for the time being, it gave me the encouragement I needed. It offered the necessary insight to keep practicing — nonattachment to results. Let go of trying to make something happen. My already restless mind was getting stirred up by my attempts to calm it down and worsened by my frustration with not being able to do it. I was trying too hard to get somewhere, when what I needed to do was simply be present. Just to sit.

The blessing of that wisdom saying has remained with me for decades, making it possible to meditate on days when I feel like meditating and days when I don't. I often think of my morning practice as an opportunity to just sit in what I experience as "the grace-bestowing presence" — allowing my heart and my mind to be filled with the renewing peace and bliss of divine Consciousness.

Meditation is not a cure-all. It won't get us a job, pay the bills, or heal a broken marriage. It will, however, enhance our ability to do any of that, and more. Meditate deep enough, often enough, and long enough, and we see. Everything improves when we become more aware. Instead of blindly speeding through life with the velocity of self-centered motivation, the wisdom light of Oneness comes on. We slow down. We become present. We see what we could not see before. We see our self, everyone, and everything as it is.

Eleven

How to Meditate

Whenever one does anything,
one has no success whatsoever without practice.

— YOGA-VASISHTHA

Meditation is easy and natural. We can make it difficult by trying too hard, having unrealistic expectations, or approaching it haphazardly, but at its core, meditation is simply being awake and aware — mindful. I sometimes tell students that I can't teach them how to meditate, but I can teach them how to prepare for meditation to occur. Luckily, they already know how to meditate. I say this because it's true. We all know how to meditate. We've done it before, even if we have never tried a formal practice.

Meditation is a heightened state of consciousness; it is distinct from the ordinary waking state or the sleep state. We all know how to fall asleep, how to change our consciousness from the ordinary waking state to the sleep state. If I were to offer a "how to sleep" workshop, I would not be able to teach you exactly how to fall asleep. You already know how to do that. But I could explain the most-conducive conditions for making the change in consciousness from waking to sleeping. I might give a pillow-fluffing demonstration and provide a list of helpful actions that assist the journey toward sleep, such as turning off electronic devices and lights.

It's not so different with meditation. Remember, you already know how to meditate. Long before we come to a formal practice, we've experienced many moments of meditative awareness. Often such moments of clear awareness come when we are relaxed and alert, perhaps taking a walk on the beach or through the forest. Our incessant mental chatter quiets down and the peace of the soul is revealed. If we don't realize that the origin of that inner peace is within us, we may go back to the shore or the woods to find it again. Meditation practice is our way of reliably finding mindful awareness wherever we are. Here's how to do it.

How to Practice

There are four basic stages to meditation practice — like the four movements in a beautiful symphony, they flow together in a great concert of higher awareness. Within these four general stages, Patanjali's eight limbs provide specific practices.

A simple guide to the stages — my four-part formula — for meditation practice is this: foster, focus, flow, and finish.

> FOSTER: Establish a conducive environment, both externally and internally. This includes posture, breath awareness, and internalization of attention.
>
> FOCUS: Use a concentration technique to focus attention on a single point.
>
> FLOW: Let go into the peak experiences of meditation and Oneness.
>
> FINISH: Consciously bring your attention back to mind and body with a sense of appreciation, renewal, and empowerment.

Foster

The first stage is arranging conditions that are conducive to meditative awareness — both internally and externally. To meditate, choose a quiet place where you will not be disturbed — shut the door, turn off the phones and computer, sit down, and intentionally direct your attention within.

As a beginning meditator, one of the first challenges I faced was my fear of being alone with myself! Sounds strange, yet when I look back, I can see how it took a while to settle in and get comfortable with the deep, and raw, connection that meditation brings. Don't get me wrong; I have always enjoyed being alone. Yet by continually staying busy doing something, I remained distant from myself. Meditation was different. Finding the willingness to be undistracted and uninterrupted — to be truly alone with myself — took courage. I had lived for decades distracted from my Self, disconnected from what I truly felt and what I deeply knew to be true. But divine grace has a way of bringing us back to our Self, helping us rediscover our wholeness. When I was ready, meditation provided the way.

Hesitation to be alone with oneself can show up in subtle or obvious ways, like leaving the phone just out of range — in case someone important calls! Or, taking a problem to be solved with us into meditation. Thus, the first stage in meditation is fostering or cultivating an environment conducive to letting go of such distractions and embarking on the inward journey.

Create Privacy

Ideally, find a private space where you can meditate — whether that's a room dedicated to meditation or a shared space that can be reserved for, or kept private during, meditation. In this space, consider setting up a simple altar, one arranged with anything that helps to elevate and quiet the mind — a candle, incense, photos of your teacher or the saints. Whenever we catch fire with determination to meditate, we find a space for it.

One determined student I knew lived with roommates in a full and active household. Where was he going to find any quiet space? He set up his meditation altar on the dashboard of his car. Every morning, he went out to meditate in the garage, where he would not be disturbed. After getting clear about your intention to set aside time to meditate, and arranging a suitable environment, turn your attention to your posture.

Sit

When the sage Ramana Maharshi was asked about the best posture for meditation, he replied that it is the posture in which the mind is still. When the body moves, the mind moves. Find the posture that is best for you, one where you can easily remain still for an extended period. This is Patanjali's third step, posture.

Meditation can be practiced seated on the floor, on a cushion, or in a chair. The posture should be relaxed but firm, with the spinal column straight. Sitting still with the spine straight and head erect encourages vital force to flow upward into the higher energy centers and helps us remain alert. An upright posture also reflects the quality of mind that is most conducive to meditative awareness — a firm intention to experience God or Truth, balanced with peaceful surrender to divine grace and timing.

The sage Patanjali notes that our meditation posture should be one that is "steady and sweet."[1] Say goodbye to any stereotypical ideas that your meditation posture needs to be some foreign form of bended legs, leaving you more conscious of the body's aches and pains rather than freeing you from bodily awareness. Be comfortable. Be still. That is the advice of the sages.

Kindle the Light of Awareness

> *Let us meditate on the radiant light of Supreme Consciousness.*
> *May it purify our hearts and illumine our minds.*
> *May it guide and inspire us.*
>
> — GAYATRI MANTRA[2]

After being seated — gently, mindfully, and lovingly close your eyes and draw your attention within. Offer a prayer of attunement, acknowledging the presence of Spirit, the saints and sages, the divine nature of all beings, and the spiritual nature of your own soul. Most importantly, *feel* your connection to Ultimate Reality and to all of life. Inwardly walk through the temple door of God's omnipresence and experience yourself praying "in" God rather than "to" God. Know that divine Ultimate Reality is nearer than your heartbeat; indeed, it's the essence of your being.

Breathe

The next step of practice is conscious expansion of vital force through regulation of the breath. Breath is intimately tied to vital force. Vital force is the connecting link between body, mind, and spirit. By enhancing our awareness of vital force, we can follow the energy flow into deeper aspects of our being. Breath becomes our vehicle.

Notice the easy and natural sensation of inhalation through your nostrils. Along with the physical perception, intend to draw your awareness within. As breath moves into your body, feel as if you are pulling your attention within, diving into the infinite ocean of divine consciousness. With the out-breath, let go of any distraction — clinging to any external disturbance or thought activity. Don't resist external disruptions or thoughts; simply let them be. With each breath, draw attention more deeply within. This is Patanjali's fifth limb, introversion of attention by withdrawing the senses from their objects.

To meditate, the mind must turn back upon itself instead of flowing outward toward involvement with sense perception. To help us continue that inward journey, we introduce an anchor for our attention. We are ready for the second stage of practice. We focus.

Focus

Concentrate

With concentration, bring your attention to a single point of focus. When your attention wanders from that focus, gently bring it back.

There are many different techniques for this stage of meditation. We can focus our attention by observing the flow of our breath; inwardly reciting a prayer; offering a prayer word or mantra; contemplating a scriptural passage; focusing attention at one of the chakra centers; visualizing a deity; or many other practices. The purpose of introducing an object for concentration is to give our attention something to land on — to interrupt the mind's normal tendency to wander and move restlessly between thoughts and perceptions.

We're familiar with the mental field growing quiet when we concentrate deeply, such as when reading a good book, listening to a concert, or even threading a needle. We become absorbed in what we are concentrating on. Awareness of what we are focused on is heightened, and we become impervious to other things happening around us. We apply knowledge of that skill in this stage of practice. We intentionally introduce something uplifting and captivating to concentrate on. Something soothing to the mind, not stimulating.

We direct our attention to that, and when our attention wanders off, we redirect it (again and again).

This stage of practice is likened to the flow of a stream of water. If you look closely, you'll see that many drops bounce out of a running stream. We try to concentrate, but attention bounces away with stray thoughts. When this happens, return to the inward-flowing stream.

Despite your attempts to concentrate, your attention will naturally wander. Especially at first, don't expect your attention to be unwavering, or you may become frustrated or disappointed. One of the first things meditation teaches is the relentless, restless nature of the mind. Training the mind to focus in meditation is like training a wild horse. Be firm but gentle.

An easy, natural, and readily available tool for concentration is our breath. Here's how to use it: As you inhale, notice the feeling as cool air moves through the nostrils, touches the back of the throat, fills the lungs, and expands the abdomen. Observe the tiny peak of the breath as it changes, almost imperceptibly, from inhalation to exhalation. Then notice changes during exhalation, as your abdomen gently contracts and warmer air exits the nostrils. Stay tuned to the breath. Follow it. Watch as it becomes slower and subtler. You'll notice that when the breath becomes quiet, so does the mind. When that happens, you're ready to meditate, and you will naturally move from focus to flow, the third stage of practice.

Flow

A time will come when the mind will stick to one point alone,
like the continuous sound of a church bell. This is meditation,
the fruit of constant and protracted practice of concentration.
The joy will be indescribable.
— Swami Vishnudevananda[3]

Concentration naturally becomes meditation. After a while, breathing slows down, becomes subtle and shallow; thought activity decreases; and moments of calm, pure awareness are revealed.

Meditate

Sages have compared the difference between concentration and meditation to be like the difference between a stream of water and a stream of oil. A stream of water has errant bouncing drops taking side trips away from the flow, while oil flows in an integral, steady stream. There is a *palpable* shift in our mental field when we move from concentration to meditation.

Watch for It

With concentration, there is some effort required. We use our will to continuously return our attention to our point of focus. When attention becomes steady, it begins to flow; no effort is required to hold it on point. Watch for this natural shift. Notice when it occurs and what it is like. Awareness flows, and expands, in a steady stream. It is peaceful and effortless.

This is meditation: a conscious, one-pointed, undisturbed flow of attention and awareness.

Stay

As the experience of peace deepens, let go of watching the breath and rest in the heightened awareness that is superconsciousness. Look within, listen within. Be open, receptive, and curious. *Contemplate your essential nature.* Steadiness in meditation naturally flows into Oneness — samadhi — or identification with what is contemplated. Consciously rest in being.

When the attention wanders to thoughts again, you can return to the breath, and refocus, or begin to conclude your meditation by bringing awareness back to body and mind to enter the final stage of practice.

Finish

It's not advisable to eat a lovely meal, then jump up from the table and run around. Better to take a little time to savor the experience and begin digesting. In the same way, sit for a few minutes after meditating to absorb and enhance its benefits. Before concluding, make a conscious effort to deeply feel the peace you experienced within. Invite the soul's peace with its healing influence to pervade the mental field and the body, taking time to feel it.

The conclusion of your meditation is the best time to pray for others and our world. From our peace, we share peace. We see others in the light of Spirit and call forth awareness of their wholeness. Rather than give attention to any changing condition, problematic as it may be, we bring our attention to unchanging spiritual Truth and affirm the activity of divine grace. We consciously affirm the graceful unfolding of divine purpose and the highest good for all. *All is well, all will ever be well.*

Refreshed, renewed, with peace as our companion, we carry the effects of meditation with us.

Best Practice Is Steady Practice

*Focus your attention within. You will experience new power,
new strength, and peace in body, mind, and spirit.
All bonds that limited you will be vanquished.*

— Paramahansa Yogananda[4]

Ideally, meditate each morning soon after arising, before getting involved in the activities of your day. Morning is ideal because we are usually refreshed after a night's rest and the mental field will be relatively quiet. If morning is not possible for you, then set aside a dedicated time later in the day or evening. The main thing is consistency.

Briefly tend to your morning routine, and then go directly to your meditation space. Light a candle or some incense and offer a prayer. Be conscious of the goal of your practice and the technique you will use. Know how much time you will dedicate to your practice. Establish a routine that works for you and stay with it.

The recommended amount of time for beginners to meditate is twenty to thirty minutes. That's because it usually takes that long for the earlier stages of practice — sitting still, conscious breathing, withdrawing attention, and concentrating — to quiet the mental field and for meditation to begin. Ideally, we have enough time to sit in the mindful, flow state of awareness for a while. Some beginners stop short of reaching meditation and remain in the concentration stage. This is helpful training for our attention, but not as restorative or transforming as even a few minutes spent in meditative awareness. Even a little taste of the soul's bliss has a lasting effect.

Observe your own practice and see what works best for you. Some people find that shorter periods of time, repeated throughout the day, are more beneficial. The most important thing is steadiness.

Nothing takes the place of daily, disciplined, surrendered meditation. Dedication is even more important than technique. Daily practice of meditation accomplishes several things: It establishes spiritual realization as our priority; clarifies our awareness over time; provides discipline that enhances our self-esteem; removes stress from the body and mind; awakens our intuitive ability; and opens our heart and mind to divine guidance, inspiration, wisdom, and compassion.

Sporadic practice does not effectively make the deep, conscious connection with the higher true Self that is necessary to thrive.

Make a commitment to meditate every day — to meet your divine Self in the inner sanctum of surrendered devotion. Vow that you will not miss a day no matter what, and you won't. If you set up a regular time, it's easier to keep this commitment. If you miss that time, you don't have to miss your meditation. Do it later that day. The small self will suggest, "Tomorrow, you can meditate tomorrow." Today is always the day to realize our potential.

Always today, never tomorrow. Always now.

Twelve

Discipline:
Do What Pleases Your Soul

Who could live, who could breathe,
if that blissful Self dwelt not within the heart?
It is That which gives joy!

— TAITTIRIYA UPANISHAD

O ver many years of teaching yoga philosophy, I have discovered certain words are sure to cause students to cringe. No sooner has *that* word come out of my mouth than the body language in front of me shifts — arms cross, shoulders rise, head moves down, eye contact is lost. One of those words is *discipline* — self-discipline. While there are some vigorous types who love that word, and who can't wait for the next arduous assignment, most have an instantaneous cellular memory that translates self-discipline as suffering, pain, and ultimately, failure. Understandably, they don't want to sign up for it.

I acknowledge that they may associate religious or spiritual self-discipline with asceticism, mortification (which even sounds bad!), or all manner of punitive self-denial. And failure, let's not forget that. We set out with high hopes of becoming holy, and then falter, giving up altogether on that 4 AM meditation along with the promise never to be angry again. Lots of nodding heads.

Then I offer this instruction: *Spiritual self-discipline is doing what pleases the soul.* There is an audible sigh of relief, a little nervous laughter, and some incredulity mixed with recognition — the flicker of a light inside.

I explain. Doing what pleases the soul means living in deep integrity — aligning our thoughts, speech, and actions with the true Self. Self-discipline is how we cooperate with divine power and grace, how we prosper by expressing our highest potential and live in joy. It's the way we turn our life toward fulfillment by purifying our heart, mind, and body so the inner Light of divinity can lead the way.

Self-discipline is essential for accessing higher awareness, realizing true freedom, and experiencing the soul's bliss and the abundantly blessed life that accompanies it. All spiritual paths point to the necessity of discipline. Why, then, do many of us either avoid it altogether or struggle with implementing it on a regular basis? We have two misconceptions to overcome. Both errors involve an incorrect view of self-discipline for spiritually conscious living. The first error is confusing discipline on the spiritual path with the "no pain, no gain" model for physical exercise. The second error is misunderstanding what brings us delight.

The yogic way of self-discipline is in harmony with its purpose — the means are inseparable from the end. The purpose is soul freedom, joy, and the delight of thriving — the soul fully and freely expressing itself. Therefore, to reach freedom, joy, and the delight of thriving we must travel the path of delightful thought, speech, and action. Spiritual self-discipline has us trade in anything that brings suffering for what brings lasting joy and soul happiness. We exchange lower drives — behaviors that are inconsistent with the truth of our being and out of harmony with dharma — for higher knowledge and behavior, that is, living in a wise and compassionate way. We raise our game. The Bhagavad Gita says it perfectly: "Raise your self by your Self."[1]

Freedom through Self-Discipline

For Self-realization and Self-actualization, practice self-discipline....
— YOGA SUTRAS[2]

Self-discipline is the first practice that the sage Patanjali lists as defining Kriya Yoga, the way of spiritually awakened intentional living. The Sanskrit word is *tapas*, which means austerity, or focused discipline. Its root meaning is "to burn or to give off heat." The "heat" of tapas refers to two things: the ignited aspiration of a spiritual practitioner and the energy of resistance that arises when we make intentional changes. Think of your practice of self-discipline as this fire energy that can burn through obstacles and light up your path — because it can, and it does. To experience that, we need to see self-discipline with the right perspective, in accordance with its purpose.

After stating that self-discipline is the initial foundational practice of spiritually conscious living, Patanjali clarifies that its purpose is to remove any obstacle that would interfere with the realization and actualization of our essential nature. This is a critically important point that makes all the difference in how we approach self-discipline. If we think that our discipline is for self-improvement, or to make ourselves "spiritual," then our approach is off base. This incorrect assumption exacerbates the error of thinking we're separate from the Source and can infuse self-discipline with self-punishment or even self-hatred. It certainly can take the joy out of it and ultimately make it hard to maintain. Fortunately, there's another way to walk the path of discipline, a way that is easier to sustain and brings freedom each step of the way.

The True Purpose of Self-Discipline

That which is unbounded is happy.

— CHANDOGYA UPANISHAD[3]

The purpose of self-discipline is to purify the body and mind, thereby creating a clearer pathway for the inner light to shine. What does this mean, really? It means when obstacles to Self-realization are removed, we can experience the awakened consciousness that is samadhi and live an awakened life. It means that we do whatever is conducive to peace, balance, overall well-being, and clarity. We make choices based on these criteria. When we do this, the light of inner guidance can shine more freely into the mind, making it easier to discern the next right action. Our path is illumined.

A spiritually focused practice of self-discipline builds energy, confidence, and resolve. It's useful to start with one area you know needs to be better aligned with your well-being. This might be a change in your diet, exercise routine, meditation practice, speech habits, or recreational activity. It can be anything you decide needs changing from something that is not currently in your best interest to a different behavior that you know is right for you now. How will you use your energy in a more positive way?

The heat energy of tapas, or intentional self-discipline, comes into play here. It takes resistance to stop an unhealthy or unwanted behavior and begin something we know is beneficial, such as regular exercise or daily meditation. Like braking a moving car, it requires attention, intention, and disciplined action. It causes friction and creates heat. That heat is energy. In the practice of positive self-discipline, we recognize that energy as potential, as life force that can be used in another way. We can do something else with it, and the more we learn to redirect our energy like that, the stronger and more self-confident we become.

With spiritually centered self-discipline, we are "flexing our soul muscles," doing what may be difficult initially but ultimately brings us greater freedom and delight. Choose something that feels achievable for you — a stretch but not a hyperextension! Yoga is moderation. What you are looking for is a gradual enhancement of your overall well-being. Use discipline to intentionally lean toward freedom, toward vitality, toward expressing your full potential.

Always Start with Enough

The successful formula for spiritually guided self-discipline is to always begin with "enough," with awareness of wholeness. From the healthy perspective of innate sufficiency, we make adjustments inwardly and outwardly because we are fine-tuning our expression as the divine being we are. We discipline ourselves to express our fullness, to let our radiance shine through our thoughts, words, and actions.

Ego thrives on the "not enough" lie — it constantly reinforces the belief that we are not good enough, don't do enough, don't accomplish enough, and aren't spiritual enough. A little discernment reveals that this belief system is inherent to the false self. To maintain the sense of being separate from the all-sufficiency of the Source, it is necessary to continually proclaim: *Not enough!* Remember that ego's default position is lack. Can you imagine for a moment a wave rising from the bosom of the ocean, looking around at other waves, comparing itself to them, and declaring: *I am not enough, not good enough, not pretty enough, not wild enough, not big enough.* All the while, it is obvious to the onlooker that the wave is nothing less than the entire ocean expressing itself.

This erroneous belief is the source of great suffering; it sends us around and around the same unfulfilling track, seeking to be more and better. It underlies the negative, punitive, hamster-wheel approach to self-discipline. When we buy into "not enough," no matter what we do to satisfy that lack, "enough" will always escape us. Always start with enough by remembering who you are, coming from your fullness, and seeing through and refusing to adopt that misguided idea of insufficiency. This sets us on a prospering course of delightful discipline and a life emanating the soul's joy.

The Discipline of Choosing Delight

When you do things from your soul,
you feel a river moving in you, a joy.
When actions come from another section,
the feeling disappears.

— RUMI[4]

The core of delightful discipline is developing our ability to see beyond immediate gratification to the longer-range effects of our choices. I use an exercise I call "drawing the circle" to heighten my awareness of my choices by bringing attention to how I begin something, carry it out, take it to a conclusion, and consider the implications of my actions along the way. When we draw a circle, we begin at a point, then extend the line to shape our arc, continuing to move it around until it meets once again and connects at our starting point. Pondering my choices with the circle metaphor brings several things to my mind, not the least of which is the law of karma. My intentions and actions will always return to me in some form in accordance with their nature. It also reminds me that my action doesn't simply move out from me as a singular, linear, disconnected event in time and space. What we think and do always takes place in the circle that is wholeness — our actions affect others as well as the planet we share.

In this exercise, we look at where the circle begins with our intention and desire, how that moves into action, and then imagine what the potential impact may be. We try to discern the whole picture, not just what we want in any given moment. We contemplate and consider the likely outcome of our choices. What may seem delightful initially can turn out to be debilitating instead. And what seems difficult initially may turn out to be delightful. It depends on our motivation and where the potential result will lead. We need to look.

Everything is contained in the rubric of "drawing the circle" discipline. Where does our choice originate from and where will it lead? It is a powerful practice for our choices — whether regarding our intentions, things we say, or actions we take. Besides taking better care of our body and mind and our intimate relationships, imagine how we could improve as environmental stewards by applying "drawing the circle" contemplation to our lifestyle choices, considering more deeply how our individual choices will impact the well-being of all. Spiritually based self-discipline includes our care and concern for the planet, that all may thrive.

A few years ago, I purchased one of those rechargeable liquid soap dispensers for our kitchen. It seemed like a good idea — measured dispensing of soap meant less waste, less mess with different people using it, and less effort. Just put your hand under it and poof! There's your soap.

After serving us well for some time, the dispenser died. It quit dispensing and wouldn't recharge. It was done. When I contacted the company, they said the warranty had expired, and the dispenser couldn't be repaired. They offered me a discount on purchasing a new one. *I stopped there.* What would I do with the old one? The dispenser was a combination of plastic and metal — not readily recyclable, not to mention the dead battery. I realized in that moment of contemplation that I had initially made a self-indulgent choice. The dispenser was delightful while it lasted, but I hadn't drawn the full circle. Then I was faced with the difficult reality that this item I had purchased was going to end up in a landfill with a mountain of other self-indulgent electronics. Instead of repeating that error, I found great joy in reinstating a simple glass jar with a pump handle, which requires only a little push of the hand to squirt the soap. Easy to use, great longevity with no electronic parts, and easy to recycle should the necessity ever arise. I drew the circle this time.

Our ability to be compassionate and caring naturally increases over time as we awaken. As we become more discerning, more committed to true prosperity, and regularly rein in the misguided, self-serving motives of ego, life's prospering, evolutionary, creative impulse rises in us. Spiritually conscious self-discipline makes us strong, wise, and ready to cooperate with this divine impulse. Our viewpoint shifts from feeling like a powerless victim at the mercy of outer circumstances to being a powerful, dynamic agent for positive change. Seemingly intractable global problems are seen in a new light — as creative challenges to be met with resources we already have, as we discover how to use them.

My small soap-dispenser dilemma is multiplied millions of times daily in households around the world. We have so many choices to make, and it seems increasingly difficult to consider the global impact of those choices. When we are ready to look, there is a way. We discover there are people everywhere finding new ways to draw their circle large enough to consider the effect of their actions on the planet and on future generations — diet, energy sources, materials we use, waste management, technology, and more. There is no reason why we can't turn up the light of wisdom and compassion rooted in spiritual awakening. We're here for that. It's our time to shine.

Have a Vision, Make a Plan, Arrange Conditions

Happiness is skillful means. And happily for happiness,
this is aligned with your deepest nature: awake, interested,
benign, at peace, and quietly inclined to joy.

— RICK HANSON[5]

To embrace self-discipline as our path to living in the highest way, we hold a vision of how we want to live the soul life, we make a plan to carry it out, and then we arrange conditions for success. Instead of focusing on our lack of discipline or past failures, it is more helpful to turn our thoughts to our vision of possibility.

Choose an area of your life that will benefit from more focused, delightful discipline. Begin by reflecting on this choice. Envision it. Call to mind what it will look like, what *you* will look and feel like as you follow this discipline. What will it require? How can you best prepare? What obstacles have you faced in the past? What will you do to overcome those challenges? Start by seeing the end result. See and *feel* what it is like for you to live in the highest way, following the soulful path of discipline you know is right for you now and will be beneficial in the long-term.

Once you decide on your discipline, make a plan. Consider how to make a conscious beginning and how you will carry it through over time. Remember, in the beginning, to bring delight into your thoughts, speech, and action. Let go of the "no pain, no gain" model and instead hold a vision of delight throughout, from beginning to end. Even if your plan includes some difficulty, which discipline very often does, it is still possible to delight in doing it. We simply delight in the choice we are making.

Perhaps you decide to get up earlier to have enough time to meditate. The initial experience of getting up earlier may not be pleasant. What can be pleasant right away is how you feel about yourself with the choice you are making. Pay attention to that instead of focusing on the discomfort. When we stay in bed longer than we intend, we have the comfort of the covers but later don't feel very good about the choice we made. If we follow our program of discipline and get up when we intend to, the initial ache of leaving the comfort of sleep will be far outweighed by the good feeling we generate by following through, which will continue throughout the day ahead.

Use the "drawing the circle" contemplation to help you arrange conditions for success with your program of discipline. For example, I notice that my best plans for healthy eating can fall asunder if I have not thoughtfully prepared for the end of the day when I am likely to be tired and hungry. If I want to follow a program of healthy eating, I must draw the circle for my entire day. What will I need to do in the morning before I start work (or even the day or night before) to support my success?

At the end of the day, instead of focusing on failures, reflect on your successes. This is a crucial component of soulful discipline — enhancing positivity. It trains our brain to remember and look for the joy we found in discipline, which in turn supports our ability to follow through. Remember what was delightful and reflect on how it felt. Recall the feeling. Help all the cells in your mind and body relive that joy. What went well? Why? What contributed to your delightful discipline? What incremental progress did you make?

Self-discipline is our way to shine. Polishing the body and mind, we allow our innate radiance to pour through. In its wake is the soul's delight.

Be Inspired and Be an Inspiration

He was a burning and a shining light.
— Christian scriptures[6]

What is your vision of a self-disciplined person living their fullest potential? Is there someone you know, or know of, who is a role model for you of positive, soul-inspired disciplined living? What does that look like? If a disciplined, purposeful approach to life supports thriving, we can identify several things when we look at those who do it. First, a thriving person exudes vitality; they are vibrant — fully engaged with life without holding back. Their energy flows freely. In alignment with that free flow of energy is their natural tendency toward generosity. A thriving person gives and gives consciously — in the right way, at the right time, to the appropriate person or cause. Observation of a thriving, disciplined person will reveal a dynamic balance of activity and rest. There is no need for extremes. No need to overwork or do too little, just a natural expression of right action. Such a life is lived intentionally — thoughts, speech, and actions are harmoniously aligned with the truth of their being and a view to the oneness of all life. With the ability to know the oneness of all life, there is a keen sense of prudence, a far-sighted pragmatism that values resources and avoids waste.

When we consider what a disciplined, thriving life looks like, we can reflect on how we currently live and see if there is anything we may want to change. Here are a few questions related to self-discipline. Add your own, based on your vision of what it can be.

> How is my vitality? Do I experience an abundance of energy? If not, why not? Do I allow situations or personalities to "get the better of me" and drain away my vital force? Or am I good at setting necessary boundaries to maintain my energy and positive resolve?

AM I GENEROUS? Do I regularly look for small and great opportunities to contribute to life? Am I happy when I am invited to give? Do I see giving as an opportunity to be in the flow of life, or do I consider it a burden? Is giving easy and natural for me? Am I able to give in a balanced way, so that my gift is in alignment with the needs of the occasion and consistent with my means?

DO I WORK HARD AND REST WELL? Is there balance in my life with action and stillness? If I don't take breaks or get enough sleep, what is the reason for that?

ARE MY THOUGHTS, SPEECH, AND ACTIONS IN ALIGNMENT? Do I consistently do what I say I will? Am I on time? Do I keep my commitments to myself and others? What do my actions say about my integrity? Am I a prudent person or do I tend to waste time, money, or energy?

Embrace Change

Changing any habits or behaviors that are not consistent with living to our fullest potential requires discipline. First, we discipline our mind to engage in introspection for greater understanding, then we discipline our speech and actions to conform to a new behavior, one that satisfies our vision of a fulfilled life. None of it has to wait for anyone else. Whenever we are ready, we can discipline ourselves to change.

When we notice where our thoughts, speech, and actions are not consistent with our view of a thriving person, it brings the opportunity to make a change. First, we can analyze the belief system behind any behaviors we want to change. For example, if you're someone who is consistently late, see if you can discern why. What does being late offer you? We may perpetuate such a habit for many reasons. Sometimes we're poor time managers and fail to allow ourselves enough time to arrive when we should. Perhaps we get too involved in doing one thing and don't give enough attention to what comes next. Or sometimes we are chronically late because we enjoy the attention it brings, the strange power play of keeping others waiting for us. There can be many reasons. If we sincerely inquire into our behavior, we can discover the belief system holding it in place. We can then change the belief and the behavior along with it.

If you can't discern what the belief system is that sustains a behavior you want to change, just change the behavior and stay open to learning why. You will likely discover more about it in the process of making the change.

The Heart of Spiritual Discipline

Even as a mirror stained by dust shines brilliantly
when it has been cleansed,
so the embodied one, on seeing the nature of the Soul,
becomes established in oneness and is freed from sorrow.
— Svetashvatara Upanishad[7]

If we consider the heart of spiritual discipline and are clear about its purpose, it becomes obvious that simply doing what is in harmony with the true Self is what is called for. And doing what is in harmony with the Self will be delightful — imbued with the soul's bliss. Not the rigidity of a results-oriented approach to discipline or the laxity of anything goes, but the generous, kind, deepest expressions of Self-care — that is, discipline harmonious with nurturing the soul life. Once we understand this and set our goal to live a soul-directed life, we can immediately experience the subtler but longer-lasting delight that comes from resisting what is not useful for our higher purpose and embracing all that is.

When it comes to spiritual discipline, imagine that your practice is permeated with joy, that you are drawn again and again to the delight that emanates from your soul. See yourself gladly turning your awareness to meditation or prayer, compassionately restraining the senses from any tendency toward injury or harm, being drawn to self-inquiry with curiosity, and willingly cultivating an attitude of surrender — letting go of any sense of being separate from the Source. Envision your days filled with sweet inspiration and bold confidence in your divine life.

A Natural Discipline Ensues

A novice asked the Buddha, "What is goodness,
and what is greatness?" The Buddha replied,
"To follow the Way and hold to what is true is good.
When the will is in conformity with the Way, that is greatness."
— SUTRA OF FORTY-TWO SECTIONS[8]

The experience of self-discipline naturally progresses. First, we turn away from or actively release what no longer serves our thriving life. As the Buddha said, we "follow the [dharmic] way and hold to what is true." To do that, we use our wisdom-guided will to make positive changes in harmony with the truth of our being. We *practice* self-discipline by implementing constructive thoughts and behaviors. We use our practice to orient our life toward its highest potential.

Once our disciplined life bears the fruit of sufficient clarity in mind and body, and we are established in Self-realization, then discipline no longer requires will. It is simply the spontaneous expression of our true nature. We naturally do what is right — make wholesome choices and live wisely and compassionately. We naturally thrive. The soul sings with joy and goals are met effortlessly as the out-picturing of a contented heart and mind.

PART IV

Clarity

⤴

Overcome Obstacles and Thrive

Thirteen

Ten Prospering Promises

For this pattern which I give you today is not hidden from you,
and is not far away. It is not in heaven, for you to say,
"Who will go up to heaven and bring it down for us, so that
we can hear it and do it?"...But the teaching is very near you,
it is in your mouth and in your heart, so that you can do it.

— HEBREW SCRIPTURES

The pendulum swings. Even when we know better, we run, everyone runs, top speed it seems, in search of fulfillment through material wealth — the world before us a shining bauble, an abundance of things, the lure of name, fame, and the promise of happiness with the next acquisition. Time to double down our efforts, update our social media platform, show up at the conference and the networking meeting. Here we go again, searching for the next specialist to cure our ills, the next dating scenario to meet the companion we yearn for, the latest diet and workout routine to get us in shape. Soon enough, we grow weary and the world grows dull with the never-ending quest for more, for something else. A turn follows, the pendulum swings toward searching for deeper values, lasting happiness, the real meaning of prosperity. Off we go on retreat, trek to the mountaintop, head for the intensive at the ashram.

Back and forth it goes. Back and forth we go — searching for happiness and security in the world, then giving it up — only to jump back into the fray after we find a little peace.

> Into deep darkness fall those who follow the immanent.
> Into deeper darkness fall those who follow the transcendent.

— Isa Upanishad 1:9[1]

Ancient Vedic wisdom in the Isa Upanishad warns there is darkness for the person who sees only the manifest world as real, who searches there exclusively, and vainly, for fulfillment. There is confusion, disappointment, and sorrow to be found for us when we seek fulfillment exclusively through action and the things of the world at the cost of our inner life. We might expect that from a scripture. Most of them say that in some way — in the world we're going to have trouble. But this Upanishad takes an unexpected turn and says the situation is worse, even darker, for those who withdraw from the world and cling only to the reality of the inner life. That's a surprise, isn't it?

According to the Isa Upanishad, considered by many to be the crème de la crème of Vedic teachings, neither withdrawing from the world nor sole engagement in it is an illumined path. Both lead to the darkness of insufficiency, whether through the door of meditation and inner contemplation or through action in engagement. Either avenue falls short of wholeness. When we really look, we can see that the way of spiritual fulfillment is right in front of us. It is neither in the world nor beyond it; it is *through it*. It is Self-knowledge born of action *and* of meditation, *both*. In and beyond find their meeting place in *through*. The Isa Upanishad offers the supreme secret, the way to free ourselves from the debilitating swing of the pendulum, our endless search for happiness in transcendence or chasing it down in the world of relationships and things. This is it: *Reality dwells in the hearts of all.*

A line from one of my poems says, "Why look for the key when you're inside the shop?"[2] The teaching for how to live an awakened, prosperous life is near us; it is within us, as the divine Self is within us — in our heart and our mind, revealed in our speech and action. Our insight and knowledge from spiritual study and meditation practice is honed — fine-tuned — in the temple offerings of daily life and the sanctity of every relationship.

We can look to yoga's eight limbs of practice for a timeless, premier tool for tending the delicate balance of immanence and transcendence — action and meditation. Many look at the eight limbs and see only a ladder — a step-by-step guide to transcendence. They do provide a progressive guide to interiorization and subtilization of our awareness, seemingly directing us ever inward and upward. Yoga offers a way to clarify awareness and shift our perception and identification from outer relationship — into and through the physical body, senses, and mental field — to that which is beyond them all. However, if we follow that trajectory alone, we are back to the pendulum. Start with the world, withdraw from it, then transcend it. Then what? Where do we go from there?

The path of fulfillment is not linear. It is circular — immanence and transcendence are inseparable, one contributes to and enhances awareness of the other. Our very being, our life itself, the Self, mirrors the eternal collusion of Spirit and matter. We are the place where heaven and earth meet and embrace. To abandon one for the other, or to put one above the other, is the grave error of ignorance that drives humanity, the earth, and all beings connected to us into sorrow. Bringing those two seeming opposites into right relationship through Self-realization and spiritually conscious action makes our heart sing with joy, and all of creation along with us. Once we go beyond the either/or pendulum, we see. It's basic: Action and meditation support and enhance one another. The eight limbs show us how to bring them together, how we can live as spiritually realized beings.

Principle, Practices, Promises

To get off the pendulum, we need a clear way through — a way that circumvents the "either in the world or beyond it" error and, instead, takes us directly into the heart of spirituality to recognize the divine Self right where we are. This is what yoga's ethical and spiritual guidelines — the five restraints (yamas) and five observances (niyamas) — do. They are a systematic method for clarifying our awareness, waking up to the divine Self in our midst, and living our fullest, most creative, thriving life. Let's return to these ten restraints and observances now, with a closer look at what they can tell us about prospering: nonharming, truthfulness, nonstealing, right use of vital force, nonattachment, purity, contentment, self-discipline, study of the nature of consciousness, and self-surrender.

Each of the ten restraints and observances is based on a spiritual principle or law that helps us see into the nature of mind, consciousness, and manifestation. Paramahansa Yogananda said, "The laws of life can teach us to live in harmony with nature and all aspects of life. When we know what the laws are, and conduct ourselves in accord with them, we experience lasting happiness, good health, and perfect harmony."[3] By contemplating spiritual law, our awareness is clarified. We begin to wake up and discover how to live in harmony with divine order — how to cooperate with the Infinite. We understand we cannot fully prosper without that — we see how thriving stems from authentic being, which is grounded in the Source.

As we engage in the practices that each of the limbs suggest, we mature — both psychologically and spiritually. We grow up —

becoming capable of relating from the true Self to the sacred Self in all with wisdom and compassion.

When we become *established* in the principle — realize it and live it authentically — our innate divine capacities bloom and we naturally thrive. We become generative. As we are prospered by life and contribute to life from our fullness, we continue to learn, to grow, and to expand our capacities. Life is ever-new joy, the unbounded soul ever-unfolding its bliss.

At the Heart of It: Spiritual Principle

The common core spiritual principle at the heart of every restraint and observance is the great Oneness — realization of the singular foundation that sustains and supports all life. It all comes back to dharma, the necessity to recognize life as one omnipresent Ultimate Reality and see all that we do in relation to that.

Each restraint and observance is a metaphysical formula for enlightened awareness and activity. Through overarching themes like nonviolence or truthfulness, they reverberate into the health and well-being of all our relationships and every area of our life. The way the principles, or spiritual laws, work rests on the seamless connection between mind and matter, consciousness and manifestation. What we hold in consciousness — what we believe, act from, and experience — will be reflected back to us. For example, if we steal from someone else to increase our wealth, we will ultimately experience lack, not prosperity. It's not possible to circumvent spiritual law; we cannot live and act outside of the reality of Oneness. What we think, say, and do resounds through the world, travels the circle that is unity, and returns to us. Sometimes it returns instantaneously, but more often it takes longer — weeks, months, years, or as some believe, incarnations. This is the basic law of karma.

To get the most out of our exploration of the restraints and observances, we practice self-inquiry. We look at each one and contemplate: What is the spiritual law that this principle rests upon? When it comes as revelation, it is ours, something connected, something we have insight into, have seen and known. What I offer here can be seen as priming the pump as you bring forth the "living water" of your own deeper contemplation.

While every restraint and observance draws its verity from dharma, the cosmic law of harmonious right relationship, each points to a specific area of life we can focus on. Here's a list of underlying principles in the yamas and niyamas seen through the lens of enlightened prosperity:

NONHARMING: We cannot harm another without harming ourselves.

TRUTHFULNESS: Aligning thoughts, speech, actions with the Truth of our being connects us with divine prospering power.

NONSTEALING: The principle behind nonstealing is the law of abundance. Thinking we have to steal from another reveals an underlying belief in lack, which negates our ability to prosper.

RIGHT USE OF VITAL FORCE: Appropriate use of our vital force keeps us consciously connected to the Source and its prospering flow of energy.

NONATTACHMENT: Greed is a misdirected quest for fulfillment that cannot be found through outer acquisition.

PURITY: A clarified body and mind and a lifestyle focused on higher purpose make us fit vehicles for spiritual realization and a thriving life.

CONTENTMENT: Only a peaceful, satisfied mind can reveal

inherent supreme happiness — realization of our innate abundance.

SELF-DISCIPLINE: Body and mind are divine vehicles — through self-discipline, Self-realization and Self-actualization are possible.

SELF-INQUIRY: Because we are divine beings, we can experience and know Truth directly.

SELF-SURRENDER: Ultimate realization is beyond mind and matter. It cannot be reached by effort or will.

Living It Every Day: Spiritual Practice

The restraints and observances for spiritually conscious, prosperous living are given to us as a broad stroke in the Yoga Sutras, which doesn't specify how to apply them to everyday situations. Patanjali gives us the life principles, but he doesn't delineate all the practices for the yamas and niyamas — those are learned from one's guru, or through personal study, contemplation, and implementation.[4] That is where our practice of self-inquiry comes into play. It's up to us to discern how to put each principle into practice.

When I was a young woman, I enrolled in a self-defense class. Week after week, I lined up with an assortment of women — different ages, ethnicities, backgrounds, economic status — who shared a common goal. We wanted to be free from fear. We wanted to know that we could defend ourselves against physical violence if we ever needed to. The instructor gave us some good basic information — when to run, when to yell, how to stand our ground if we needed to fight. We paired off and practiced — one of us on the offense, the other defense. He instructed us how to stand and face each other, showed defenders how to dodge a blow or put up a block. I graduated from that introductory course with enough information to know what I didn't know. I was pretty sure I could defend myself if my attacker stood right in front of me and reached out exactly as my practice partner had done. But what if someone came from another direction? I had no idea how to meet that challenge. Obviously, more study and practice would be needed. The restraints and observances are no different; they are a work in progress. We learn more about them, and about ourselves, as we engage in real-time life experiences.

The practices for each of the restraints and observances have an arc that runs from the outer physical level to inner, subtle levels, including speech and thoughts. They begin with the obvious. For example, nonviolence on the basic level instructs us not to engage in physical harm. Refrain from harming — don't kill or injure self, others, or the environment. Even at this level, which seems clear enough, we will soon find ourselves asking important questions about how to live. Does that mean we should not kill animals for food? What about fish? What about plants and trees? What if someone attacks us, or we witness an attack: Is harming another in self-defense acceptable? And so it goes.

Once we address nonviolence on the physical level, we contemplate our words and stop harmful speech — meanness, hatred, or unkindness in our conversations. Gossip and sarcasm must go. Then we consider our thoughts and catch ourselves if we wish harm to another or hold hateful, vengeful, or mean-spirited thoughts.

During our practice, it is always helpful to remember that we are not engaging in a never-ending list of dos and don'ts. We're not practicing for sainthood. We are adjusting our thoughts, speech, and behavior to align with the enlivening power that runs the universe. We are setting ourselves up to thrive, and everybody else along with us.

Below is a brief overview of practices. The usefulness and power of the practices comes with personal insight and implementation. We test them in the laboratory of daily life as we contemplate their comprehensive effect. Adjusting one attitude or changing one behavior will often reveal the next steps we must take to bring our life in alignment with higher purpose. For instance, the five yamas, or restraints, first involve abstaining from behaviors that are not in harmony with an awakened, thriving life. Then each progresses to cultivating positive behaviors that are in harmony. For example, the first imperative of nonviolence is to refrain from causing or condoning harm, but fulfillment of the principle is to act compassionately.

> NONVIOLENCE: Refrain from harming self, others, or the environment through any form of violence — action, speech, or thoughts. Cultivate compassion.
>
> TRUTHFULNESS: Speak only truth. Live with integrity, in harmony with the true Self.
>
> NONSTEALING: Refrain from theft or envy. Live authentically; do your own work.
>
> RIGHT USE OF VITAL FORCE: Use your energy wisely and consciously. Refrain from sexual misconduct. Live intentionally with higher purpose.
>
> NONATTACHMENT: Reduce unnecessary desires. Live simply; cultivate discernment.
>
> PURITY: See to cleanliness of body, mind, and environment. Cultivate a peaceful, uplifting environment both inwardly and outwardly.
>
> CONTENTMENT: Discern what brings lasting happiness. Abide in soul awareness.
>
> SELF-DISCIPLINE: Refrain from whatever does not serve your highest good; do what is in harmony with your soul.
>
> SELF-INQUIRY: Contemplate the nature of reality — meditate, study scriptures and the book of your life.
>
> SELF-SURRENDER: Release the false idea of being separate from the Source. Let go of attachment to outcomes. Be open to divine grace.

Realizing It: The Promises

While Patanjali does not provide details about specific practices of the restraints and observances — that is left to the gurus, scholars, and all of us who test them out in the laboratory of daily life — he does shine a bright light on the promise of each one as they are realized. Each yama and niyama is described in the sutras by its culmination or fruition. They spell out what can be expected or observed when a person is *established* in that virtue — when inner realization and outer action are in complete accord with the spiritual principle. Because this accord brings us into complete harmony with the divine Self, spiritual power is released; it flows unobstructed into our life and through us into the lives of others. Those sutras are what I call the promises — the word *promise* being, according to the American Heritage Dictionary, an "indication of future excellence or success" or that which "afford[s] a basis for expectation."

Here I have paraphrased traditional interpretations of the sutras to highlight the ten prospering promises they contain:

1. Cultivate nonviolence and experience the entire world as your friend (2:35).
2. Be completely truthful and your words will have creative power (2:36).
3. Take nothing from others and experience prosperity and good fortune (2:37).
4. Let nothing distract you from right living and experience great vitality (2:38).
5. Free yourself from greed and see life clearly (2:39).
6. Cultivate purity and experience even-mindedness and true joy (2:40, 41).
7. Be content now and realize unshakable happiness (2:42).
8. Always do what pleases your soul and experience perfection of the body, mind, and senses (2:43).

9. By study of scripture and Self-inquiry know the reality of God (2:44).

10. Surrender to God — realize absolute Oneness and freedom from fear (2:45).

A Promise and a Prompt

Why are we successful in some aspects of our life but not others? What holds us back in the areas that are not working well? Exploring the promises will yield valuable insights, usually surprising ones. The prospering promises of the restraints and observances can be used, not only as goals we strive for and are inspired by, but as prompts for practice in areas where we have challenges. Just as we can contemplate them as guideposts showing us how to arrange conditions for the highest good, we can also look to them as markers for course corrections along the way.

Contemplating the promises as prompts for course correction is both straightforward and intuitive. First, we look to the specific area where a challenge is occurring. Then we examine the promise related to that area. We inquire about our *integrity* related to that promise by quieting the mind, raising the question, and simply being open to insight. It may not (usually does not) come in one sitting. More likely, we inquire and the answer is revealed to us later as an insight that arises when we are open and relaxed. The inner light of intuitive perception comes on, and we see the connection between the promise, the spiritual principle, and our area of inquiry. Once we see it, we know what to do to make the necessary change. We can make the adjustment — make amends where it is needed, take positive action, turn toward wholeness, and bring our life into higher harmony with spiritual law.

Let's look at how it can work. Let's say there is an undercurrent of discord in a primary relationship. The initial inquiry is simple enough — we inwardly ask whether we are out of harmony with any of the principles. We examine our conscience. In the instance of relationship challenge, we look first to nonharming, since it connects specifically to harmonious relations. Have we said or done anything that was harmful to the other person? Have we lacked forgiveness, kindness, or compassion? Are we holding a resentment?

Harmlessness and truthfulness always work together, so the next place to look is truthfulness. Have we been honest with this person? Told the truth or withheld it? Lacked self-honesty by saying or doing things that were inauthentic or insincere? We can also explore our integrity, or lack of it, with any or all of the eight other principles. How might this relationship trouble reflect lack of harmony with each principle?

While being out of integrity with any principle will short-circuit our thriving and affect our relationships, this process for clearing up trouble spots is usually most efficient when we look first to the principle directly related to the problem. Relationship trouble? Start with nonharming. Problem with realizing goals? Truthfulness. Can't seem to prosper? Nonstealing. And so forth. Look at the difficulty and consider which promise most closely relates to it. Trust your intuition and your self-inquiry to guide the process. Remember, you are not looking for some external validation. At the deepest level of our being, we always know the genesis of any inharmony and what we need to do to make a course correction. This self-inquiry process supports the inward journey necessary to reveal what we know and bolsters our courage to make important changes.

Our lives are seamlessly whole; everyone and everything is connected. To work with the promises as tied to spiritual principles, we approach them holistically. We don't look only at the immediate situation where the challenge is occurring. We take a broad view, a whole-life view. For example, we may experience a challenge in our primary relationship at home and can't figure out how lack of compassion connects because that seems to be in order. Love and compassion are there. But if we do a whole-life scan on the topic of harmlessness in relationship, we may discover another relationship where we are resentful, lack compassion, or are outright hostile. Maybe it's a conflict with a friend or a coworker, including some harmful conversation playing out with others. That tear in the fabric of life's Oneness may be affecting the relationship at home. Why wouldn't it? We don't live in isolation; there is no wall between who we are in one relationship and how we are in another. It's worth exploring. This arena is where spiritual realization comes to life — in our heart, in our mind, on the ground where we live every day.

The Great Promise

Yoga's ultimate promise of the spiritually awakened, thriving life is liberation — a life of freedom lived in the spontaneous joy of the soul. The great error of ego-driven motivation is removed through Self-realization. We no longer live to get and devour. We live to give and create; ours becomes a generative life, one that overflows with blessings for all. The ten prospering promises are the ways we turn our life in that divine direction. We live by grace, life's inherent irrepressible support, and not by self-effort alone. Freed from the taints of shame and blame, we are fully empowered to transform our lives and contribute to the well-being of others.

Fourteen

Overcome Obstacles

*On this path, effort never goes to waste, and there is no failure.
Even a little effort toward spiritual awareness will protect you
from the greatest fear.*

— Bhagavad Gita

Will I succeed? It's a logical question as we consider how to live fully, to thrive and prosper. At times, we experience steady progress as we move in the direction of fulfilling our goals and thriving along the way. Living in balance and having resources to meet our needs flows effortlessly. With discernment and regular spiritual practice to keep our heart, mind, and motives clear, we move ahead with the winning combination of personal effort and divine grace. Abundance is at hand. We meet the right people at the right time who are drawn to be part of things unfolding harmoniously. Life is good! Then, there are those times when we approach what is before us with similar discernment and preparation, but lo and behold, right in the pathway of successful completion of our worthy goal stands an obstacle.

Sometimes it's clear that the obstacle is minor and temporary. In that case, we can simply wait patiently or take necessary steps to move it aside. But there are also obstacles that appear formidable. They seem unmovable, and dealing with them can be challenging. In this situation, I have seen people do all sorts of things to try to find their way through. Some will give up on their project or dream, fold up their energy and intention, and let the obstacle declare for them that it "wasn't meant to be." Others will pray and wait, or contemplate, inwardly seeking to discover any connection to the obstacle in their own consciousness. Some will try tools — create an affirmation, offer a chant, or engage in a ritual action that signifies the process of moving through the barrier. Still others will double down their efforts or reach out and ask for help. Any method we choose to apply can potentially be useful, if it also facilitates a change in consciousness. Any lasting success at transforming obstacles before us must come from within. Recognizing the inner component and connection is invaluable; it's a natural preventative against similar challenges appearing later. Without discerning the subtle cause of the obstacle or our connection to it, we may move through it only to meet it again in another form just down the road. We also run the risk of missing any gift of awakening it brings.

Since life is one reality and we are not separate from it, we are empowered to move through obstacles by first making any useful inner adjustments. We often work so hard on the outside, literally wearing ourselves out trying to change things, when it's much more efficient to do the inner work first. This allows us to be clear about what action needs to be taken, if any. Sometimes the obstacle simply falls away in the light of insight and a change of consciousness.

From the spiritual perspective, however formidable an obstacle may appear, the operant word is *appear*. At the heart of our ability to get beyond obstacles is the deeper understanding that conditions are always changing. Not one of them is permanent. Yoga philosophy refers to conditions — which include everything in manifest creation, everything in nature — as maya, or illusion. Conditions are real, but they are constantly changing and have no independent Ultimate Reality. They appear, move, change, disappear, reappear — a constant dance of energy in motion. Obstacles become more difficult to deal with if we see them as permanent and give them a solidity that they do not have. As the Buddha said, "All things arise and pass away. But the awakened awake forever."[1]

We learn to see through obstacles by remembering their impermanence, their ephemeral nature. That's the first great insight in our tool kit for dealing with obstacles. The second is remembering that divine resources are always available to meet real needs because life itself continually moves in the direction of thriving, prospering, and fulfilling its higher purposes. With clear understanding and with faith — which is opening to the flow of life's abundant resources — no obstacle can long prevail.

Not only can no obstacle long prevail on the path of awakening to our full potential, there is no such thing as failure. How can that be so? Failure only comes into play when we see success as a final product. True thriving is not a result and does not depend on meeting goals, even though we set them and pursue them with intentionality and vigor. Living from the inside out, all the way to thriving is thriving. Working toward goals is always in the spirit of learning, growing, awakening, and serving life along the way. Anything and everything that occurs is grist for the mill for thriving in accordance with spiritual principles. Dealing with obstacles is a vibrant part of it. How else would we learn and grow? How else could greater abundance arise without breaking down the limiting barriers of our expectations?

The promises that no effort is ever wasted and no obstacle can long prevail do not mean there will be no losses, setbacks, or difficulties. On the contrary, they imply that success always includes them. When we learn how to have a more expansive view of victory, we find that seeming reverses, setbacks, and obstacles are all integral to our highest success.

Go Ahead, Shine

There's a way to turn
without losing your balance...
raise your self by your Self
at dawn. Go ahead.
Shine in the morning sky.

— Ellen Grace O'Brian, "The Moon Reminded Me"[2]

There are times when, even though we know what we are called to do for our own divine expression — for healing or thriving — we hesitate to commit. We lack an expansive enough vision of who we are and what success really is. We may say things like, "I have failed so many times before. I don't want to fail again, so I won't even try." Or, sometimes, we say, "Because I have been defeated in my efforts before, I won't put myself into it completely. I'll just try and see what happens." The "I'll try" approach without a full-on commitment to succeed is an affirmation of lack before we even begin.

What's the secret to living our fullest life as we strive to reach goals? Recognizing the higher goal of Self-knowledge, Self-realization, and Self-actualization. When we know that working toward our commitments in order to prosper — to be healthy, to experience loving relationships, to succeed with our careers, and to be productive in our creative endeavors and our ability to serve life — is a pathway to unfolding our highest potential, we can embrace both so-called failure and success. Both are steps along the way of the soul's journey and can be recognized as the learning opportunities they are. There is no end to failing and succeeding! When we see this play of failing and succeeding as integral to our awakening, we can engage fully in our soul's calling and live in the ever-new joy of our divine potential unfolding.

Five Core Obstacles

The obstacles are ignorance, ego, desire, aversion, and clinging to life.
— Yoga Sutras[3]

At the root of our sorrows and troubles, we find what yoga calls *kleshas*, which means afflictions, impediments, or obstacles. There are five of them — ignorance, egoism (I-am-ness), attachment, aversion, and confusion about birth and death (clinging to life of the body-mind). These are the major obstructions in the mind that block the experience of yoga, realization of the true Self. Our spiritual practice is aimed at removing them, clearing the way for the inner light of the Self to shine.

These obstructions have a twofold purpose. They allow Spirit to become involved with the enlivening influence of nature, which brings forth creation, innovation, and the manifestation of individuals. The limiting influence of the kleshas allows Spirit, which is unlimited, to express in discrete ways — as you, me, and an infinite number of others throughout time. The diverse beauty and complexity of creation becomes possible; the One becomes many. This is awesome. At the same time, if we are unconscious of the obstacles that make creation possible, they become binding for the soul — the primary impediments to our liberation and ultimate freedom. This is a problem.

The first obstacle, *avidya* or ignorance, is the cause of our troublesome case of mistaken identity. While our true Self is unlimited, spiritually conscious being, we mistakenly and tenaciously believe we are the limited body and mind we occupy. Ignorance of what we really are gives rise to the second klesha, *asmita*, the sense of "I-am-ness." This sense of individual self becomes ego when the power of perception is wrongfully attributed to mind, instead of credited to the Seer, the divine Self that illumines the mind. With that identity theft, ego then sets up its own camp as the false self, which it maintains with the help of the following two obstacles: *raga*, attraction, and *dvesha*, aversion. Our mistaken identity then creeps beyond the body and mind, into relationships, possessions, accomplishments, or the roles we play — things we erroneously allow to define and confine us. We begin to identify who we are by what we like, what we don't like, what we do, or what we have. This grand charade is topped off by the obstacle *abhinivesha*, instinctual clinging to life in the body-mind. Now we have avidya in full bloom.

These five are the major obstacles Patanjali identifies as obstructions to samadhi, or superconsciousness. We can also see how they impact and impede our ability to thrive. Ego, by its very nature, is limited — a blind, narrow superimposition on the unlimited, unbounded Seer, the true Self. Our frames of likes and dislikes color our perceptions, and if we are not aware of them, they obscure our ability to be open to possibility.

Abhinivesha klesha, or clinging to life, refers to the instinctual fear of death. This obstacle is rooted in the belief that our existence is limited to the body-mind identity. Identifying with the mortal body and mind brings fear of death in its wake. While the instinctual fear of death is an accurate understanding of abhinivesha, another way to look at it is clinging to the past or trying to hold on to life as it once was.

Clinging to the past often occurs at the major life junctures where we are called to let go and grow. It can manifest in young people who have trouble moving from the student stage of life into accepting full responsibilities of mature adulthood. They still want to live at home and be taken care of. Or parents may cling to their old identity as they try to direct the lives of their adult children, who have grown and left home. Parents may also resist seeing how their marriage must evolve now that the task of parenting is complete. We can also observe it in those who reach elder years but seem to only look back, not forward, spending their days regretting or reminiscing instead of responding to life's current call to awaken. If we are not afraid to let go of former roles and responsibilities, our elder years can be the time to embrace our most important spiritual stage of life.

Anticipating Obstacles

I asked a friend the other day how his new focus on healthy eating and exercise was going, and he said, "Well, when the stress mounts at work, all of that goes out the window." Allowing our resolve and inspiration to cave in when obstacles arise can lead us to feeling that we are victims of circumstances, certainly not masters of our destinies. Obstacles are likely to arise. Without mounting a defense against imaginary foes before we even get started, how do we prepare ourselves in a positive way for the difficulties we may very well encounter?

There is a small creek in my backyard. I enjoy watching how the water moves around the rocks in its path, which then becomes a regular course. If you throw in a new rock, the stream doesn't stop; it finds a way around it and changes its course. The stream's flow and flexibility is a good example of how to respond when we encounter obstacles. We can recognize obstacles as intrinsic to any journey as well as a valuable part of it.

One of the greatest obstacles we can put in our way is the idea that we won't have any. Fueled by initial enthusiasm, we may venture forth thinking that the way ahead will be a straight course without interruption. That's rarely, if ever, the case. The pathway of success doesn't look like a drainpipe — a straight line from here to there. A truly fulfilling life looks more like a creek with the beauty of natural twists and turns made by the water's encounter with obstacles.

Meeting Obstacles as Opportunities

On the spiritual pilgrimage, all obstacles are created by the very subjective and objective worlds in the seeker himself; his attachment to the world of objects, emotions, and thoughts are alone his obstacles.

— SWAMI CHINMAYANANDA[4]

Even more important than recognizing that life offers opportunities for growth is knowing that the opportunity (aka obstacle), and the necessary inspiration for meeting that opportunity, arise from within. Remember, what one person sees as an obstacle, another may clearly see as opportunity. We see situations or conditions as "obstacles" only when we're attached either to a particular way of moving forward or to a specific outcome. Remove that attachment, replace it with openness and curiosity, and the onus of the obstacle vanishes. Our sword of discernment transforms it into an opportunity.

When those opportunities for growth arrive, they can serve us well as a point of reflection — a time for discernment, expanding our consciousness, and opening to possibility. They encourage us to pause and ask questions: *How important is it to persevere through this? Is there another way to meet my goal? Is there a different way to view this?*

Instead of looking at how the situation must change, we can often find the most powerful breakthrough when we ask questions like: *What needs to change in me? How might this obstacle connect to my belief system? Am I ready to change?* And, perhaps even more significant: *Is it possible that life is trying to bring even more prosperity to me in this moment than I am ready to receive? Can I see beyond the confines of narrow particulars to the expansion of greater possibilities? If divine love has something to do with this, what might that be?*

Here are three things we can do to meet obstacles as opportunities for growth and greater good:

ANTICIPATE OBSTACLES AS OPPORTUNITIES. Remind yourself at the outset of a new endeavor or setting a goal that obstacles are an integral part of growth. Decide to see them as one of the ways that life shows us capacities we didn't know we had or reveals potentials in a situation we couldn't see before. Often, we only recognize this in hindsight. How many times have you heard someone say, "If only I had known this was going to work out for the better, I wouldn't have spent my days and nights tied up in worry about it." Anticipating obstacles as opportunities in disguise keeps us from falling into that trap. Wonder can take the place of worry.

GET CLEAR. When obstacles arise, there's a tendency for the mind either to kick into overdrive or to deflate with heaviness or despair. Instead of those default reactions, we can let the obstacle remind us to stop, reflect, and allow insight and inspiration to arise. This is the moment to tap into life's prospering inclination. Be willing to wait for inspiration and a new way to be shown.

LET GO. An event, situation, or circumstance becomes an obstacle that feels formidable when we are attached to things being a certain way. If you encounter an obstacle, consider that it is an obstacle principally because you allow it to be one. Ask: *What can I let go of that would transform this situation? What would it be like if I let that go?* Imagine that; see what that freedom reveals.

Greeting obstacles as opportunities helps us hone our skills of introspection, deep listening, and opening to possibility. There is no reason we can't thrive along the way, just as the stream continues to flow around a rock. The softness of water meets the hardness of a rock and flows around it, charting a new course. That flowing quality of flexibility and receptivity helps us see things with fresh eyes and open to new solutions, possibilities, and greater prosperity.

When I first began my study and practice of Kriya Yoga, I had an opportunity to travel with my spiritual teacher. At one point, we were stuck in an airport waiting on a delayed plane. It was a long journey and I was tired. Many years later, I still remember the poignant life lesson he offered in response to what I saw as an annoying obstacle. I said to him, "I hate waiting in airports." For no real reason other than seeming inconvenience, I was making myself unhappy. He responded gently, "The way I see it, we always have to be somewhere." The question for us is: *How? How are we being where we are?*

What Is Ours to Do

*It's better to do one's own duty, even if imperfectly,
than do that of another, even if perfectly.*

— Bhagavad Gita[5]

We can't do everything. In our fast-paced, technology-driven, hyper-connected times, it's increasingly apparent that we can't do everything that comes our way, even if it appeals to us. There is simply too much. We must become "masters of determination" who skillfully wield the inner sword of discernment to cut away nonessentials in order to focus on essentials. As we live full lives, it's easy to say yes to too many opportunities and not make appropriate boundaries. Pretty soon our lives are full, but not necessarily full of what truly matters to us. Truly fulfilled living requires us to continually and clearly discern our "yes" and our "no" — the beautiful boundaries that support focusing on what is ours to do and letting go of what is not.

Life is inherently abundant. Nature continually creates and re-creates. We are all blessed with the inner power to attract opportunities for expression. As we grow spiritually, the appearance of opportunities increases because our inner magnetism increases. We may once have felt bereft of potentials or possibilities, but even a little sincere engagement in spiritual practice and inner development shows us another way. Once we begin to cooperate consciously with the infinite power of the universe, we meet opportunities at every turn. Instead of seeking opportunities, our inner work becomes honing our discernment about what is ours to do and what is not.

Clarity about our duties and responsibilities, our life purpose, and our goals is essential for being a "master of determination." How can we determine what's useful for us, or not, if we haven't specifically identified what is ours to do? Duties and responsibilities in life change over time, requiring regular periods of reflection. What was once a key responsibility may change dramatically as we grow older, change jobs, enter a new relationship, or deal with challenges. We must examine what we have done, what we dream to accomplish, the trajectory of our life, and the needs of the time we are living in — all in light of the soul's joy.

Be a Master of Determination

You have no greater friend and no greater enemy than yourself. If you befriend yourself, you will find accomplishment. There is no law of God preventing you from being what you want to be and accomplishing what you want to accomplish. Nothing detrimental that happens can affect you unless you sanction it.

— Paramahansa Yogananda[6]

Life mastery is a fascinating journey of continuously taking charge and repeatedly letting go. We are fiercely intentional with our resolve, determination, and focus to live fully, while completely surrendered to life's insistence on the soul's joy as the key to thriving. Skillfully determining the course of our life requires calibrating that balance again and again as we welcome obstacles like an aikido master — working with the energy of what comes and being transformed along the way.

When an obstacle appears, here are six steps to follow for greater understanding, insight, and self-mastery.

1. MEDITATE. Clear your mind. Sit quietly. Simply notice your breathing until thoughts and feelings settle. Remain for a time in the awareness of your essential nature as spiritual — beyond thought, change, or phenomena. Affirm and feel that your mind is clear, your discernment is keen, and your intuition is awakened.

2. CONTEMPLATE. After meditation, remain for a time in tranquil, insightful awareness. Use your discernment to objectively view your situation and any obstacle you face. Remind yourself that whatever the obstacle is, it is only a condition, and all conditions are subject to change. Nothing in the manifest realm is permanent. Everything is continually changing. Free yourself from seeing this obstacle as permanent. Know, and affirm, that divine order prevails in your life.

3. INQUIRE. Further, use this time of contemplation to inquire into any connection you have to this obstacle. This inquiry works best if done in a nonjudgmental way. Try to simply be curious. Ask yourself some friendly questions, like, *How might this obstacle be useful to me?* Sometimes we discover that we have called it forth, or welcomed it in some way, because it either serves a purpose for us or is consistent with some belief we have. Once we see our relationship to the obstacle, we can change our thinking and release it — either let

go of attraction, of clinging to it, or let go of aversion, of fear of it. Whatever the obstacle is, it is not ours; it never belonged to the true Self.

4. AFFIRM. An affirmation that can be used after the inquiry is: *All obstacles are removed in divine order.* Or, simply: *All things are now in divine order.* When speaking these words, connect with their meaning and the feeling the meaning evokes. Rest assured that all things are moving according to divine plan and purpose. Believe that any obstacle will not long prevail; it will be removed in the right time and in the highest way. Feel that the highest good is now unfolding for everyone concerned. It is also helpful to recognize that the obstacle to be removed might be our own viewpoint or behavior. What needs to change might not be the circumstance — it may be us. Be willing to make any necessary changes.

5. WAIT. Following this inner work, wait with faith. Wait with positive expectancy and act when the right steps are revealed. Neither pushing the river, nor neglecting our duty, we respond appropriately when new insights arise and when opportunities are presented.

6. BE GRATEFUL. Cultivate contentment and gratitude as your consistent state of mind. This attitude keeps the mental field clear and allows us to stay open to further inspiration.

Beautiful Mistakes

...and the golden bees
were making white combs
and sweet honey
from my old failures...
— ANTONIO MACHADO[7]

When we recognize the source of thriving as the unbounded, spiritual core of our being, this brings an expansive viewpoint for embracing our successes and failures, the obstacles we encounter, and the gifts of grace we receive with unparalleled equanimity. That equanimity, with its openness to possibility, becomes our greatest asset for moving through life with abundant joy and grace. We can step back from the noise and fray, from fear or anticipation, excitement or anxiety. As we view and experience the landscape of our life where everything changes, we can take a breath and acknowledge the unchanging perfection at the core. We can appreciate the moving twists and turns that make life beautiful, all the while abiding in unmoving Absolute Reality.

I have always been interested in the beauty and grace of the Japanese tea ceremony, so when I got an opportunity to learn about it at a local Zen center, I jumped at the chance. Before tea, the Zen priest teaching us the fundamentals of the ceremony had us spend a significant amount of time cleaning the tea room and the implements. The metaphor of "preparing the way" was not lost on me.

When she demonstrated how the actual ritualized service of the tea and sweets was to be done, I became overwhelmed. There were too many precise movements to remember. Bowing, placing the implements, showing the beautiful cups, appreciating — all sorts of things took place before the tea was even poured! How could I possibly remember everything she had instructed us to do? I wanted to do it right and noticed I was feeling anxious. I asked her, "What if I forget what I am supposed to do? What if I make a mistake?" She said, "How would it be to make a mistake?" I said, "Terrible. I don't like to make mistakes. I'd be embarrassed." She said, "Perhaps there is another possibility to consider about mistakes. Try to imagine a world without them — a world without any mistakes."

Offering a graphic example, she continued, "Think of an oak tree. If a tree had no obstacles or mistakes in its growth path, it would grow completely straight and tall. Everywhere we look, trees would be straight as an arrow, with every branch uniform. But instead, when we look at the oaks on the hillside, their beauty comes from their curved branches, their response to every obstacle they encountered. Every place they turned was a 'mistake' from their original growth path, but every turn ultimately became their beauty."

This contrasting image — of an obstacle-free world with only row upon row of rigidly straight trees versus the living wonder of trees gracefully bending their boughs in response to life's obstacles — became my introduction to beautiful mistakes.

I am, you are, we are, life is, perfectly imperfect.[8]

Fifteen

Optimize Success

You can only become truly accomplished at something you love.
Don't make money your goal. Instead pursue the things you love doing
and then do them so well that people can't take their eyes off of you.

— MAYA ANGELOU

*C*an we truly succeed without love? Prosper without the soul's joy? The old paradigm of success at any cost stands revealed for the outdated, misdirected strategy it is. Stories and evidence abound of those who single-mindedly pursue their goal and lose what is truly meaningful to them along the way. Another way shines before us now — both ancient and timely.

The Vedic path of fulfilled living has not one but *four* essential aims: purpose, prosperity, pleasure, and freedom. Live with meaning and higher purpose; thrive and prosper; enjoy life; and realize true freedom. The imperative to prosper is for the sake of the soul, not at the expense of the soul. Pursuing any one of the life aims exclusively without the ameliorating influence of the other three, we cheat ourselves. The price we pay is our aliveness — missing the fullness of joy that life can be.

The formula for success that yoga offers is stated in Patanjali's sutra 1:22: "Progress is in accord with intensity of practice, whether mild, medium, or extremely intensive."[1] This verse is about progress toward experiencing samadhi, or superconsciousness, but it can also be aptly applied to progress toward our worthy goals. At first glance, the temptation is to read this verse as familiar — something along the lines of "the harder we work, the greater the gain," sounding a lot like the "no pain, no gain" model for success. But that's not it. Here, "intensity of practice" doesn't refer as much to *effort* as it does to *intentionality*.

The stronger our focus, the more intentionally we live, the greater our success.

Regarding this verse, Roy Davis comments, "Practice is extremely intensive when nonessential matters are disregarded and attention and actions are concentrated on the purposes to be accomplished."[2]

The spiritually based formula for success is clear focus, intentional living, and steadfast commitment to *complete* well-being — allowing body, mind, and soul to thrive as mighty instruments for life's prospering power. This formula points back to the necessary collusion of effort and grace, requiring our complete focus on what is ours to do and complete openness to the beneficence of the universe along the way. The greatest successes are gifts of grace. They come to us within the sphere of our highest intentions but recognizably beyond the scope of personal effort. We know grace when we experience it. We are amazed, astounded, awed. Expanded.

Get Centered, Stay Centered

Environment is stronger than willpower.

— Paramahansa Yogananda[3]

A successful, thriving, spiritually aware life is best supported by a healthy lifestyle that includes a wholesome diet, sufficient rest, regular exercise, daily meditation, loving relationships, and positive thinking. Caring for body, mind, and soul-life is essential. Without self-care, we are prone to experience the debilitating effects of stress and revert to old destructive habits that undermine our progress. The times we engage in thoughts or actions that aren't useful are usually connected to being overstressed by poor nutrition, lack of exercise or sufficient rest, worry, or neglecting to meditate regularly or to spend time with nurturing relationships.

As Paramahansa Yogananda insightfully noted — *environment is stronger than willpower.* Established habits are readily triggered by our surroundings. This works in our favor if the environment is in alignment with our goals, and this works against us if the environment triggers old habits we are trying to change. If we're tired, or otherwise off balance, we're more likely to respond to the environmental trigger, even if we had previously intended to behave differently. To stay the course of establishing new behaviors that are consistent with thriving, we must arrange an environment conducive to success and recognize self-care as essential, not a luxury.

Self-care helps us get centered and stay centered, supporting our resolve to make positive changes. Below is a formula I developed with the acronym CENTER, which stands for "consider, establish, nurture, think, enjoy, remember." CENTER can be used to arrange conditions for success.

CONSIDER YOUR INTENTION AND CLARIFY YOUR GOALS. Clarity supports focus and intentional action. Begin by considering your overarching intention. What is your purpose? What will it serve? State your intention, then your goal or goals that support it. Write this down and keep it where you can see and refer to it regularly.

ESTABLISH A CONSCIOUSNESS OF SUCCESS. Envision your goal already accomplished. Feel or imagine the experience of succeeding. Let that feeling permeate your mind and body. We work on the subtle "blueprint" level of our goal when we do this. Then, do at least one thing every day that's consistent with your vision and supportive of your success.

NURTURE YOUR BODY, MIND, AND SOUL. Identify any adjustments you will make that are supportive of your well-being. Keep it simple. Remember that too much stress combined with lack of self-care undermines the resolve to implement new, positive habits. Poor self-care is self-sabotage. Take charge by taking care.

THINK POSITIVELY. Learning to cooperate with divine grace, following our wisdom-guided intuition, and remaining steadfast with new positive habits are skills we develop. It is a living, learning process. It takes time for something to manifest from the inner, subtle realms to the outer, physical realm. The time it takes is our learning curve, a period of transformation. We rise to meet our goal as our inner powers are unleashed. Success is a process, not an event. Hold positive thoughts about yourself as you grow and change.

ENJOY YOUR LIFE AS YOU COOPERATE WITH YOUR UNFOLDING POTENTIAL AND HIGHEST GOOD. Don't put off joy, thinking of it as a result. Joy is a quality of the soul. When we're in touch with that, we're in touch with our soul nature. Pay attention to what brings you joy, peace, and contentment. Include that. Love yourself, love others, love your life along the way.

REMEMBER YOU ARE A DIVINE BEING. Achieving our goal doesn't change what we are. We are already whole and complete. Nothing can take that away or improve upon it. Be anchored in your innate wholeness. That anchoring allows us to remain centered when powerful waves of change are moving through our life.

Consider. Establish. Nurture. Think. Enjoy. Remember.

Ask yourself the following questions each day as part of the CENTER formula checklist. Make any adjustments needed to stay on course.

C: Have I carefully *considered* my intention and clearly stated my goals?

E: Have I taken time today to adjust my mind and consciousness to be *established* in success?

N: Am I *nurturing* my body, mind, and soul by practicing good self-care?

T: Are my *thoughts* positive?

E: Am I *enjoying* life?

R: Do I *remember* my true nature?

Arrange Conditions for Success

There's much we can do to realize our innate potential by cooperating with the infinite and its grace-filled prospering power. The positive changes we make on the physical, mental, and spiritual levels of our being all clear the way for that power to express in and through our life. We can't make realization occur, nor can we guarantee success, but we can cultivate the most conducive environment for both to occur. Arranging conditions for our success, along with inspired right action, makes all the difference.

Fine-Tune the Environment

The influence of environment is hard to miss. An afternoon spent in a quiet forest grove on a sunny day, or walking along the seashore, will clear our mind, renew our energy, and facilitate inspiration rising to the surface of our awareness. Sitting bumper to bumper on a crowded freeway surrounded by toxic fumes and frustrated drivers, or walking into a dark, smoky bar with lonesome blues music playing, surely affects us differently. Say hello to tension, heaviness, fatigue.

The physical environment that surrounds us is an extension of our body-mind. A continual interplay goes on between our external environment and our physical body, mind, and soul. We can recognize the potential impact of the external environment and make wise choices about where we go and where we'll stay. We can take special care in our immediate surroundings — the personal space of our home and place of work — to facilitate the most conducive environment for overall well-being, creativity, and thriving.

According to the teachings of yoga, our environment should be peaceful and uplifting. This is considered the best way to allow innate peace to surface and our creative, nurturing capacities to be unveiled. It's good for our health as well as spiritual development. Cleanliness, order, and spaciousness is generally recommended as supportive of thriving, but what that looks like can vary widely. The main thing to consider is what you experience as uplifting. What brings joy to your heart and peace to your mind? Cultivate and enhance those aspects. Choose carefully what you allow in the door of your home or office. Let your choices reflect your intention to succeed — to live, love, and thrive in the highest way.

While it's essential to make changes in mind and consciousness, sometimes it can be energizing to start at the physical level. Pick a space to transform. Think about how that space could more fully support your success. Identify two or three things that you could do *immediately* that would make a positive change. Sometimes, something as simple as clearing our desktop, or bringing in some treasured artwork, can offer a sense of possibility.

After you've done those simple things, notice their effect on your mind and body. How does it feel? Do you notice any change? Consider what you can do to maintain this change and further arrange your environment to support your ability to prosper.

Change Thought Patterns

When the mind is disturbed by negative thoughts,
one should dwell on their opposites.

— Yoga Sutras[4]

We arrange conditions in our mind conducive to success by changing any thought patterns that are not consistent with thriving. Most of us have debilitating self- or other-critical thoughts that arise (either occasionally or frequently). If we consistently focus on these negative inputs, or allow them to run in the background unchecked, we undermine our ability to lift ourselves up and connect with spiritual power within us. We have a powerful choice to make. When we notice negativity pervading our thoughts, we can pause, consider what the opposite would be, and then introduce that opposite as a new, more useful thought into the mental field.

This is an ancient, time-tested method of yoga practice — countering thoughts and emotions that are not useful to our higher purposes by contemplating ones that are. We counter feelings of hatred by contemplating love or loving-kindness. If we notice frustration, we think about patience. When we are anxious or worried, we remedy that with faith or contentment. We bring the positive thought to mind, contemplate it, and notice the bodily felt shift. Stinging with jealousy? Try the healing balm of appreciation. There is no end to the inner resources available to change the content, and the climate, of our mental field through this strategy.

Some argue that we shouldn't attempt to change our thoughts and emotions because they are essential to our authentic expression. Thoughts and feelings are important and should be honored. The purpose of this process is to purify the mental field into a clearer, more effective vehicle for insight and transformation. The goal is to see more clearly, which we can do skillfully if we are not debilitated by negative thoughts and afflictive emotions narrowing or confining our perception. With this process, we don't miss important information, lessons, or insights that thoughts or emotions bring. We can effectively see their origin and potential influence by introducing luminous, expansive thoughts and cultivating a positive mental atmosphere.

> *...the master directs*
> *His straying thoughts...*
> *It is good to control them,*
> *And to master them brings happiness.*
> — SAYINGS OF THE BUDDHA[5]

To change our thoughts, we step back from them as the conscious witness. This strengthens the awareness that we are not our thoughts, no matter what they are, positive or negative. The goal is to transform the mental field by increasing the quality of luminosity. We do two things: We seek insight into the meaning of the new, more uplifting thought through contemplation, and we cultivate the positive feeling it evokes. For transformation to occur, both discernment and feeling need to be engaged. This transformation doesn't happen simply by pretending we are happy when we are sad or friendly when we are angry, such as insisting through gritted teeth, "I'm not angry!" This is simply denial. Rather, through this practice, our thoughts and feelings are actually transformed. They become congruent, aligned with our essential Self.

You might find that, while the process is simple, it isn't necessarily easy. Negativity can be tenacious, with roots in old beliefs or inaccurate ideas about what we are. No sooner do we introduce that new, positive thought than the old judgment slips back in, perhaps arguing that the old thought is true or the new one is false. Now we not only have a negative thought, we have an inner conflict. Thankfully, it's a conflict readily overcome.

One of the best ways to have our new uplifting thought "stick" is to combine or associate it with a positive action we have already taken. To do this, simply recall an uplifting action or experience that relates to your new positive thought. There are many positive things we experience and do every day, and it can be something simple. For example, if a thought negatively affirms, *I'm so lazy I won't ever succeed*, then counter it with the thought, *I'm moving forward every day*, and recall something active you have done, like taking a brisk walk that morning. Connect your positive thought to something you've already accomplished — not something you plan or hope to do. Consider this action validation of your new positive, successful way of thinking and being.

Move Beyond Thought

Besides the discipline of changing our thoughts to bring forth our potential to prosper, we arrange conditions for success in our consciousness through daily superconscious meditation. To fully open ourselves to possibility, we must soar beyond *any* thought. Positive thoughts are more supportive than negative ones, but our highest potential is accessed in the essential Self beyond *any* boundary of thought, emotion, or form. Infinite, unbounded spiritual consciousness is our essential nature. Meditation allows us to be consciously aware of that essence. When we consciously immerse ourselves in our unbounded essence in superconscious meditation, that expansive awareness pervades our consciousness throughout the day. It helps us stay open to insight, remain centered, release attachment to outcomes, have a more expansive view, and be guided by grace. This is the "highway" of arranging conditions.

With regular experiences of superconsciousness that purify the mental field, we frequently find ourselves "in the right place at the right time." We effortlessly discover that we are in the flow of life's supportive influences and the uplifting qualities of nature. This appears as a clear contrast to times when we feel we are "in the wrong place at the wrong time" — when the connection to our divine Self is obscured and we feel out of sorts with the universe. Nothing ensures being in the right place at the right time like the regular, deep, daily practice of superconscious meditation — every day, opening our heart and our mind to the Source.

What We Really Love

A successful life, a fully prospering life, is only possible with the soul's joy, never without it. This joy is not a heady happiness, an emotional reaction to life experiences. The soul's joy is life-giving refreshment. Like a bubbling spring that rises from the deep ground of our being, it continually refreshes our life with the crystal-clear waters of Self-knowing. It's the experience of being fully alive, in love with life, eager to greet each new dawn wearing the colors of possibility.

To succeed
Optimize your life
Sanctify your days
Make a sanctuary for the soul
Build it with love
Light it with peace
Invite everyone in.
Center your self in your Self
Nourish your body
Open your mind
Honor your soul
Change your thoughts
Soar beyond them.

Sixteen

Mine Your Inner Resources

Following the preceptor's advice
I have steadied my mind.
And I now collect diamonds there
Which I locate, and find.

— KABIR

O ne dark night the mystifying sage Mullah Nasruddin is outside his house frantically searching the ground under the
streetlight. He's digging around, sighing, looking up, wip-
ing his brow, then returning to look again. His friend walks up and
asks, "What are you doing out here so late at night?" Mullah replies,
"I'm looking for my keys." His friend says, "Where did you last see
them?" Barely looking up from his search, Mullah answers, "In my
house!" "I see," says his friend, "if you last saw them in your house,
why are you looking out here?" Mullah replies with exasperation,
"Because the light is better out here!"

No matter how many times I tell this well-known story of Mullah
and his lost keys, and whether people have heard it many times or
not at all, laughter is the natural response. We recognize our own

foolishness and the frustration of looking for what we have lost in all the wrong places.

This amusing and poignant tale can be seen as an allegory of our loss of Self. We have all, at some point, lost our proverbial keys to the kingdom — the essential insight we need to prosper. We are trying to figure out how to thrive, and like Mullah, we're "out on the street" looking for what we can only find inside. Why do we look externally, out there, for the key to an abundant life? Because we are conditioned to look outside of ourselves. We have learned that from an early age — the light is better out there. It's easier for us to see the things of the world than to recognize the subtle inner light of consciousness, the real key we need.

The house represents our consciousness. We know the keys are there, but we aren't inclined to look there because we think it is "darker" inside. We don't know *how* to look within, how to mine our inner resources. That is, until the friend comes along. In spiritual stories, the friend is the spiritual teacher, the one who points to the right direction for true fulfillment. The teacher asks, "Why don't you look in your own house?" That's the question of the true guru of the ages. Once our error is exposed, the inner journey of awakening to the gems of Self-realization begins. Once we know where to look, we can start learning how.

Mining the Mind

Countless are the waves of ocean
So are waves of mind,
When waves abate and mind steadies
Diamonds grow there to find.

— KABIR[1]

On our journey of realizing our innate fullness, mind can be our greatest friend or our greatest enemy. If we don't understand what the mind is, how it works, or how to use it, we'll be subject to its default setting, which is limited. We'll use the mind as a tool exclusively to explore the external world of thoughts and things, all the while limiting our perception and knowledge to what the mind can discover. We'll swirl round and round with thought activity, trying to figure things out, while the most important question awaits our attention: *Who, or What, is thinking? What is That, by which all thought and perception is made possible?* When we ask that question, we've made the life-transforming turn toward finding the key in our own house.

Yoga philosophy gives us a map for navigating the territory of the mind. Prior to waking up spiritually, most of us imagine we are the mind, if we think much about it at all. It's pretty clear that we aren't the body (though we do cling to that identity as well). We watch the body change over the years and see it as an object of our perception. What escapes us, until we start to investigate, is that we are also observing the mind. We are not the mind, we are the Seer. We are that Supreme Consciousness that illumines the mind, making perception possible. Our brain is the physical organ of the mind, and mind is the subtle instrument of the soul or the Self.

The mind, which is a portion of universal Mind, is made up of four components — the mental field, where various forms of cognition take place; sense-mind or thinking mind, which responds to sensory input; intellect or faculty of discernment, which weighs and judges input; and ego, the false sense of individual existence that claims experiences and perceptions as its own.

Here's the key we've been looking for: Mind, with its different aspects, is not sentient — only with the inner light of the Self is mind able to be aware. Realizing the spiritual Truth of our being is an experience that is necessarily beyond the limitations of the mind. Thinking mind can conceive the possibility of what we are; intellect can deduce, infer, and intuit it; but only the direct experience of the Self beyond the confines of mind brings full knowledge and realization.

Spiritual practices are for clarifying the mental field so that the inner light of the divine Self can shine through it. When the mind is calm, not obscured by waves of restless thought, knowledge of the Self is revealed. We experience the "diamonds" of Self-knowledge and the gems of inspiration that pour forth from that diamond mine. We can be guided by the promptings of the soul, rather than the patterns in the mind based on past experiences. It's a new day, with the rich possibilities of Spirit open before us.

The Colors of Perception

Our mind is a part of nature, of manifest creation, which is made possible by three qualities termed *gunas* in Sanskrit — luminosity (*sattva*), activity (*rajas*), and inertia (*tamas*). These qualities are always found together in a dynamic, ever-changing interplay. Nothing in nature is free of their influence. Nothing — not the food we eat, the car we drive, the television we watch, the weather, our relationships, our mental field, our bodies. Knowing about these influences makes it possible for us to work with them — to skillfully identify, mitigate, and moderate their influence, then move beyond being influenced by them at all in what is called the supremely free state.

To use the power of our mind to meditate, contemplate, affirm, or visualize, it makes sense to first recognize how our state of mind is currently being colored by the predominating guna influence. The following verse from the Bhagavad Gita gives us some clues to look for: "When the light of wisdom shines from the portals of the body's dwelling, then we know that sattva is in power. Greed, busy activity, many undertakings, unrest, the lust of desire — these arise when rajas increases. Darkness, inertia, negligence, delusion — these appear when tamas prevails."[2]

Once we are aware that these influences exist, we can pay attention to how they affect our bodies and our minds, color our perceptions, and influence our choices. We can select environments and influences that are most supportive of our goals and make appropriate adjustments. We can learn how to observe when a particular influence is predominant, when a change is needed, and how to facilitate that change.

As a rule, those on a spiritual path are advised to cultivate environments and lifestyles that are infused with sattva, uplifting qualities that contribute to clarity in body and mind. We do this by paying attention to what we surround ourselves with and what we consume or take in through all our senses — this includes food, conversation, media exposure, and so forth. Sattva is a purifying and peaceful influence that allows the innate radiance of the soul to permeate the body and mind.

If we want to bring more lightness (the quality of sattva) to the body, we select fresh, whole foods — fruits, vegetables, and grains — for our diets. We select moderate, restorative, and calming forms of exercise, such as walking in nature or gentle yoga postures. To increase sattva in the metal field, we can use pranayama to purify the mind, prayer or devotional practices, meditation, and uplifting time in nature.

If the heaviness of tamas guna predominates in the body and mind, then it can be useful to call upon rajas to help make a change. Literally, we must get moving — go for an invigorating walk in nature, take up a task we've been putting off, turn off the TV and stretch. The active quality of rajas can help us transform the pervasive dullness of tamas guna. Then we can temper the rajas guna with sattva guna.

One thing to remember about the gunas is that they are always in a state of disequilibrium; that is their nature. They are changeable and constantly in flux. We are not going to achieve some frozen state of sattva! All the gunas are necessary for the life functions to continue. We need them. But we also need to avoid being under their sway. Instead, we can become conscious participants with nature. It's amazing what we can do to make a change in our life by paying attention and taking positive action. We do not have to be taken hostage by changes occurring in nature, either around us or within us. We can make adjustments that allow us to be at our best and be fruitful with our inner work.

Affirm Your Soul

Personal circumstances invariably correspond to your mental states and states of consciousness. What you think, feel, or know yourself to be capable of experiencing manifests circumstances and events, attracts them to you, or enables you to perceive them as being presently available.

— ROY EUGENE DAVIS[3]

Once we are aware of how the mind works and what influences it, we're ready to use its power. The use of affirmation is one of the easiest and surest ways to change our mind and change our circumstances. It doesn't take long to have an experience of how effective affirmation can be. In fact, change comes immediately. As soon as we use the tool of affirmation correctly, our consciousness shifts from lack to abundance. The first change that comes is how we feel and how open we are to opportunity. Those inner changes are not only the most significant, they are the root of all the outer changes that will follow.

I still remember, decades later, my first experience with using affirmation as a spiritual tool. I was astounded with what unfolded. I was a new student on the path of yoga and metaphysics, and I had never really considered how my thoughts, beliefs, and states of consciousness affected my experience of life and my circumstances. When I needed to make a change, I did whatever I needed to do outwardly to facilitate that change. The practice of affirmation showed me that this singularly outer way of making course corrections was neither the most efficient nor the most effective method. While it seemed I was fairly successful at doing what I wanted or needed to do, what remained out of my purview with this outer-oriented approach was what I *could* do and what my potential was. An entire vista of possibility opened to me once I began to open my mind.

When I first delved into the practice of affirmation, I did not have a specific goal. Most every area of my life needed improvement, so I began with an affirmation that covered it all. Because I affirmed it daily, learned it by heart, experienced its truth in consciousness, and saw the results it brought forth, I remember it to this day.

Here it is:

> I am now in my right place. I am happy, healthy, and prosperous in all ways. I live in the constant awareness of the presence of Spirit.

Within three months, my job changed, I moved, and I became involved in a new relationship. The important thing to note is that I wasn't aggressively trying to change any of that. It unfolded from within and the changes came quickly. I began to have a living faith, developing confidence in the infinite Ultimate Reality as the supportive power and presence at work in my life. This made all the difference.

What did I do to discover such a dramatic result? I took the teachings to heart. I meditated and studied every day. After meditation, I would first read aloud, then silently remember my affirmation. *I would sit with it until I felt it to be true, as my current reality.* I wrote it down on several pieces of paper and posted it around my home as a constant reminder to stay anchored in this new awareness.

Besides the joy of discovering how my mind is connected to universal mind, which was immediately responsive to my change in consciousness, I discovered the principle itself. Now the tool of affirmation is available to me anytime.

Stay the Course

If you continue with your mental affirmation, and go still deeper, you will feel a sense of increasing joy and peace. During the state of deep concentration, your affirmation will merge with the subconscious stream, to come back later reinforced with power to influence your conscious mind through the law of habit.

— PARAMAHANSA YOGANANDA[4]

Here's an important tip for working with affirmations: *Stay the course.* That's being steadfast with your spiritual practice and doing everything you know to do to cooperate with divine grace, the supportive influence that permeates life. Because this work is subtle and we don't always see immediate outer results, we can be tempted to think it's not working and fall back into old thought patterns. However, when we use the tool as directed, we experience immediate inner change. It's a matter of knowing how to identify that change and continuing to be faithful to the practice. The immediate change is a change in consciousness. This is an inner experience — subtle, but perceptible and essential to our success.

When you work with an affirmation, notice how it feels to call forth your innate wholeness, infinite potential, and divine qualities and accept it as true now. Sit with it. Work with it until you experience a change in how you feel about yourself and about your life. This is the key to success with affirmations.

If thoughts of worry, lack, or limitation creep back into your mind when you are engaged in daily activity, gently remind yourself that you have experienced an inner change that is already at work in your life. Recall the words of your affirmation. Recall the positive feelings. Inwardly smile, knowing that you are in partnership with the Source.

The Spiritual Practice of Affirmation

Both spiritual and scientific insight into the processes of creation reveal a continuum of energy in expression — from subtle to gross manifestation. Absolute Reality expresses in infinite ways all that is, from the transcendental field through manifest creation, from rocks to trees to galaxies, from thoughts to things and the magnificence of every being. The effectiveness of the spiritual practice of affirmation rests on this awareness of life's creative process. With spiritual affirmation, we consciously use our thoughts and speech to connect to the creative energy and power of Spirit. The great yoga master Paramahansa Yogananda introduced this dynamic process of affirmation, based on ancient Vedic insight into the spiritual laws of manifestation, to thousands of students in America when he came to the West in 1920. He encouraged everyone to use affirmation to draw upon their inner, divine resources, saying, "Affirmations repeated understandingly, feelingly, and willingly are sure to move the Omnipresent Cosmic Vibratory Force to render aid in your difficulty."[5]

Rightly understood, spiritual affirmation is a statement of truth, a statement that reflects the essential truth of our nature as infinitely resourceful and creative. Sometimes people are puzzled by the process of affirming something that may not initially be seen. How can we affirm "I have everything I need" when we are keenly aware there is no money in our bank account? How do we make sense of that? Is the use of affirmations just "positive thinking"? It is positive thinking, but positive thinking with spiritual awareness and the intention to draw upon the soul's innate power to create or bring forth whatever is needed.

It may be factual at a point in time that the bank account is empty. However, we use our discernment to see that such situations are outer conditions that are continually in flux or subject to change. When we affirm in the face of that changeable situation that "I am happy, healthy, and prosperous in all ways," we are seeing beyond current conditions. Instead of allowing conditions to determine our state of mind and situation, we draw upon the true nature of the soul as full, infinitely prosperous. It's simply a true statement about the soul. By affirming in this way, we begin to live from the soul level of our being, overriding the ego's grip of scarcity thinking.

What Happens When We Affirm

When we create an affirmative statement based on spiritual truth, we immediately begin to draw upon our inner creative abilities and resources. We change our internal conversation from lack to abundance. "Like attracts like" is a basic spiritual principle. We cannot expect to thrive if our mind is occupied day after day with thoughts of lack and limitation. To bring forth abundance and experience the fullness of life, we start by accessing it within us. We change our thoughts. We change our internal conversation. We change our speech. And we change our viewpoint — our way of looking at the world and interpreting our experience. Affirmation gives us a new way of seeing.

A spiritual affirmation is based on the truth of our being; therefore, using the words "I am" is often most effective. The phrase "I am" is a declarative statement of eternal existence and, along with that, inherent divine potential. Because we are expressions of the one Absolute Reality that is commonly called God, all the potentials of God exist within us at the soul level of our being. Our affirmative phrase that begins with "I am" is a way of declaring this truth and beginning, in that very moment, to draw upon the infinite power and potential within.

Because affirmations are statements of spiritual truth, they are unconditional and thus occur in the present moment. The strength, resources, and power we draw upon when we affirm are already within us. These divine potentials are not dependent upon any external circumstance. They exist now. We call these potentials forth by affirming them. The full expression of these potentials requires our cooperation, but in no way does that negate their present reality.

The phrase "I will" is not recommended because it sets a future time frame for accepting our good. To simply declare "I am happy, healthy, and prosperous in all ways" brings our affirmation into the now moment, where it is experienced. This is important because experience, with feeling, is essential to manifestation. We state the truth as a present reality. We feel it to be so and we accept it. Remember that the reason for using affirmation is to adjust our thoughts, and our states of consciousness, to be in tune with higher truth.

We discern and experience the truth of our affirmation by reflecting on the truth of our being, remembering we are one with the unbounded Source of all that is. We recall that infinite creative possibility exists within us.

After writing an affirmation using the "I am now" formula, we speak it aloud several times. We reflect on it. We contemplate our affirmation, turning within to consider our soul nature as we do. We allow our thoughts to settle. We imagine or feel what it is like to experience that affirmation fully. We experience and feel our innately divine nature. This is possible once our thoughts settle, so sit with your affirmation until you experience this shift in consciousness.

Take It into Daily Life

Live with the affirmation. Refer to it as you begin the day, ideally contemplating it after meditation in the morning and just before you fall asleep at night. Return to it throughout the day as you are inclined.

Our thoughts and speech have creative power. Are they in line with our affirmation? If not, a course correction is needed. Working with the energy of affirmation is like building a fire that can illumine our way forward. If our inner work is followed by negative, constricting thoughts and careless speech, it's like pouring cold water on that fire. We keep the fire burning bright by adjusting our thoughts and speech. Notice how you talk about yourself and others. Let your speech express creative power and blessing. You will notice real evidence of a changed life immediately, when you change debilitating habits of thought and speech.

By following a regular practice of writing, speaking, and reflecting on our affirmation, it takes root in our mental field, replacing former thoughts of lack, negativity, limitation, or fear. Even when we're not consciously working the affirmation, it rises to the conscious level of mind and shines a light of positivity and possibility upon our path, helping us make any needed course corrections.

Stepping into What Is Ours

Breaking out is following your bliss pattern,
quitting the old place... following your bliss.
— Joseph Campbell[6]

Using affirmation alone rarely makes the changes we seek. Rather, the practice helps us call forth and be receptive to opportunities that arise. We still need to cooperate with the good that comes our way. We must consider what is right for us and what is not. When an opportunity arises, just because we're using an affirmation doesn't necessarily mean it's the right choice for us. Discernment is always needed.

The practice of affirmation introduces a new way of thinking and of living. First, we start with the technique. We create a personal affirmation and use it. We work with it throughout our day. We begin to experience changes in how we approach life and our openness to possibility. New awareness of opportunities and creative inspirations arise. Ultimately, we learn to naturally think, speak, and act affirmatively because this is most consistent with the truth of our being. We step into the life that is ours, the soul life that has been waiting for us.

Seventeen

Intend, Declare, Vow

*I'd made a vow: for an entire year, I'd get up at the same time
every day.... As soon as the alarm went off, I'd get up. Instead of
complaining to myself how sleepy I was, instead of questioning
the value of the vow, I'd get up.... I'd meditate. I'd pray. I'd write
in my journal. I'd practice waking up a little more.*

— SY SAFRANSKY

What makes the difference between what we say we want to accomplish or realize and what comes to fruition? Take a moment to remember an important goal you set for yourself and accomplished. What was it? How did you do it? Usually what we find is a winning combination of clear focus, commitment, discipline, and grace — the ways we've experienced support beyond our personal effort. There are often numerous things we say we want and far fewer that we truly commit to. But when we determine we're ready and truly commit ourselves, breakthrough becomes not only possible but predictable.

We can mobilize the power of our determination by setting an intention, making a declaration, and offering it as a sacred vow. An intention is an aim or a goal. Its Latin root means to stretch toward, to direct one's mind to. A declaration is a statement that affirms our intention. A vow is a promise we make, an inner process of dedication that energizes our will. A vow becomes sacred when it draws upon our deepest desire, is connected to our life purpose, and serves the greater good.

Often the process of setting goals has us think about what's missing or "wrong." We think about needing to lose weight, be more disciplined with our work, or find a way to fully prosper. This perspective says, "I am not now, but I want to be." It can be difficult to overcome that negative mindset of insufficiency. Spiritual insight offers us a more positive way to approach goal setting. From the spiritual perspective, we start with our inner resources. We affirm what we are and the potential we have, rather than focus on what's missing. This perspective says, "I am." It draws upon our ability to claim and express our potential. We affirm what is possible and call it forth. For example, if your intention is to be more loving, to experience healing and greater harmony in your relationships, your intention might be expressed as "I am a loving person. I experience harmony in all my relationships." This affirmative statement becomes your declaration.

How can we declare what we have not yet experienced? Think of your intention as stretching forth from your innate divine capacity. The moment we earnestly intend something, it draws upon our inner resources and begins to express. We can immediately experience it. This is an important key to realizing our intention. Think of an archer. The "goal" is to hit the target. We consider hitting that target as success. But success is in every step. The actual hitting of the target is but one step. The intention to hit the target, the engagement of the imagination, the vision and felt sense of it, the preparation for it, physically pulling back the bow and its release — recognize this as "whole" and you will understand how you can declare your intention as a present reality and why it is important.

What do you deeply desire to bring forth? What is essential to your fulfillment? What will not leave you alone? What do you know you should do or be? Are you now willing to make that your intention? What would the realization of that intention require of you? How does it call you to develop your innate potential? Our intention and declaration express our innate potential as the present reality it is. Say we intend to experience greater abundance and blessing in our life. We can truthfully affirm "I am abundantly blessed" because we are each innately an unlimited being. Any specific goals would then connect to that affirmation of innate potential. "I am blessed. I have fulfilling work. I am abundantly compensated and generously share my resources with others."

The final step of making a sacred vow requires us to examine our intention in the light of our life purpose and our connection to the well-being of all. Does our intention serve life? Is it constructive? Does it make a positive contribution to others as well as to our own good? Life continually supports the thriving, developing, and fulfilling of its purposes. When we align our goals with serving the whole, we open the floodgates of grace-filled support. Our vow is a way to dedicate our intention, declaring our place in the Oneness of all things. Once you have determined your intention, stated it as your declaration, and discerned that it is in harmony with higher good, then offer it. Offer it on the higher altar of illumined consciousness with a prayer that it may serve life.

Use the Science of Mantra to Set Your Intention

Mantra is a profound tool to purify the mental field, help prepare us for superconscious meditation, and align our mind and consciousness with Spirit. It can also be used to bring awareness and energy to an intention or sacred vow. Mantra practice energizes our will and strengthens our determination by clarifying the mind, awakening vital force, and focusing our attention. When mantra is used to gal-vanize our focus toward realizing a goal, it is first offered to create a prayerful beginning in harmony with the highest good. Meditation and prayerful use of mantra opens the highway for divine grace to be revealed to us. It is not a magic incantation to create anything; rather, it's a way we align our intention, declaration, and vow with the forces of divine nature and of Spirit.

Mantra is a sacred sound, word, or word formula that connects the vibration of sound to the primal energy of creation. Scientists, as well as mystics of many spiritual traditions, have discovered that what we see manifested as solid objects are condensed forms of en-ergy. The "big bang theory," which assumes our universe began with an explosion of energy, correlates with insights of the ancient Vedic seers. They realized the universe is an emanation of cosmic power, signified by the primal sound or mantra "Om." Our entire universe, on every level, is made up of this energy. It is expressed by sound as vibration.

Sound permeates all the realms of creation with the power to influ-ence matter. Some of the effects of different sound frequencies upon the body and the mind can be experienced and measured. The im-pact of music is a common example that most of us are familiar with. Research with premature babies in neonatal intensive-care units has shown that live music, played or sung, helps to slow infants' heart-beats, calm their breathing, improve sucking behaviors important for feeding, aid sleep, and promote states of quiet alertness. On the other end of the human experience, we have countless accounts of elderly, agitated Alzheimer's patients who haven't spoken in years but who calmly sing every word when they hear a song from their youth. The sound of music is truly powerful.[1] In the same way, by using mantra, we intentionally tap into the power of sound and its subtle meaning to transform the mind and enliven prana, which is our vital force, and bring about beneficial changes in the brain, physical body, and environment as well.

What Mantra Is

Such key concepts as the five elements, the seven chakras, and the three gunas are part of a mantric tapestry, linking us back to the cosmic mind and our true Self beyond name and form. Mantra is the essence of the great yogic teaching as well as its primary practice. It turns teaching into practice and allows our practice to directly teach us, as the mantra gains its own life and consciousness in the very ground of our being.

—Dr. David Frawley[2]

The Sanskrit term *mantra* means a spiritual tool for the mind, a formula for reaching higher states of consciousness. This sound or word is not only powerful as a vibration of energy but as a condensation of knowledge or insight. Just as an aphorism or a sutra reflects an entire teaching in a condensed statement, so a mantra carries essential meaning through vibration. Mantra practice liberates the mind from the confining structure of thought form. It frees the mind from the constraint of concepts and allows it to be a vehicle or conduit for higher understanding and insight.

The most effective forms of mantra are derived from sacred languages, such as Sanskrit, Latin, Hebrew, Arabic, and various indigenous languages. Ancient sacred languages were initially used to express spiritual knowledge, and they continue to resonate insights into the nature of reality that were realized by their originators.

The energetic influences of certain mantras are known to have specific effects on the mind. A mantra may be given by a guru at the time of initiation into a tradition to assist the seeker with meditation practice and to support subtle, energetic attunement to the spiritual lineage. Some gurus may suggest specific mantras to help overcome difficulties. Many Sanskrit mantras are chanted today and known for their general beneficial value. Those who study and practice them discover the deeper significance of these mantras and the power contained in them to support positive change. Here are some of the more familiar Sanskrit mantras today: "*Om Namah Shivaya*"; "*Hare Krishna, Hare Rama*"; "*Om Dum Durgaye Namah*"; "*Om Gam Ganapataye Namah*"; "*Ham-sa*"; "*Hong sau*"; "*So'Ham*"; or even simply, "Om."

Often prayers or phrases from the scriptures of religious traditions are used as mantras, both as support for clearing the mind and opening the heart for meditation and for energizing or spiritualizing an intention. Here are some examples of prayers or scripture verses used as mantras: "The Lord is my shepherd, I shall not want"; "Be still and know I am"; "*Shema Yisrael, Adonai Eloheinu*"; "Abba, Father"; or "*La Ilaha Illa Allah.*"

Different Types of Mantras

There are three types of mantras: *saguna, nirguna,* and *bija.*

SAGUNA MANTRAS: These mantras refer to divine qualities. They are connected to a deity, a specific form that is invoked and meditated upon — Hare Krishna, for example. Saguna mantras are said to carry the energy symbolized by deity forms — all of which can be understood to be different expressions of the one eternal Absolute Reality.

NIRGUNA MANTRAS: These don't reference qualities and are not related to a specific deity form. They are sacred sounds connected to the Source of all creation, such as "*So'Ham,*" which means "I am That."

BIJA MANTRAS: These are single-syllable "seed" sounds with vibratory power and an inner mystical meaning. These seeds do not have precise meanings but carry connections to spiritual principles. "Om" and "Shrim" are bija mantras.

Properly understood, any word or word phrase that has a positive energetic influence on the body and mind can be used as a mantra to prepare for meditation or to energize an intention. Prayers and prayer words in English may be used, as long as the necessary devotion and focus is maintained.

For a beginning practice, if you are new to mantra, the mantra Om can be used. It is the mantra recommended by the sage Patanjali in the Yoga Sutras to remove obstacles in the mental field in preparation for superconsciousness. The most ancient of all mantras, Om represents the primal sound, the energetic conjunction of divine consciousness and power moving into creation. It is the "Word," the primal energy at the beginning of all things, pervading all things, connecting us to the divine Presence. Contemplate Om as you chant it. Feel that you are connecting to the Lord of the universe, the divine One expressing as all that is, yet ever remaining unmoved by it all.

How to Practice

May you become in practice all that you are in potential.
May the love that informs every cell in your body permeate
every thought in your mind.
— THOMAS ASHLEY-FARRAND[3]

Mantra practice is called *japa*, which means repetition. Depending on the purpose of our mantra practice, japa may proceed differently.

When used as a technique to purify the mind to prepare for meditation, we stop the mantra when we enter a meditative state of consciousness. The work of the mantra for that occasion is done, except to momentarily recall it whenever attention becomes distracted. It then acts like an anchor, returning awareness to the depths of our being. If we're using a mantra to energize an intention or to engage in a longer-term process of healing or purification, then practice is done for a prescribed number of repetitions.

The traditional number of repetitions for Sanskrit mantras is 108, a symbolic number said to refer to 108 divine names or to the 108 subtle energy pathways leading out from the heart chakra. Thus, 108 is the traditional number of beads on a *mala*, or string of prayer beads, used for meditation. Malas, or rosaries, are used to count the number of times we say the mantra. Most yoga malas have either 108 beads or a division of this number, such as 54. There are malas or rosaries in other traditions with a different number of beads, chosen according to the symbols of the tradition they represent. Any mala or rosary that is meaningful to you can be used for your practice.

The structure of a traditional japa mala includes the beads used for counting the repetitions and a central bead that is usually larger and set apart from the others. This bead is called the "guru" bead or the "meru" bead. "Guru" means teacher; it can refer to the Supreme Teacher of all, which is God. "Meru" is a sacred mountain that signifies the mystical inner summit of supreme realization. On a japa mala of 108 beads, one begins at the bead adjacent to the meru bead and stops there when it is reached. It is not included in the count. If the mala is shorter and several repetitions are needed to reach 108 (or if you are practicing an additional round of 108), then turn back at the meru bead. One does not cross over this bead. This brings an added element of respect and awareness to practice.

Follow these steps to use a mantra to energize your intention to thrive:

1. Write your intention on a piece of paper. Read it aloud. Place it on your altar where you can see it, or fold it carefully and place it in a container you keep on the altar or other dedicated space.

2. Determine the mantra you will use — any prayer, word, or phrase that is familiar, uplifting, and useful for you. Use the same mantra every day, and practice for a minimum of thirty days. Ideally, chant the mantra daily for forty days.

3. Before you begin chanting your mantra, take a moment to contemplate its meaning. Think of your sacred vow or intention and the power in your own divine being that is being invited forth by the mantra. Prayerfully hold your mala at your heart center, ready to begin.

4. Offer the mantra 108 times at the same time each day. Chant the mantra before or after your meditation practice.

5. Mantra can be chanted audibly or mentally. When chanting aloud, you can adjust the volume and tone of the chant to provide variety and keep the mind engaged. To chant mentally, use your willpower to repeat the mantra inwardly. After chanting audibly and mentally, inwardly listen to the mantra as it spontaneously emerges in the mental field.

6. Mantra should be "listened to" as well as chanted. This takes two principal forms. First, inwardly hear the mantra as it resounds in the mental field after your audible and mental chanting concludes. Then, also be aware of the mantra as it naturally arises in the mental field throughout the day. The mantra will take on its own

energetic life and do its purifying work beyond your formal time of practice. The power of that spontaneous practice is enhanced when we tune in — when we become aware of the mantra rising above our mundane thoughts and purifying the mental field.

The second form of listening to the mantra is to pay attention to any changes in our perception of subtle energy as we chant or after we conclude. Keen observation of insight and inspiration that arises is also an important form of listening to a mantra. By paying attention to changes in energy and deepening of our understanding, we tune in to the power of the mantra.

It can be useful to track your practice of mantra in a journal, noting any observations and insights you have.

Going Deeper with Mantra Practice

Mantra is now in the mainstream of Western culture. The word itself is loosely used in blogs or news stories to indicate someone's latest motto. An internet search for Sanskrit mantras brings up more than three million entries in half a second. Blogs and books about mantra practice abound. We can readily study, learn, practice, and experiment with this ancient tool and benefit from it. For deeper understanding and profound spiritual transformation, learning and receiving a mantra from one's spiritual teacher is ideal. The mantra is then taught to us with guidelines for practice, insights into its esoteric meaning, and most significantly with the direct transmission of the teacher's knowledge and experience of the mantra. It is given to us as a potent, energized seed, one that given the right conditions can take root and blossom into spiritual insight.

Vow to Prosper

The deep parts of my life pour onward,
as if the river shores were opening out.

— RAINER MARIA RILKE[4]

Our affirming, declaring, and vowing is a recognition of our relationship with the Source. It's lifting our self by our Self — deciding to let the soul lead with the luminous mind as its support. It is a way we acknowledge the divine Presence, recognizing the grace and beauty of the great cosmic dance of creation we are living every day. It's a way to live it full on — conscious, fully awake, and ready to prosper — declaring our place, not settling for less, and giving our all.

We place our hands over our heart center and bow our heads before we take the next step. It's a gesture that says, "This life is holy. I bow to the divine that is in me, in everyone, and in everything around me. With a full commitment to life's prospering energy, I vow to live fully."

PART V

Generosity

≈

Live the Prosperous Life

Eighteen

Radical Prosperity

Eternity is at our hearts…warming us with intimations of an astounding destiny, calling us home unto Itself. Yielding to these persuasions, gladly committing ourselves in body and soul, utterly and completely, to the Light Within, is the beginning of true life.

— Thomas Kelly

Viewed through the Vedic lens of spiritual awareness, prospering is to serve higher purpose. Paradoxically, living that purpose requires both getting into, and over, our self. Getting into our self is the spiritual exploration we undertake to discover the true Self, to remember who we really are. Getting over our self is releasing remnants of the false self with its separate, limited, personal agenda. Full-on thriving necessitates a bigger agenda, one that exceeds small self-interest and individual capacity. It's an agenda that involves surrender and the expansion of potential and possibility that only surrender brings. It's a radical approach to fulfillment — radical prosperity through serving life.

The term *radical prosperity* is drawn from the deep meaning of the word *radical*, which the American Heritage Dictionary defines as "arising from or going to a root or source; fundamental; basic."

Our prosperity is radical like a seed is radical — carrying within it the energy and blueprint to thrive that is inherent to its essence. *Radical* also means, according to the dictionary, "carried to the farthest limit; extreme; sweeping; favoring or effecting revolutionary changes." True prosperity is also radical in this sense — a revolutionary approach to thriving, a way to live that is at once innovative, groundbreaking, and unconventional. The abundant, soul-guided life is inwardly, rather than outwardly, directed. It is not guided by the marketplace; it is nonconforming to ordinary drives for name, riches, or fame. Yet it may produce any or all of that, which is of little or no concern to the one following this prosperity path — a radical life of self-giving lived in harmony with spiritual principle. Thriving that arises from spiritual awakening — dedicated to the well-being of all — carries the revolutionary potential of selfless love with its power to transform hearts and minds. Our eyes are opened. Where we once saw only intractable problems, abundant solutions to our personal and global ills appear.

Our Big Foolish Project

Start a huge, foolish project,
like Noah.
— RUMI[1]

Our big foolish project is our divinely inspired life, our response to life's invitation to serve. There's a tendency to think that living a higher purpose by following a divinely inspired idea must be some grand project or monumental task, but that is not necessarily the case. *We, ourselves, are the divinely inspired idea.* The astounding destiny we are called to is the fulfillment of our purpose — the authentic expression that is our life. We thrive when we take up this "big foolish project" of becoming who we are through serving life, contributing what is ours to contribute.

Consider the timeless story of Noah and the ark — a demonstration of radical prosperity. Noah followed his inner guidance to serve life and be a bold and courageous agent of transformation. He wasn't building a yacht for himself. No doubt he was subject to the ridicule of others and the barbs of his own self-doubt, yet he persevered on the journey of becoming. Metaphysically, the story is one of transformation — the flood signifies the purification process that accompanies surrender of self-will. The ark filled with animals, Noah, and his family represents mind with all its creative potential responding to divine direction. Leave the old consciousness — old ideas and habits that no longer serve your prospering path — leave all that behind and head for higher ground, a more spiritually evolved outlook. Noah's destiny is tied to doing what is his to do, according to his gifts and potentials. So is ours.

According to Our Gifts

We must follow our own nature....There are those whom God has willed that after gaining wholeness they should do things for other human beings. There are others whom God has willed to simply be, which is a very, very important manner of serving mankind....And there are other human beings whose vocation is to make; that is, people who are artistic.

— SEYYED HOSSEIN NASR[2]

Once we discover our innate wholeness, the only way open to us is one of serving life. From that awakened viewpoint, what else would there be to do? When we are free of the troublesome personal need to gain anything, the lighted path opens before us, which is offering our gifts in harmony with the truth of our being. What we must do is that which frees the soul to express. This is the great prospering path of becoming. The wisdom traditions point to it with their universal signposts on the way of awakening. In the Bhagavad Gita, Krishna says, "It is better to do one's own work and fail in the attempt, than to do the work of another and succeed."[3] Surely a radical definition of success! We readily grasp its wisdom when we know our success is soul-actualization. Then it is obvious that the only way to thrive is to do that which is guaranteed to draw out our divine potential. The teachings of Jesus in the Gospel of Thomas echo this prescription for fulfillment: "If you bring forth what is within you, what you bring forth will save you."[4]

The ancient and ever-new call for radical prosperity brings us to the threshold of "how." How do we offer our gifts? How do we line up with life's prospering intention? How do we begin to serve life? We begin by offering. We offer the inclination of our heart in harmony with who we have always been; we offer our talents — whether raw or developed — in accordance with our nature; and most significantly, we offer ourselves to serve life. We release ideas and expectations about our service based on the lives of others. While we may be inspired by them, our path of prosperity will have its unique turns and terms — its individual lessons and requirements.

Who we are is what life is looking for. We've already been accepted into life's prospering program.

So often we imagine selfless service as a project and gear up to do something truly worthy or inspiring. Do something! Open a soup kitchen, a shelter for abandoned animals, or a school — yet, that is not it. It may be something, or nothing, like that. Our particular path of service brings forth the puzzle piece we are holding — our unique offering to the expression of life's wholeness. It may be a project, the seeds of which have been germinating in our heart for years. Or it may be a fully conscious life, harmoniously and simply lived, where wholeness shines forth to bless all humanity. Or it could be creating something new — technology, art, gardening, cooking, science. The possibilities are endless, each according to one's own nature.

Getting Out of the Way

The primary skill required for serving life is the ability to get out of the way, to remove the constricting stops of the small self and open to a greater vision of possibility. This begins with examining our intention, the motive behind what we desire to do. Our deep motive must shift from "me" to "we." We stop looking to find what is going to make us prosper. We stop asking: *How can I be successful? How can I be taken care of? How can I be happy?* Getting out of our own way is letting go of that conversation. The new conversation begins with: *How can I serve? How can I contribute to the happiness of others?* We stop seeking personal gain and seek the good of all. We forget about our small self. This is a "stretch prayer" of spiritual surrender — "not my will but thine be done." *Use me, Lord. Let me be of service.* The prayer is: *Let me serve Life.*

I have seen many people attempt a half step here instead of the full leap. Instead of letting go of the small self and opening willingly to life's greater plan, their prayer attempts to invite in Spirit's prospering power with ego still in charge. This prayer goes like this: "Dear God, please bless my lottery ticket. Bless my dot-com. Bless my stock portfolio. Make my creative idea prosper. I plan to use them for good purposes. I offer them to you. Bless them, and I will tithe to my spiritual home. I will give to charitable causes. I, I, I..." Most people praying this way are sincere. They hope to do good works. They just can't yet see that they have written failure into their prosperity plan. Inviting God as our project manager, or subcontractor, is a backward approach. It's not destined for total success because it is self-serving.

To align ourselves with divine will, we open ourselves to a new and greater possibility. The prayer is different: "Spirit, how can I serve? What is the highest idea for my life? Sign me up for that! How can my gifts and talents be useful to your purpose? I offer them to you. Let me always be guided by your will, not mine." We align ourselves with divine will, with life's prospering power, through our humble willingness to serve. Not intending personal gain, but with the heartfelt prayer to be useful and serve others in the highest way.

Everything That Is Needed Appears

I set about…to see what a penniless, unknown human individual
with a dependent wife and newborn child might
be able to do effectively on behalf of all humanity.

— R. Buckminster Fuller[5]

In the early 1980s I was fortunate to hear Buckminster ("Bucky") Fuller speak before he passed from this realm in 1983. His life story, work, mission, and example resounded like a temple bell, inviting all who had the ears to hear to awaken to a vision of possibility — to see a world where everyone's needs could be met. While some saw him as a genius, others saw an impractical dreamer. He was certainly a man of vast imagination, vision, and talent who inspired an entire generation of global thinkers. He was perhaps most famous for his design of the geodesic dome and his visionary call to see ourselves as fellow passengers on spaceship earth, but what interested me most about him was his mission and approach to life — radical prosperity at work.

During a profoundly difficult period in his life as a young husband and father, Bucky Fuller had an insight that changed the course of his life. His situation was dire. Following the tragic death of his and his wife's three-year-old daughter, Alexandria, and the birth of their second daughter, Allegra, Bucky lost his job. With no savings to fall back on, he feared for the well-being of his young family and considered suicide, thinking the insurance money from his death would provide for their support.

He had been trying so hard to prosper — working to provide for himself and his family, but one obstacle after another arose. The housing company he founded with his father-in-law failed, and he felt he had, too. During this dark hour of contemplation, Fuller became inspired to take another route. He was, after all, an inventor with a scientific mind; he became curious and decided to make his life an experiment. He believed in the resourcefulness of nature, and it appeared to him that life took care of itself — which it does. What if he tried to discover what would serve life and did that above all? With that revelation, his life turned a prospering corner.

Buckminster Fuller went on to flourish as a research professor, inventor, architect, futurist, author of more than twenty-one books, and inspiration for the awakening of a global perspective. His mission says it all: "To make the world work for 100 percent of humanity in the shortest possible time through spontaneous cooperation without ecological damage or disadvantage to anyone."[6]

Will It Serve?

For thirty years I used to say, "Do this" and "Give that";
but when I reached the first stage of wisdom, I said,
"O God, be mine and do whatever You want.
— ABU YAZID AL-BISTAMI[7]

When we recognize our wholeness, become willing to prosper, and are open to a thriving vision, life responds. Life sends the people and resources to bring that vision to fruition. I've seen it. When our community got ready and declared its prospering vision for a home for our meditation center, life responded to us abundantly. When the funds became available to purchase the property, finally providing the home we had prayed for, I had a new consideration to deal with, a new question. There it was before us, the property we had dreamed of (in its fixer-upper form), a place where we could welcome people who were ready to learn to meditate and live a dharmic life. But was it the *right* place?

After visioning, setting an intention, and opening to possibility, if we are not mindfully aware, we can get caught up in the sheer momentum of life's prospering response and be tempted to embrace the first thing that comes along, the first hint of the universe responding. It's useful to pause and take a good, discerning look at what's before us. I have witnessed people put forth a vision for a healthy, spiritually oriented relationship, and then they get involved with the first person they meet, thinking she or he is life's answer to their prayer. This isn't always wise. It's not divinely ordained just because it shows up.

Sometimes, bringing forth the highest good requires another adjustment of our consciousness. We may not be aware of what we left out of our vision until what is before us falls short of our dream. The initial showings, the first manifestations of our vision, can be like the first spurt of water from a long-neglected well. That water is tainted with sediment and residue. It takes a few more pumps before the water runs clear. In our visioning work, what shows up first for us may carry some "residues" of old ideas that are no longer useful. Say you envision finding a partner who is kind, doing good work in the world, and prosperous, and then someone shows up who is all of that but does not believe in committed relationships. If that's not right for you, then it's time to clarify the vision and wait. We must use our prayerful heart and our wise mind to discern if what shows up is truly right for the vision we hold.

Although the potential property for our meditation center looked and felt right, many questions still needed to be answered, so we took the time to discern what was right. We had managed renting two rooms in an office complex, and now we were contemplating purchasing property on an acre of land in the city with overgrown gardens and three large, beautiful, but aging buildings. When I showed the property to my father (ever the practical man), he said, "Who's going to mow all those lawns?" I hadn't thought about that exactly, but I had considered what it would mean to take on such a great responsibility with our small staff and budget. It was daunting. However, my question was not my father's practical one: Could we do it? Could we maintain and care for it? My question was: Is this the right place for the work we are inspired to do? Is this the place that will bring peace to hearts and minds? Is it dharmic — in divine order — in harmony with divine will? *Will it serve life?* I knew if I could find the answer to *that* question, the "could we" question would be taken care of. I prayed.

I placed the offer for the property, our statements of vision and purpose for the center, and photos of the place on my altar. I lit a candle. I sat and looked at the papers in front of me and contemplated the possibility before us. I closed my eyes and paid attention to my breath. I let my thoughts settle and my mind become quiet. After sitting in the silence for a time, I floated the questions in my mind: *Is this the right place? Will it serve seeking souls?* A response bubbled up from within me, clear and strong. A phrase resounded in my heart and mind: *Many souls will come to God there.*

The response was clear to me — life's compassionate, evolutionary plan for spiritual awakening would be served. My doubts were removed and my hopes were affirmed. We would move forward with this place, which was destined to become a spiritual home for hundreds of souls and a teaching center to serve thousands worldwide.

The answer to my prayer was typical of how higher guidance comes. Rarely involved with mundane details, soul guidance shines a light on the spiritual essence, the heart of a prayer. The response that came to me was not a yes-or-no directive about buying the property. It didn't address the real estate deal; it didn't advise what the financial offer should be or reveal how we were going to repair the foundation or maintain the overgrown gardens. The response came only as a peace-filled assurance that it was in divine order; *it would serve.* All that was and would be needed for that divine purpose would be provided on time and in abundance. It's the way of life to prosper itself.

> *Says Kabir,*
> *I have cleansed my mind*
> *Pure like Ganges water,*
> *The Lord now runs after me I find*
> *Calling "Kabir" "Kabir."*
>
> — Kabir[8]

The prosperity we seek is seeking us. We discover it once we get out of the way.

Nineteen

Keep Your Soul

The entire world is the garment of the Lord.
Renounce it. Covet nothing.
Be free.
Enjoy.

— Isa Upanishad

Renounce. Be free. Enjoy. It's the time-tested formula for how to live a fulfilled life without losing your soul in the process. This same formula was offered by Mahatma Gandhi when a journalist asked him to summarize his philosophy of life. He replied with the now-famous three-word motto: *Renounce and enjoy!* It's a concise synopsis of Vedic wisdom for living a happy, healthy, spiritually awake, soul-centered, abundant life, the one found in the Upanishads and the Bhagavad Gita. How is renunciation connected to enjoyment? Most people consider the opposite to be true — indulge in pleasure to be happy or acquire and possess as much as possible to enjoy life fully.

What should we renounce to fully enjoy life? Are we to renounce possessions? Goals? Sensory pleasure? None of that sounds like a pathway to enjoyment or even success, for that matter. That sounds more like a joyless austere life that could be both dull and difficult — a common misperception about the spiritually disciplined life.

Once when I was teaching a class about yoga's discipline of renunciation — practicing dispassion, or nonattachment, to quiet the mind and be guided by the soul's wisdom — a woman in the class blurted out, "It's too difficult! I'll have to change everything." I responded that the way we ordinarily live — without the discipline of renunciation — is really the most difficult way because it predictably brings conflict, sorrow, and suffering in its wake. It may seem easier on the surface, until we take a more comprehensive look at its cost. I asked her, "How joyful is your life now?" "Not very," she admitted. She was feeling the natural pull of the soul, its desire for a clearer path of expression. This is the real purpose of renunciation and living a disciplined life. We practice renunciation to "keep our soul," to maintain contact with the divine Self in the whirl of restless desire and its faithful companion, suffering. What we renounce is distraction that leads to loss of soul and the suffering that follows.

Given the choice, not many of us would argue against renouncing needless suffering. The teachings of yoga insist that we can and, in fact, we should. Patanjali's sutra 2:16 says: "Future suffering is to be avoided."[1] When I first encountered that sutra, I thought, *Well, yes, of course. That's obvious. All of us want to avoid suffering!* On further examination, I realized what it meant. Future suffering *can* be avoided. That's a life-changing proposition that has us sit up and pay attention.

The Secret to Our Joy

Joy must lie inside oneself. In order to realize this inherent and untainted joy, which indeed we experience every night when the mind is subdued in deep dreamless sleep, it is essential to know oneself.

— RAMANA MAHARSHI[2]

The world, everyone, and everything in it are of Spirit and belong to that numinous Source. Everything comes from it, lives in it, and returns to it. How can we own any of it? Anytime we think we do, we are mistaken. Sure, there are things we have and even relationships that are "ours." But a deeper understanding is realizing that it all existentially belongs to Spirit; we are but stewards or caretakers. This is true even of our own body. We inhabit it, care for it, and hopefully enjoy it, but all the while knowing it's not truly ours. There is nothing, not one thing in this vast creation, that we can ever permanently hold on to or take with us when we leave this realm. Ever wonder why it seems so hard for us to grasp that? Why, when the awakened ones of every enlightenment tradition throughout time have proclaimed it? Even when those we know tell us much the same as they prepare to make their transition from this realm? What really matters? It's a short list: *love, compassion, presence.* The Vedas teach that the only thing we can keep with us is our degree of spiritual awakening — only realization of that which we are remains.

Just to be alive is awe-inspiring when we can see, or even glimpse, the way things truly are. This helps remove our tendency to attempt to own and objectify others, nature, even our own body or mind. A prayerful verse from the Svetashvatara Upanishad says: "Lord of All, you are hidden in the hearts of all beings.... You are woman. You are man. You are the boy and the girl, too. You as an old man totter with your cane. You face every direction...abiding through your omnipresence."[3] The verses proceed to poetically point to that Ultimate Reality manifesting as all that is — the dark blue bird, the green parrot with red eyes, the lightning-filled cloud, all the seasons of time and the seas that cover the earth — and always concluding: It is you, the One, the divine Self that is the Life of all. Whatever we think it is, it is the Self that dwells within that we love. Once we realize the indwelling Self as the Self of all, we are free from the lingering sorrow of inevitable loss.

How can we ever lose that which is all pervading? The secret to our joy lies here.

This joy of the soul is the tender poignancy of Self-knowing. It is insight into what is real and what really matters. This realization frees us from the soul-robbing sorrows of ignorance without incapacitating our feeling function. Grief and delight still have a place in our heart, and either can become a doorway to divine love.

An enlightened Zen master faithfully taught his students about the transitory nature of phenomena, how seen in the light of impermanence, everything we perceive is "unreal," an illusion. It will all change and pass away. One day, the Zen master's young son died. His close student came to his home only to find his beloved teacher in tears. The student was taken aback and couldn't comprehend the seeming gap between what this teacher had taught him about the nature of reality and his obvious grief. "Roshi," he said, "I don't understand. You have taught us that all we see here is an illusion, yet you are grieving. Why?" His beloved teacher replied, "Yes, it is true, all this changing phenomenon is an illusion. And the death of one's child is the most painful illusion of them all."

There is profound soul freedom in seeing that we cannot own anything in this creation, this divine dance of Spirit. And to make matters even better for us, it turns out we can't control outcomes either.

Five Factors of Action

Why is it that some things work out and others don't? What's going to succeed? What will fail? While there is no lack of business or fitness gurus with a no-fail formula for success, Vedic teachings offer some wisdom that can transform our awareness of success and our way of approaching it.

Teachings in the Bhagavad Gita identify five factors involved in every action: a place for the action, an agent or doer of the act, the instruments of the action, the effort itself, and the unknown.[4] To identify these five factors, let's consider a farmer and the planting and harvest of her crops. The place is the field. The agent is the farmer herself. The instruments are both subtle and gross — the skills (both physical and mental), the mind and sense organs of the farmer, as well as the shovel and other tools she uses. The fourth factor is the effort or energy expended in selecting the seed, planting, weeding, watering, harvesting, and so forth. The "unknown" fifth factor is identified as divine will, destiny, or even luck. In this example, the fifth factor might be an unusual turn in the weather, for good or for ill, which completely changes the outcome. An unseasonable drought might devastate the crop, or an unexpected abundance of mild, sunny days might lead to a bumper crop. Either way, the unknown can change the course of our intended action. If we're rigidly attached to an outcome, then we're not ready for what *might* come our way and may suffer as a result.

With discernment, we can see that not one of us, no matter how skilled or powerful we are, can fully control any outcome. Truth be told, we cannot control whether or not we will breathe our next breath. Some find that awareness unsettling, but the wise find it supportive of conscious living. With this realization, working in the highest way is doing what we do with integrity, doing the best we possibly can, and then letting go of the outcome.

We still set goals. We still open ourselves to every form of success; we work for it and strive for it. However, we cease to be attached to outcome. Instead, our focus is on our relationship with life. We do what we do with an inner harmony, an awareness of our true nature as one with Spirit. How well do we cooperate with the infinite? Do we work with integrity? Do we cultivate an attitude of surrender that allows divine energy to flow through us? We trust that working in harmony with divine will *always* yields success, sometimes in the way we envisioned, other times in surprising ways we could not have anticipated. Sometimes, we may need time and further insight to discover and understand the nature of success.

Our degree of attachment to things and to outcomes can be a ready measure of our spiritual progress and degree of realization. We may be proficient at spiritual practice, but if we need things to be a certain way to be content, then the goal of practice is not yet realized. Only through the ability to let go of attachments can we experience consistent peace of mind. Without renunciation, we're elated when things go the way we planned and we're despondent or angry when they don't. We imagine we're successful when goals are met or things are acquired and consider ourselves failures when they aren't. All the peace gathered on the meditation cushion in the morning can be blown away in the afternoon wind of an undesired outcome.

With the practice of renunciation, we take refuge in the Self and do not identify ourselves with the forces of nature and the dance of change that is its way. We rely on Spirit, trusting the divine order of things. Beneficially contributing to life demands that we hone our awareness, that we strengthen our resolve and our faith. We learn to "see in the dark" — to see beyond current conditions and obstacles with the vision of what our choices and actions make possible. We choose to do what we know is right, sometimes in the face of opposition, often without any visible result or assurance other than our inner realization of truth or justice. This ability to trust life, which is learning to trust our Self, is fundamental to peace of mind and overall well-being. Without this deeper trust, the mind reels at every turn in the road. When the mind is restless, there is no inner peace. When there is no inner peace, there can be no joy. Without joy, what's the point of success?

Free to Live in the Soul

[One] whose mind is disciplined who moves in the world with the senses under control and is free from attachments and aversions is established in tranquility....For the uncontrolled person, discriminative intelligence, power of concentration, and inner peace are absent. How can there be happiness for such a one?

— BHAGAVAD GITA[5]

When we renounce these two ways of approaching life — freeing ourselves from the idea of possession and the illusion that we can completely control outcomes — what we free ourselves from is stress. When stress inevitably arises, it can be a helpful reminder to return to our commitment to "renounce and enjoy!" When we feel overly stressed, we can discern the reason for it. Does it have to do with an attachment to an outcome? That is usually the case. If so, ask yourself if you can let that attachment go. Imagine what it would look and feel like if you did let that go. What would it require to give yourself fully to the work before you, without attachment, focused only on surrendered integrity?

When we free ourselves from unnecessary stress caused by misunderstanding the true nature of things, we're free to engage fully in living our higher purpose. We're free to work without worry, love without trying to own or control, play without holding back, experience pleasure and all that life can offer, set goals and aim high, miss the mark and learn from our mistakes, and become a powerful force for good, a generative instrument for the well-being of all.

We are free to live, and to give, fully. That is our greatest success.

There's Good and Better

Perennial joy or passing pleasure?
This is the choice one is to make always.

— KATHA UPANISHAD[6]

Once we begin to renounce what was never ours to begin with, and anchor our awareness in that which we truly are, life takes on a new glow of ease and delight. Where there was formerly struggle, we find a quality of effortlessness. To sustain this way of grace-filled living, an essential discipline must accompany it: discerning between lasting benefit and passing pleasure, while consistently choosing that which serves our highest goals.

A popular phrase today is "It's all good!" It's a great affirmation of life itself and a useful reminder to elevate our thoughts and moods through positivity. Those on the path of spiritual awakening will take it a step further and say, "There is good and there is better!" What is initially pleasant and enjoyable may not, in the long run, prove helpful. At times, what is difficult in the beginning can turn out to have lasting benefit and bring joy in its wake. The Sanskrit terms for these two choices are *preyas* and *shreyas*. Preyas is merely pleasurable or pleasing, while shreyas is good and truly beneficial.

Preyas and shreyas are woven into the fabric of our everyday life. From morning to night, we encounter them and decide which we will choose. Think about food. "Snack" or "convenience" foods are manufactured to be pleasurable and readily available. They are often full of salt, sugar, and unhealthy fats, which taste pretty good (at least until our palate is purified). Eating a bag of potato chips may seem easy and delicious, but ultimately it's neither good nor beneficial. The long-term adverse effects of processed foods are well known. Eating a salad of organic greens takes effort to prepare, and it won't be filled with sugar and salt, but it's both healthy and beneficial in the long run.

Everywhere we look — what we choose to eat, the company we keep, what we read or listen to, the environment we occupy, the activities we engage in — the choice between good and better presents itself. If we truly want to thrive and fulfill our innate divine potential, it's essential to be well-acquainted with these choices.

The Pleasurable

People fancy they are enjoying themselves,
but they are really tearing out their wings for the sake of an illusion.
— Rumi[7]

One of the markings of preyas is that we often choose what's pleasurable without considering the long-term consequences or effects. This teaching doesn't say we must completely avoid what is pleasurable, but instead it encourages us to look carefully at what we truly want, what something actually is, and what its effects are. One challenge of preyas is that its pursuit can be ongoing. Pleasure-seeking can consume our time and energy, and without restraint, it can ultimately take over our life. That same energy of desire, if redirected, could instead foster the growth of our "wings," our capacity for higher knowledge.

If the answer is not to simply "avoid the pleasurable," what is it? How do we navigate these sometimes-perilous decision-making waters? The answer involves committing to both discernment and moderation. The first part is simple — look before you leap! Look at the choices and ask, "What is merely pleasant and what is truly beneficial?" We can make choices that are both pleasing and beneficial to our well-being once we decide to include this assessment in our choice-making process. To discern the best choice, we keep our commitment to the soul life in the forefront of our awareness as we consider the long-term consequences of each possibility.

At times, we know a choice is purely pleasurable. Is there space for that on the spiritual path? The sages say yes, but it depends on our ability to manage our appetite and keep our desires in check. Moderation is the way of yoga, freedom from either compulsive attraction or aversion. Sometimes even the goal of moderation can get lost in compulsive thinking. For example, some yoga students become fanatical about food choices, thinking they are adhering to the way of shreyas or the truly beneficial. But this rigidity gives too much power to outer conditions. What we are as spiritual beings is superior to mind and body. There is no need to be rigid. Just be wise.

Of course, abandonment of all discipline is another problem. If we allow our desires alone to dictate our choices, we'll find ourselves on a never-ending quest to satisfy the desire of the moment, which rarely leads to long-term fulfillment.

Truly Beneficial

Shreyas is that which is *comprehensively* beneficial — a choice that contributes to enhanced awareness and overall well-being. At times, a choice includes both pleasure (preyas) and lasting benefit (shreyas), like a walk in nature. However, more often preyas and shreyas are at odds with one another, or the distinction varies depending on the circumstances. The "quick fix" of instant gratification is clearly preyas, but in many situations, we are tasked with invoking our faculty of discernment and inquiring: *Necessary? Sustainable for the earth? Beneficial? Preyas or shreyas?*

A simple way to think about these two options is that preyas is led by the senses and shreyas by our faculty of discernment. Using our ability to discern short-term pleasure from long-term benefit helps us make wise choices. We live skillfully and generatively — our choices measured by their benefit not just to the small self but to the Self of all.

Besides considering short- or long-term benefit, we can also consider the qualities of nature that pervade our choices and where they will lead. We go deeper by examining the instrument of choice-making, discovering how our discernment is colored by the three qualities.

Three Kinds of Happiness

There are three kinds of happiness. By sustained effort, one comes to the end of sorrow. That which seems like poison at first, but tastes like nectar in the end – this is the joy of sattva, born of a mind at peace with itself. Pleasure from the senses seems like nectar at first, but it is bitter as poison in the end. This is the kind of happiness that comes to the rajasic. Those who are tamasic draw their pleasures from sleep, indolence, and intoxication. Both in the beginning and in the end, this happiness is a delusion.

— BHAGAVAD GITA[8]

As I outline in chapter 16 (page 193), the gunas, or qualities of nature, pervade the mental field and color our perception. This can influence our discernment between what is truly good or useful and what may not serve us in the long run. The Bhagavad Gita offers a description of the kinds of happiness we experience based on the influence of these three fundamental qualities of nature — whether stimulated by sattva guna, which is illuminating; by rajas guna, which leads to restlessness and greater desire; or by tamas guna, which darkens the mind with inertia.

The Gita verses tell us that sometimes what is truly good may seem like poison in the beginning, but in the end, it is like nectar. How can that be? A good example is establishing a new morning meditation or exercise routine before you leave for work. If you're not accustomed to arising early, willing yourself out of bed can seem like poison, but finishing your meditation or exercise routine provides nectar. Conversely, sometimes what feels like nectar at first can be like poison in the end, such as when we give in to immediate gratification and desire without fully considering the consequences. An apparently innocent flirtation with an office mate might seem sweet like nectar, but over time, it could create a lingering distraction, and a twinge of conscience, that brings disharmony in our primary relationship, which is not intended or positive.

Although all three gunas are always present and each can serve useful purposes, an ongoing predominance of either rajas or tamas guna proves problematical for those on a spiritual path. Yoga philosophy teaches us to cultivate the quality of sattva in all areas because it brings peace, clarity, and illumination to the body and mind. This body-mind clarity allows us to access the inner wisdom of our essential Self and properly use our faculty of discernment. An illumined mind has the capacity to wisely make difficult choices — choices that require discrimination and willpower. When we are calm and clear, we can decide to do what will provide long-term benefits, rather than taking "easier" shortcuts that cost more later with diminishment of our well-being and disconnection from the soul.

When rajas guna (the quality of passion and restlessness) dominates the body and mind, we're more inclined to follow the whim of the senses rather than the light of clear discernment. This is because rajas guna clouds the faculty of intellect. Just like clouds that block the sun, the restless nature of rajas blocks our access to the inner light of awareness. We may be momentarily aware of the higher way, but due to the nature of restlessness, we give in to the call of the senses and let them lead instead. When we allow this, we sometimes rationalize or justify the behavior, saying to ourselves: *I've been working so hard, I deserve a treat!* Or, *I know this isn't really that good for me, but tomorrow I'll get back on track with my plan.* These are the choices that we fool ourselves into thinking are "good" but later realize are not. Typically, when we let rajas guna dominate our choices, we later experience guilt or regret — the poison at the end.

When tamas guna, with its quality of heaviness and dullness, prevails in the mind and body, there's very little, if any, light of discernment coming through. It brings a depressive state of mind that tends to perpetuate itself. The addictive cycle that comes with using drugs like alcohol or marijuana is an example of how the ongoing dominance of tamas guna instigates desires for happiness that are delusory.

Why not really be as happy as we really are? After all, the essence of the soul is bliss. To experience this higher happiness that is fully available to us, we cultivate the clarity of sattva. With an illumined mind, we are better able to discern the desires that will serve in the highest way. We can see what is not so good, what is good, and what is even better.

Choice after Choice

Live your life as a great bliss adventure. Be willing to follow what has heart and meaning. Choice after choice we determine the direction of our lives. The moment of choice is a moment of soul-culture, an entry point for Self-actualization. Let go of attachment to how you think things should be and allow the soul to lead.

We consider each choice in terms of its potential future trajectory, and this is wise, but we can also see that choice is ever a *now* moment. It's a declaration we make of who we are. It's stepping into the divine possibility of being what we are in fullness when the soul leads. We discover how powerful our ability to choose really is and what a difference it can make to choose well. It matters — not only for us, but for others, and future generations as well.

Twenty

A Grateful Generous Heart

*Every time I say thank you
a new gift appears at my door.*

— Ellen Grace O'Brian, "Lark Singing through the Night"

A grateful heart is a magnet that draws to us what is harmonious and good. This idea is reflected in a playful metaphysical adage: not, "We see things as they are," but, "We see things *as we are*." In other words, our state of mind and consciousness color our perception and determine how we see and experience things. Taken a step further, this dynamic explains how we also then draw to us what corresponds with our consciousness. When our hearts are grateful, when we approach others and life itself with gratitude for all that is given, we generally reap more of the same. The opposite is true as well. When we're down and depressed and can't see much good anywhere — that experience will tend to compound itself.

Life in the manifest realm is mixed — light and dark, hot and cold, day and night, up and down, fast and slow, and so on it goes. But beyond all duality and changing phenomena is the unchanging

Absolute Reality that we can know as good, as whole and completely supportive of its divine purpose. Isn't it better for us to call forth the good in every situation? To call it forth in every moment? We can do this through training our mind to extract what is good, what is praiseworthy or useful, and gratitude is one way to do that. Simply look deeply into any relationship, or any situation, and ask what there is to be grateful for. There is always something. When we find it, and call it forth, our heart opens and we become more receptive to the presence of divine grace at hand.

Which comes first, gratitude or grace? They seem to arise together. Gratitude is our natural response to the gift of grace, and gratitude itself opens us to the awareness of ever-present divine support. When we work hard toward something and accomplish it, or desire something and attain it, we generally feel good, and along with that we feel some relief — a kind of "job well done!" out-breath. A very different feeling arises when we become aware of the powerful presence of divine grace that has allowed us to experience more than we ever could have without divine support. On those occasions, we feel something else. We feel awe. We are amazed, inspired, and yes, grateful.

The distinction between relief and awe is a good indicator. It gives us a glimpse into how expansive our life is, how awesome it is or can be.

Gratitude Practice

When we stop complaining, we will be in paradise.
— KABIR HELMINSKI[1]

Gratitude stretches us to be bigger, to expand our consciousness, to open our hearts and our minds more fully. When we begin the practice of cultivating gratitude, we often notice that it's generally easier to feel grateful for what we like, for what we want or find pleasant. It's more difficult to experience gratitude when what comes our way is unwanted.

I once worked with a woman who had an amazing gratitude practice. It was so pervasive that it was contagious. I found myself feeling grateful for her because her grateful attitude made our encounters so pleasant. Her responses frequently surprised me and helped me to expand my perspective. This was her practice: Whatever I offered her, she responded with a genuine "Thank you!" Her response was always the same. If I offered her my praise and gratitude for something she did well, she would thank me. If I let her know that she had made a mistake or that something was not done well or right, her response was still "Thank you!" This was the key that made this practice so effective. She was truly grateful, her words accompanied by a genuine smile. She never gave one of those "thank you" nods accompanied by a smirk. How did she do that? I never asked her, but my guess is that she was a natural at cultivating spiritual awakening through selfless service. She did what she did as an offering, as her way of worship. She was grateful when it went well, and she was grateful when it did not because that gave her an opportunity to learn.

Being able to say "thank you" to what comes, both pleasant and unpleasant, is unconditional gratitude. "Thank you" can be said aloud when appropriate, or silently as a prayer, but let's say it! We can practice offering gratitude for something or someone that has pleased us and for something or someone that has not. The first is easy. The second, not so easy. It becomes easier as we hold that whatever comes into our life and experience always brings an opportunity for us. What will we do with that opportunity? When we meet it with gratitude, our potential to prosper and grow in love is multiplied.

Living from Overflow

The master can keep giving
because there is no end to her wealth.

— Lao-tzu[2]

Gratitude and generosity are devoted friends; they go everywhere together. Once our heart opens with gratitude for the abundant mercy and grace-filled gifts of the One that pour into our life, we cannot help but overflow. We cannot hold back the tide of abundant generosity. Ever conscious that infinite potential indwells us and flows through us, we approach life with the willingness, intention, and natural inclination to give. We give because we are abundant. We give because it is the nature of the infinite Source to give. We give because it is *our* nature to give.

If there are times when it seems that abundance is lacking, the first thing to do is adjust our thinking and beliefs. We transform thoughts of lack to the awareness of abundance by remembering the highest truth about life. We recall what is true about us as spiritual beings and then act in accordance with that truth. There is little value in affirming that we are full, unless that fullness is expressed as generosity, as "overflow." Putting our fullness into action is the best way to stay in the generous flow of life. A stream that is cut off from its source and does not flow soon dries up. So it is with us. Giving from the conscious awareness of overflow is a sure way to affirm our connection to the infinite abundance of Spirit. H. Emilie Cady wrote, "Every man is an inlet, and may become the outlet, of all there is in God."[3]

A student once observed that whenever her Zen master placed a dipper into the stream to gather a drink of water, she left some water in the bowl and poured it back into the stream. The full circle of receiving from the Source and giving back to the Source was demonstrated with that simple but profound ritual. We cultivate that same deep connection to life with the awareness that we are continually provided for by the Source and consciously giving back to it. This receiving and giving from the Source to the Source is true regardless of the channel through which our supply comes.

To experience living from overflow, we find ways to be both an "inlet" and an "outlet" for divine supply. We become an inlet through our prayer, superconscious meditation, contemplation of the nature of Absolute Reality, and surrendered devotion to the One. It's important to sit long enough, and be focused enough, for thoughts to settle, whether we are praying, meditating, or contemplating. When restless thoughts no longer cloud the mental field, we experience our wholeness. When we experience it, we know we are sufficient. We're free from desiring anything external to feel complete. We're an inlet, infused with divine grace, power, and inspiration.

It helps me to spend a moment at the conclusion of my meditation practice reflecting on all that is given and provided. I also find it helpful to pause several times during the day and intentionally give with the awareness that I am giving to the Source. If I am feeding the fish, watering the plants, or cooking for my family, I see it as my offering to the divine. Experimenting by serving those around us with the awareness that we are serving the one Source can bring a shift in perspective that leads us to become a mighty outlet of divine supply.

To be an outlet of divine supply, we can open any avenue for constructive giving. Money is a very common way that people share their energy and blessings received. Because money so obviously reflects our energy flow, it's important to share it — not only because it can be helpful to others, but because it is essential for our ability to live abundantly. But it doesn't have to be financial giving. We can enter the flow with any good thing we give, whether it is time, love, forgiveness, food, money, or even a smile. Paramahansa Yogananda encouraged people to be "smile millionaires." The possibilities for giving are endless. The potential for us is to experience *always* being in overflow. Not overwhelm. Overflow. Life gracefully giving to and *through* us.

We can choose giving as a natural orientation for everything we do. Instead of too much concern with the what, when, where, and how of giving, we can develop a broader, deeper, more meaningful, soul-satisfying focus.

Let the focus of giving include everything; let it be how we live every day.

What would it look like? It may not look too different on the outside. In other words, we might continue to do many of the same things that we already do, but with an intentional consciousness of giving. We tend to our job, our work, and our responsibilities to others with a giving consciousness. We release ourselves from the idea of working for a paycheck or for any acknowledgment or reward. We think of our work as serving, as giving. We do our best and let it go. We see all that we do as an offering and give it freely.

I find this practice of intentionally, prayerfully giving and serving to be enjoyable, productive, amusing, and challenging at times. Conscious giving is surely a way to enter the abundant flow of grace through surrendered offerings. The heart responds immediately with joy. Life truly is more enjoyable when we give. The whole self is engaged in giving — heart, mind, body, soul.

Other times, the practice can show us when we are not in alignment. Hands may be giving but heart is not. I find it amusing and challenging when I notice I am doing something I don't really want to do. At times like that, out of my stronger commitment to give with love, I round up my grousing, complaining thoughts and pouty feelings, clean them up, and take them into the temple of higher awareness. The commitment to give consciously as my offering to the divine Self makes me aware of being out of integrity. I am amused about it because I know there is no sense in doing things that way, with that kind of energy. Who do I think I am doing anything for? This practice shines a light on my path back to truth.

The Immediate Blessing of Pure Giving

Generosity is a sign of our reliable connection to the Abundance.

— Kabir Helminski[4]

Sometimes we forget how much the ability to give to others means to us. Imagine a life where you were not allowed to give anything to anyone. What impoverishment that would be. While we don't give expecting to receive anything in return, the blessing of pure giving is immediate and long-lasting.

An adage says that no one is as poor as the person who believes they have nothing to give. We can turn that around and affirm that no one is as rich as the person who always knows they have something to give. In truth, our wealth is measured not by what we have accumulated but by what we are able to give. The power of the practice of generosity is that anyone can give, and they can start giving immediately, no matter what their circumstances. Generosity is not a matter of material wealth. Most of us have met others who have great material resources but an impoverished spirit, witnessed by their need to hold on to what they have no matter how much it is. Then there are those who have little material goods but completely magnanimous spirits, those who willingly give you the best of what they have.

The spiritual law that connects prosperity and generosity is simple. Generosity is a practice that frees us from the constraints of the small self, the focus on "I, me, and mine" that can be a source of limitation and suffering. When we understand that to truly prosper is to be a life-giving spirit, allowing life to flow through us to love and serve others, we are freed from too much self-concern. Our own happiness is discovered as we contribute to the happiness of others.

Here's a generosity fable for all times.[5] There was once a rich woman who didn't consider the needs of others her concern or responsibility. It just didn't occur to her; she was so busy tending to her own needs and wants. However, one day as she was leaving the grocery store with her bags of food, she encountered a hungry person at the door asking for something to eat. She was rather annoyed at the interruption, but she reached into her bag, grabbed one of her organic carrots out of the bunch, tossed it to him, and went on her way. On the way home, she was involved in a car crash that she did not survive. When she arrived in the afterlife, she found herself in the lower realms of suffering and want, surrounded by other selfish people. She asked: "How can I get out of here?" A voice inquired, "How did you live?" She reflected on her life and saw that it was pretty short-sighted, filled with unnecessary self-concern. Then she remembered the carrot — her one moment of generosity, such as it was. As soon as that memory came, a giant carrot appeared before her as a vehicle to lift her out of this lower realm. She climbed onto the carrot and it rose. She was overjoyed! That is until others saw this way out and began to jump on it as well. "Mine!" she said as she pushed them off. "My carrot!" No sooner had she declared "mine" than the carrot quickly descended back to where she had started.

The truth of our being is Oneness — we are connected to the Source of life and to all that is. We cannot thrive in isolation. Once we see that, we find ways to experience that Oneness through sharing, loving, and caring for all as our Self.

Giving Every Day

Paramahansa Yogananda said, "Unselfishness is the governing principle in the law of prosperity."[6] The practice of generosity is the way
we transform our selfish tendencies into unselfish habits. At first, our
attempts to be generous and give to others may be "selfishly" motivated by our desire to work the spiritual laws of prosperity. This is
okay. It is just a stage of an unfolding journey. For a while we might
be "selfishly unselfish." But once we create new habits, and a new
orientation of giving and caring, the innately generous nature of the
soul will prevail.

Like all spiritual practices, this one begins within, in the sanctuary
of our illumined consciousness. It begins with taking the time after
meditation and prayer to be thankful for all that we have been given,
all that we have to give, and intending to give at every appropriate
opportunity. Our contemplation and pure intention is followed by
using our discernment to ascertain the highest way to give. How we
give is as important, perhaps even more important, than what we
give. Vedic teachings offer some simple guidelines for determining
the energy behind our giving and discerning how to give in the appropriate way.

Giving in the Highest Way

We're back to the gunas, the three qualities that permeate nature
and influence everything — thoughts, motives, actions, and things.
Now that we are more familiar with them, we can readily see how
they influence giving and how they can be a trustworthy guide. Is
our gift permeated with sattva guna — peace, illumination, pure
generosity? Or is it motivated by the restless, usually self-centered
greediness of rajas guna? Maybe even the resistant, less-than-con-
scious, dull quality of tamas guna?

Here are the guidelines for conscious giving from the Bhagavad Gita:

> *The gift that is appropriately given to one from whom*
> *nothing is expected is sattvic.*
> *The gift that is grudgingly given, with the expectation of*
> *reward or gain, is rajasic.*
> *The gift that is given inappropriately or to an unworthy*
> *cause, and that is given without respect, or with*
> *contempt, is tamasic.*[7]

When our giving is pervaded by tamas guna, we give inappropriately or thoughtlessly (what is not right for the person or the occasion), are resistant to helping or serving others, feel burdened by the act of giving, or arrogant about our ability to give.

When our giving is colored by rajas guna, the main motive is to get something back, whether that is recognition, appreciation, or some material gain. Giving influenced by rajas guna will be out of balance. It tends to be either too much or too little because it is based on the personal needs, wants, and aggrandizement of the giver, not on what will serve the one receiving it.

When sattva guna prevails and permeates our giving, what we offer is given freely from the heart without selfish motive or expectation of getting anything in return. It's also thoughtful, taking into account what best serves the recipient. A sattvic gift will not burden the recipient; it will be a positive, supportive contribution.

We've all been on the receiving end of a tamasic gift — perhaps it might even be one of those "regifting" inspirations people have today. Why not give someone else a gift we received that we don't want? Or we have intuitively felt the burden of expectation from us that accompanied a so-called gift. The felt sense of a rajasic gift carries that burden, and often it is weirdly inappropriate. The marks of a sattvic gift? Given with love and care, it is also received that way.

Awareness of the energy of our giving extends to all of our gifts — sentimental offerings to family and friends, offerings of service in the greater community, and our philanthropic giving. With the gunas, we have a time-tested energy meter to consider the quality of our gift. To give appropriately, freely, and joyfully — that is the way of a generous, grateful, abundant heart.

In our less-inspired moments, we may operate under the notion that as we grow in faith, we will develop a more giving consciousness. Or that we will give when we have more material resources at our disposal. That's a classic mistake. Through giving we affirm our abundance. When we refuse to give, we refuse our own prosperity. What's the formula? Give what you can. It's as simple as that. The more we cultivate a giving consciousness, the more we nourish our own spiritual growth. In other words, it isn't advisable to wait. The time to give is now.

Twenty-One

Becoming Wealth

Light the love lamp
with your heart.

— RABINDRANATH TAGORE

hen we seek the jewel of abundance within the spiritual context of the purusharthas, the four universal aims of life, we are destined to discover the truth of our essential Self, and along with that, the profound truth about wealth.

The quest for a prosperous, thriving life begins for different reasons — all of which Vedic wisdom affirms. The Bhagavad Gita (7:16) notes four kinds of seekers who embark upon the path of spiritual awakening — those who are suffering and looking for relief from their sorrows; those who are seeking wealth; those in search of the knowledge that will bring success; and those who are wise. Whatever our departure point, we set out on the spiritual path of Self-discovery, each with our own motive, in our own way and time toward a common destination. Whether we do it with dedicated focus or haphazard rambling, whether or not we initially recognize spiritual awakening as our ultimate goal, the journey of Self-realization is at hand. Whether we are seeking wealth, success, knowledge, or relief from our sorrows, the remedy is always the same: waking up to the truth of our being.

Waking up is occasionally spontaneous. As the sage Ramana Maharshi noted when asked about attaining Self-realization, "Realization is nothing to be gained afresh; it is already there. All that is necessary is to get rid of the thought 'I have not realized.'"[1] That is true. Yet for most of us, awakening is gradual, more like a sunrise — revelation of the true Self occurs as our consciousness is clarified and mistaken notions are removed. We progress along the path with the winning combination of self-discipline and divine grace.

Waking Up Chakra by Chakra

Our progress on the journey can be tracked with yoga's map of the main chakras — our seven centers of subtle energy positioned along the spinal axis. Each chakra is related to a level of soul awareness, or spiritual realization, as well as indicative of our emotional and psychological development. One useful way to think of these subtle energy centers is as *viewpoints*. When awareness is centered at a particular chakra level, it will reflect the viewpoint, or orientation to Absolute Reality, indicated by that stage of development. Our search for prosperity can be tracked with this developmental map as well. We need only examine our motives and our concerns. What is our viewpoint when we embark on our search for true wealth? How does it change as we prosper? What does it indicate about our level of emotional and spiritual maturity?

Our initial impetus may be survival, the instinct that yoga associates with the base chakra. How can I skillfully take care of my personal needs and those of my family? How can I do it in an ethical way that contributes something positive to life and isn't harmful to others? Others begin their search for prosperity impelled by their irrepressible creative urge, a second chakra motivation. How can I offer my talents to the world and prosper at the same time? Can I make enough money with my art, my services, or my invention? Third chakra awareness brings the desire to succeed using mind and willpower. How can I thrive, prosper, and succeed in life? What's the winning strategy for success? Can I succeed without losing my soul?

Jump to the fourth chakra and a major shift takes place — a change in orientation from surviving, succeeding, or prospering to sincerely asking: How can I *serve*? This fourth chakra, heart-center orientation, is the door to the inner world, a passageway to the abundant riches within our consciousness. At this point, we let go of self-serving motives and surrender our wealth — whatever gifts, talents, and resources we have — to serve life. We recognize the prospering power of our primary relationship with life, and we turn our attention to cultivating that via a rich inner life. This opens the floodgates of abundance. When we stop seeking wealth, it seeks us. Established in awareness of the divine Self, abundance finds us irresistible. We become a match for it. Verses from the Upanishads echo this insight: "Whatever world a man, whose being is purified, ponders with his mind, and whatever desires he covets; that very world, those very desires, he wins."² And there is more to come.

At the fifth (throat) and sixth (third-eye) chakras, we become established in spiritual realization, stable in our awareness and understanding of truth. The throat center is associated with truth, not only speaking it, but realizing it, living it, and becoming a vehicle for the expression of higher Truth. It is often referred to as our cornucopia of abundance. Being established in truth leads to experiencing the unobstructed flow of divine creative power. Our words acquire manifesting power. That's prospering power. It's the second of the ten prospering promises listed in chapter 13: "Be completely truthful and your words will have creative power" (sutra 2:36).

The third eye is the center of clear seeing, being established in Self- and God-realization. At this level of awakened insight, one lives in the constant awareness of wholeness, the abundant fullness of the Self. Energy of all the chakra centers then flows harmoniously and operates in balance. The so-called lower chakras are not left behind but wisely integrated, elevated by higher knowledge. We have a stable foundation of Self-awareness, free flow of creative energy, the capacity to use our wisdom-guided willpower and an open, sur- rendered heart — all illumined by spiritual realization. We are now capable of living a prosperous life without losing our soul. In the words of Sufi Sheikh Abu Sa'id ibn Abi'l-Khayr: "The true [realized person] sits in the midst of [others], and rises and eats and sleeps and marries and buys and sells and gives and takes in the bazaars and spends the days with other people, and yet never forgets God even for a single moment."[3]

The crown chakra, the seventh level, is associated with full libera- tion of consciousness, absolute freedom from the influences of na- ture or latent patterns in the mind. Untouched by the sway of nature, there is nothing that impels us. Nothing needs to be done, yet every- thing is accomplished. This is the stage where freedom is expressed as spontaneous right action. It is complete freedom, with no trace of self-interest.

Becoming the Jewel of Abundance

Like a bubbling spring that continually overflows, our life through our awakened consciousness becomes generative, a source of re- freshing abundance for others. Having become utterly transparent to the Source, we ourselves become a shining jewel of abundance.

The small, grasping self has been transformed from a needy little tyrant into a surrendered servant in service of the soul. Now that we are no longer constrained by self-serving motives, nonstealing, the spiritual principle underlying prosperity, is fulfilled. Pandit Rajmani Tigunait writes in his Yoga Sutras commentary, "For a self-aware yogi, nature's bounty is a shining gem. When we are established in the principle of nonstealing, these gems are drawn to us and we ourselves are gems."[4]

The greatest potential of life's aim of artha — wealth — is to become wealth itself.

Perhaps initially surprising, the life goal of wealth is not to *acquire* the jewels of wealth in any of its myriad forms — love, money, health, success, vitality, or possessions. Instead, the goal is to *become* a radiant jewel of life's prospering impetus in service of its evolutionary inclination for individual and global awakening.

As we prosper in harmony with spiritual principle, we evolve. We become more aware of our divine potential and our heart's desire to express it. We become life's evolutionary agents and our abundance grows exponentially. Our life gets bigger — it becomes more purposeful. Our focus changes. We are less concerned with the tedious distractions of wanting the latest thing and become keenly focused on what has heart and meaning. All the while, every useful thing we have ever desired comes to us in this stream of surrendered service. What is for us, comes to us. What is no longer needed, falls away. During it all, the heart remains full.

The quest for true wealth turns out to be nothing less than the search for the Self, the Source of all wealth. Searching for wealth, we discover that there is nothing else that will truly satisfy the heart. Everything else, wonderful as it may be, is transitory, illusive. Is it still important? Yes, definitely. Wealth is the means for fulfilling our purpose and being able to live freely, skillfully, and joyfully. We don't skip that step.

If we follow the ancient way of purposeful living based on spiritual principle, we discover how to prosper and have our needs met. We decide to thrive. We study spiritual principles and confirm their truth by putting them into practice. We adjust our thoughts and open our mind to infinite good. We learn how to cooperate with life's prospering influence. We surrender the mistaken notion that we are on our own and welcome divine support. Our abundant life unfolds gracefully. Joel Goldsmith, American mystic and spiritual teacher, describes the experience this way:

> We are no longer limited to a human mind or to a human experience. Spirit knows no limitation. Spirit just pours Itself through. It comes flowing through in such a glorious, rushing manner that we can scarcely believe it. It may flow through as an entirely new life, as new work, as new activity, or it may increase and prosper that in which we are already engaged. We become beholders of the activity of God and marvel at its munificence, its beauty, and its bounty. In that moment of heightened awareness, we know there is a high purpose for each one of us, a divine destiny.[5]

We prosper as we live skillfully with purpose. An abundant life unfolds naturally as we live in harmony with the infinite. Yet beyond skillful, prosperous living, there is even more in store for us — a more expansive life lived with higher purpose, waking up to our true Self.

It Is Right Here

It lies within the body, brilliant and full of light....
It is right here within those who see,
Hidden within the cave of their heart.
— Mundaka Upanishad[6]

Once we wake up, our orientation toward life and its wealth takes a turn, one poetically described in the Mundaka Upanishad. Two birds, eternal friends, live in the same tree. The one on the lower branches is filled with sorrow, consumed by endless craving as he continually eats the fruits of the tree. On a higher branch sits his friend, a golden bird, who witnesses in silent serenity without partaking of the fruit. When the bird on the lower branches looks up and becomes aware of the resplendent bird, he is filled with grace. It's a transforming moment of awakening. The bird beset by the hunger of ignorance becomes aware of the power and freedom of the true Self. He recognizes his own splendor and is freed from sorrow. He no longer needs to devour. He sees there's another way to live. There's another way for us to live, too.

We wake up to the true Self and are transformed from being consumers who live with a materialistic consciousness — freed from the need to devour, acquire, and achieve more and more. We recognize that true wealth is not found in our drive for external riches — things, accomplishments, or even acquiring knowledge. As philosopher and author Jacob Needleman noted, "Materialism is not a 'sin'; it's a mistake. But a mistake of immense proportions, and with deadly consequences.... Like grasping a picture of food and trying to eat it. Not only meaning, but also health, safety, service, love, and power, can be obtained only through turning to reality. The unreal world can never yield these things to man."[7]

The hunger we have for soul-satisfaction, the wealth that only realization of wholeness can give us, will never be satiated by external forms of wealth. Only the development of the inner life — realization of the true Self and ability to draw upon its riches — brings the fullness that transforms us into a generative, giving presence.

Thriving, prospering, and experiencing abundance is not only within our reach; it's the inherent nature and inclination of life itself. We can recognize the generously creative quality of life when we really look for it and do our part to participate in it. As Paramahansa Yogananda taught, "Abundance, material as well as spiritual, is a structural expression of *rita*, cosmic law or natural righteousness....Every saint who has penetrated to the core of Reality has testified that a divine universal plan exists and that it is beautiful and full of joy."[8]

The real nature of abundance is realizing that the universe is self-complete and we are one with it. It is full; lacking nothing. Life will bring forth whatever is needed for its purposes. When we let go of clinging to any idea of lack and instead turn our gaze toward the all-sufficiency of Spirit, we can see that. We experience our own wholeness, fullness, and abundance.

Breaking free from the bounds of selfishness into the light of selflessness, no longer seeking to enrich ourselves alone, we become transparent instruments of life's prospering power. We prosper and the jewel of our life shines into the lives of others. As Pandit Rajmani Tigunait notes, "Not only are we no longer wasteful, we invest time, energy, and resources in protecting and preserving the future of humankind and the planet."[9] Now our wealth is measured not by how much we have but by how much we give, how capable we are of being a generous, generative presence.

Set Your Heart on Abundance

Being generative is becoming an instrument of divine possibility — opening the space for life's prospering power to create something new, something that meets real needs, contributes to the well-being of all, and is an investment in the future of life. It is our abundance offered with an eye toward the future, the impact of our wealth beyond our individual lifespan.

Generativity is a term first used by psychologist Erik Erikson to signify the "ability to transcend personal interests to provide care and concern for younger and older generations."[10] More recently, the term has been more widely applied regarding the meaning and impact of legacy — how our life impacts the future well-being of others. It has been referred to as the "inner desire for immortality."[11]

Individuals who score high on psychological tests indicating their degree of generativity (their concern for and active engagement on behalf of future generations) tend to have an enhanced sense of well-being.[12] This is not surprising. When we view it through the lens of spirituality, it is simple. When we see beyond the illusion of the individual time-bound, body-identified small self and extend our resources on behalf of others — particularly those we will never know or see — we expand our potential. Do we become immortal as a result? We're already immortal. Being generative is living it.

When the Center for Spiritual Enlightenment moved to our new property in San Jose, one of the first things we did was tend the gardens. In place of the waist-high weeds, I envisioned a luscious, fragrant, blooming oasis of divine peace in the heart of the city — a place of natural beauty open to all. I imagined a meditation garden with evergreen shrubs, flowering plants, flowing fountains, and a variety of trees offering shade for those who would one day sit there on a welcoming bench. Surrounded by beauty, birdsong, and the gentle rustle of the golden leaves of the birch trees dancing in the afternoon breeze, it would be heaven on earth. I could see it.

I called an arborist. We stood in the garden and I shared my vision. I could tell he saw it, too. He looked around, turned his glance upward with a kind of dreamy gaze, and said, "In fifty years, this will be absolutely beautiful." I admit, I had to catch my breath. How old would I be? Would I ever see the fruition of the garden I was planting?

We're accustomed to the immediate gratification that bolsters the sense of small self: *I want. I accomplish. I get. Now.* Moving into generativity requires moving out of those small-self boundaries. That's exactly what's needed on our journey of awakening to our unbounded eternal Self.

Spiritual generativity reaches beyond the small self and its limitation of time to contribute a lasting, positive, transformative impact on the future of humanity. Spiritual generativity asks the primary question: What will remove sorrow and bring lasting peace? Helping others wake up. Only that.

The complex global concerns we have today need to be addressed comprehensively, with insight that begins with unity, the awakened ability to see the interconnection of all life. We may not see the results of what we offer, but whatever contributes to awakening has an impact in the heart of the moment that ripples into the heart of the future — it touches the eternal life that is now and the eternal life that is always.

When Paramahansa Yogananda came to the West to bring the teachings of yoga to many seeking souls, he knew that his offering for individual and global awakening would be generative; it would thrive, spread to all lands, and impact generations far beyond his lifetime. My teacher told me that Yogananda often remarked as he worked with thousands of seekers, "I was planting seeds...."[13]

A Space of Possibility

What is your vision of possibility? What is your dream? We move in the direction of our dreams by claiming them, declaring them — as outrageous or as simple as they may be. Then we support that dream with our wealth, our means.

Between the present need and where we stand is a space of possibility for life's prospering power to come forth.

We are that space of possibility.

The necessary evolutionary jump for humanity we are waiting for takes place over the chasm in our consciousness. To be generative requires us to see the need, capture the vision of what is possible, stand for it, and act on its behalf. When we hold a vision of possibility, we do not know *how* it will come to be; we just know *that* it will come to be. We take the leap.

If this sounds like faith, it is.

Faith is defined as "a confident belief in the truth, value, or trustworthiness of a person, idea, or thing." Faith is what we trust in, what we rely on. Our faith is not so much our stated beliefs as it is how we live, the basis for the choices we make. In Sanskrit the word for *faith* is *shraddha*, which means trust, belief in divine revelation, or *what is placed in the heart*. Our faith is continually revealed in our thoughts, speech, actions, and ultimately, as the life we live.

What does faith have to do with artha — our ability to live well, have our essential needs met, and our worthy dreams fulfilled? Everything.

Our Spiritual Resources

I do dimly perceive that whilst everything around me is ever-changing,
ever-dying, there is underlying all that change a Living Power
that is changeless, that holds all together, that creates, dissolves,
and re-creates. That informing Power or Spirit is God.

— Mahatma Gandhi[14]

I was listening with rapt attention to global peace activist Ela Gandhi — granddaughter of Mahatma Gandhi, and former member of the South African Parliament — speak about the struggle and the victory of the people of South Africa to overcome the oppression of apartheid and the necessity to continue to work with nonviolent methods to bring positive changes to our world today. She talked about the assassination and loss of her beloved grandfather decades earlier in India; about witnessing the brutality of the apartheid system in South Africa and grieving the death of one of her sons, who was killed during the resistance; and about being subjected to nine years of house arrest, yet, in spite of all that, continuing her work for peace.

She noted that those in power at the time had abundant wealth and resources at their disposal. I could feel my heart ache as I thought about all she had been through. It was unimaginable to me. I asked her, "How did you do it? How did keep your strength and not lose hope?" She replied, "We were not discouraged because we had spiritual resources."[15] I could hear in her voice and sense in her presence the conviction of faith that stands on the power of Truth, the divine power that can be accessed to meet every real need and bring to fruition the highest good. This is the wealth that is enduring and unfailing. Since hearing her profound testimony, that phrase has remained with me — *we were not discouraged because we had spiritual resources.* It has come back to me time and again as witness to the truth that we all are sustained by spiritual resources.

We know how to assess our material resources and to evaluate the worth of our skills and talents. A look at the bottom line on our bank statement, at our annual income tax return, or at our resume all give an indication of what we can bank on. But how do we assess our spiritual resources? What does it mean to rely on them and how do we do it? How can we rely on what we cannot see, cannot measure or contain?

There are no walls or borders in Absolute Reality; nothing separates us from the one life expressing as all that is. To rely on our spiritual resources, we realize this unity. Spirit is our life and nothing can separate us from that. Next, we admit that Spirit is infinitely resourceful — no lack can exist in God. Then it is only an insight away to realize that this infinite, unlimited creative power and unconditional love does not withhold resources. The nature of God as infinite, omnipresent, and unconditional is not consistent with the notion of lack or holding back.

It's a critical leap of faith to know that God has already released our good in harmony with the divine plan. Relying on spiritual resources is recognizing this support as constant, unfailing, and unconditional. Paramahansa Yogananda observed, "Man's forgetfulness of his divine resources (the result of his misuse of free will) is the root cause of all other forms of suffering."[16] We may not see that support outwardly; we may even wonder when we will. Yet our strength is built upon knowing it is present and will become visible when the time is right. Wisdom, guidance, and creativity all pour forth from the spiritual resources within us at the perfect time.

The greatest thing we can remember about wealth is this: *spiritual resources*. We need never be discouraged. We all have spiritual resources.

Moved by Love

The Bhagavad Gita comes to a moving conclusion. Things clear up for Arjuna. Once beset by doubt, confusion, and despair, he awakens. He is transformed through his encounter with Krishna — the seeking soul finds refuge in Supreme Consciousness, the divine Self.

After Krishna has counseled Arjuna — revealing to him the nature of Absolute Reality; the truth of his own nature; how to live skillfully, prosper, and fulfill his destiny — he tells him, "Do as you please." Isn't that how it is with us? Everything is given. The truth about the spiritual life is hidden in plain sight. We hold the radiant jewel of abundance in our own heart. Knowing that, we can do as we please. Will we choose to thrive? To prosper? To be moved by divine love and fulfill our potential?

Arjuna is ready. As he puts it, "Delusion is destroyed....I stand freed from all doubt....And nothing moves me now, except your Word."[17] Nothing will move me now but higher knowledge, nothing but inspired intuitive wisdom. Nothing but the inclination of the heart toward divine love will move me now. Free from self-doubt, from worry or the opinions of others, the shackles of fear no longer bind me. Never again will I be tossed about by restless desire or sink down under the weight of despair. I rise. I awaken. I prosper and thrive.

The Gita concludes with the promise of victory and prosperity for the awakened soul, the voice of the narrator proclaiming that "wherever there is [union of] Krishna, Lord of Yoga, and Arjuna, the archer [the seeking soul], there will surely be splendor, victory, righteousness, and wealth."[18] A magnificent, victorious, abundant life of higher purpose. Guaranteed.

The changes that last, those that truly matter, come forth from within us when the splendor of our divine nature is unleashed. Divine light shines through us and is the hope for our time, our lives, and our world. We have only just begun to imagine what is possible in an awakened world where the jewels of abundance grace every hand.

The Bhagavad Gita's culminating verses repeat a refrain rising to a crescendo:[19]

I rejoice again and again! I rejoice again and again!

Acknowledgments

The jewels of abundant blessings for this book and all it represents overflow. I'm grateful for Marc Allen from New World Library who caught the vision of artha — our prosperity imperative and what it means for our world today. His encouragement and expertise has been an invaluable support. With appreciation for the way Spirit moves through the world and connects us, I offer gratitude to my literary agent, Stephany Evans, who introduced me to Marc, and to my dear friend and colleague Acharya Shunya Mathur, who introduced me to Stephany. There are others, too, who helped shine a light on this book as it began to take form. I'm grateful to Mirabai Starr, who offered her generous blessing and assisted with the initial proposal, and to Kate Sheehan Roach, who enthusiastically helped me compile a course into a book, a task that required her family to give up their kitchen table for a time. And at New World Library, to Kristen Cashman for her inspired editing, Georgia Hughes for setting me off on the right path, and copyeditor Jeff Campbell, I'm so thankful.

A deep bow of gratitude is offered to all the students over the years who enrolled and engaged in Artha 365, my yearlong online abundant living course, and offered their heartfelt testimonies from their practice that inspires this book. That course, this book, and my work at the Center for Spiritual Enlightenment (CSE) has been profoundly supported over the years by Reverend Sundari Jensen, who has my deepest appreciation. As do all the CSE ministers, my assistant Irma Lovic, the amazing CSE staff, and the Yoga Hour team — to each of them, and to all the students of Kriya Yoga at CSE and throughout the world, I am profoundly grateful. Martin Wuttke and Dr. Stella Faerber dove into their research archives to assist with the section on habit and environment, which was a timely and tremendous support.

For inspiration and valuable assistance along the way, I am also deeply thankful to Swami Bodhananda Saraswati, spiritual director of the Sambodh Society. My pranams of gratitude as well to Paramacharya Sadasivanathaswami from Kauai's Hindu Monastery for his interest in the book and his encouragement.

To Phil Goldberg, who so generously took the time and caring to bring his writing talents and knowledge of yoga to the foreword for this book, and whose wisdom and friendship over the years I have come to treasure, I say thank you, again and again.

And the gems keep coming...Patricia McMahon, who spent patient afternoons with me in the garden to capture an author photo; Supriya Groom and Meena Corbin, who literally delivered meals to my door so I could write; Scott Kriens, who made a writer's retreat possible when it was needed most; and many dear friends, authors, and teachers who have inspired me along the way with your love and friendship and your commitment to an awakened, healthy, prosperous world.

To my husband, Michael Amarnath Scott, for all the chapters read, the wonderful late-night and early-morning discussions of yoga philosophy, and for always buying my chairs, I am forever grateful. To the flowering garden and songbirds outside my window who kept me inspired and mindfully aware of love and beauty throughout writing and revising, I bow in remembrance of Devi.

The flowers I leave at the feet of the gurus. I offer them to Roy Eugene Davis, the one who made it all possible for me, and to Paramahansa Yogananda, eternal gratitude.

Glossary

abhinivesha: Confusion about birth and death; instinctual clinging to life in the body-mind; strong desire arising from identification of the Self with the body or mind; fear of death; one of the five *kleshas* or obstacles described by Patanjali in the Yoga Sutras.

Aham Brahmasmi: I Am the Absolute (Brahman). I Am Totality. One of the four great sayings from the Upanishads regarding the essential identity of the individual and the Absolute.

ahimsa: Nonharming, nonviolence, or noninjury; the first *yama* or ethical restraint of the eight limbs of yoga.

ananda: Bliss; the innate joy that arises from Self-knowledge.

anandamaya kosha: The bliss sheath; the innermost of the five *koshas* or coverings surrounding the soul.

annamaya kosha: The physical sheath, the physical body or gross body; the outermost of the five *koshas* or coverings surrounding the soul.

aparigraha: Nonattachment, nonacquiring or nongrasping, freedom from greed; the fifth *yama* or ethical restraint of the eight limbs of yoga.

artha: Prosperity, wealth; one of the *purusharthas* or four universal Vedic goals of life.

asana: Posture, seat, a position conducive to meditation; the third limb of the eight limbs of yoga. In the Hatha Yoga system, there are various asanas for purifying, strengthening, and balancing the body and mind.

asmita: The sense of I-ness, egoism; mistaken identification of the eternal Self with the body and mind; one of the five *kleshas* or obstacles.

asteya: Nonstealing; one of the five *yamas* or ethical restraints of the eight limbs of yoga.

atha: Now, then, therefore; an auspicious moment.

atman: The divine Self, Spirit, soul.

avatar: Literally, "divine descent"; fully illumined consciousness manifest in physical form; an incarnation of God.

avidya: Ignorance, wrong knowledge of the Self; primary of the five *kleshas* or obstacles and the root cause of suffering.

bija mantra: Single-syllable seed sound with vibratory power and an inner mystical meaning.

brahmacharya: Right use of vital force, continence; literally, "walking with God or moving in Brahman." The fourth of the five *yamas* or ethical restraints of the eight limbs of yoga.

Brahman: Ultimate Reality, the Absolute without form; from the root *brh*, meaning "to expand"; the all-pervading supreme existence that is beyond concepts.

chakra: A vortex or center of energy in the subtle body. There are seven major chakras or energy centers.

chit: Pure consciousness.

dharana: Concentration; the sixth limb of the eight limbs of yoga.

dharma: The way of righteousness, purpose, duty, support, or law; the fundamental law of life; the underlying cosmic order. One of the *purusharthas*, the four universal Vedic goals of life.

dhyana: Meditation; uninterrupted flowing of attention toward an object of concentration; the seventh limb of the eight limbs of yoga.

dvesha: Aversion; one of the five *kleshas* or obstacles.

enlightenment: Having true knowledge of higher realities; liberation of consciousness from the errors of perception that cause identification with the false self.

God: Ultimate Reality, which has both a transcendent essence and an immanent expression. This Ultimate Reality is viewed differently according to culture and religious belief.

God-realization: Direct insight, experience, and knowledge of Ultimate Reality and its cosmic processes.

guna: One of the three basic qualities that permeate nature — *sattva*, luminosity; *rajas*, activity; and *tamas*, inertia.

guru: Teacher, spiritual teacher; literally, "light that removes the darkness of ignorance." Guru can refer to God, the supreme teacher of all teachers.

Hatha Yoga: A complete yogic system of various techniques, including *asanas*,
pranayama, and *mudras* designed to purify the body and mind and bring balance to the flow of *prana* supporting health, well-being, and the ability to still
the mind for meditation.

Ishwara (*Ishvara*): The divine intelligence and power that brings forth creation
and that permeates, regulates, and sustains it — the Creator, Lord, or God.

Ishwara pranidhana: Surrender to God, the Lord, or Creator; self-surrender; letting go of the illusional sense of separate existence; one of the five *niyamas* or
observances of the eight limbs of yoga; third of the three disciplines of Kriya
Yoga designated in Patanjali's Yoga Sutras.

japa: Repetition of a mantra or a name of God.

kama: Pleasure, enjoyment, or desire; one of the *purusharthas*, the four universal
Vedic goals of life.

karma: Action (especially actions that have a binding effect); the accumulated effect of actions past and present; the law of cause and effect.

klesha: An affliction, impediment, or obstacle to superconsciousness or Self-
realization; a cause of suffering. The five *kleshas* or afflictions include ignorance (*avidya*), egoism (*asmita*), attachment (*raga*), aversion (*dvesha*), and
clinging to life in the body-mind (*abhinivesha*).

kosha: To enfold, sheathe. The five *koshas* or coverings that enfold the divine Self
include the physical sheath (*annamaya kosha*), the energy sheath (*pranamaya
kosha*), the mental sheath (*manomaya kosha*), the discernment or intuitive
sheath (*vijnanamaya kosha*), and the bliss sheath (*anandamaya kosha*).

Kriya Yoga: Actions that support spiritually conscious living; purification to remove obstacles to *samadhi* or Self-realization. The path of yoga defined in
Patanjali's Yoga Sutras, which includes self-discipline (*tapas*), study of the
nature of Ultimate Reality (*svadhyaya*), and surrender to God (*Ishwara
pranidhana*).

Lakshmi: Goddess of wealth and prosperity; auspiciousness.

liberation of consciousness: Absolute freedom from the influences of nature or
latent patterns in the mind.

mala: String of prayer beads or a rosary used to facilitate concentration for meditation, often with a mantra; most yoga *malas* have either 108 beads or a division of this number, such as 54.

manomaya kosha: Mental sheath; the third of the five *koshas* or coverings surrounding the soul.

mantra: A sacred sound, word, or word formula that is used as a spiritual tool for the mind for reaching higher states of consciousness. This word or sound vibration connects to the primal energy or vibration of creation and is a condensation of spiritual knowledge or insight.

maya: Illusion; the cosmic principle of appearance, which refers to God's creative power; its qualities veil the invisible Absolute.

Meru: A sacred mountain that signifies the mystical inner summit of supreme realization. On a *japa mala*, the central bead is called the meru bead or guru bead.

moksha: Spiritual liberation, absolute freedom; liberation of consciousness from the errors of perception that cause identification with the small self. The fourth of the four *purusharthas*, the universal Vedic goals of life.

mudra: A hand pose or a gesture used to aid concentration and the flow of *prana*.

nirguna: Without form or distinction, without reference to qualities. *Nirguna* mantras are sacred sounds connected to the Source of all creation.

niyama: One of the five spiritually based observances or disciplines that support spiritual awakening in Patanjali's Yoga Sutras. *Niyamas* include purity (*shaucha*); contentment (*santosha*); self-discipline (*tapas*); study of the nature of consciousness (*svadhyaya*); and surrender of the illusional sense of separate existence (*Ishwara pranidhana*). The second limb of the eight limbs of yoga.

panchakosha: A framework delineating five coverings surrounding the soul; these include physical (*annamaya kosha*), energetic (*pranamaya kosha*), mental (*manomaya kosha*), wisdom or discernment (*vijnanamaya kosha*), and bliss (*anandamaya kosha*). The Sanskrit root *kush* is a derivation of the word *kosha*, which means to enfold; the coverings that enfold the Self or soul make physical expression, mental cognition, intellectual reasoning, intuitive ability, and Self-awareness possible.

Patanjali: Sage who compiled Vedic wisdom into the Yoga Sutras. Some historical estimates place him in the second century CE.

prana: Literally, "to breathe forth"; subtle vital energy, life force, breath. *Prana* is the connecting link between the physical, mental, and spiritual dimensions of our being.

pranamaya kosha: Energy or vital force sheath; second of five *koshas* or coverings surrounding the soul.

pranayama: Regulation or control of the breath, expansion of vital energy; the fourth limb of the eight limbs of yoga.

pratyahara: Introversion of attention and awareness by withdrawing senses from their objects of perception; the fifth limb of the eight limbs of yoga.

preyas: What is pleasurable or pleasing; worldly pleasure.

purusha: Soul or Spirit, pure consciousness, the Self.

purushartha: Literally, "for the purpose of the soul." The four universal Vedic goals or aims of human life, which include purpose (*dharma*), prosperity (*artha*), pleasure (*kama*), and liberation (*moksha*).

raga: Attraction, passion, attachment; one of the five *kleshas* or obstacles.

rajas: Activity, restlessness; one of the three *gunas* or qualities of nature.

ratna: Jewels, pearls, gems; occasionally a more general term for wealth.

Rig Veda: Ancient collection of Vedic Sanskrit hymns; oldest of the four canonical sacred texts of Hinduism, known collectively as the Vedas.

rishi/rishika: A seer of spiritual Truth, a Vedic sage; *rishi* is male, *rishika* is female. Those who received direct transmission of the Vedic hymns; a seer or realized sage.

rita (rta): Cosmic law, natural righteousness, natural order, Truth.

sadhana: Spiritual practice or discipline; literally, "to go straight to the goal."

saguna: With attributes or qualities; one of the three types of mantras.

samadhi: Meditative absorption, direct experience of the divine Self, union with the Absolute; literally, "to hold together completely." This is the final limb of the eight limbs of yoga.

Sanatana Dharma: The eternal way or religion; system of eternal values beyond human history; the basis of all order in the universe; traditional name for the Vedic philosophical principles and spiritual practices that became known as Hinduism.

santosha: Contentment; one of the five *niyamas* or observances of the eight limbs of yoga practice.

Sat: Existence, Absolute Reality or Being.

sattva: Luminosity; illuminating, purifying, uplifting influence; one of the three *gunas* or qualities of nature.

satya: Truth or truthfulness; the second of the five *yamas* or ethical restraints of the eight limbs of yoga practice.

Self: When capitalized, refers to our true nature, atman, divine Self, soul. Though we may refer to it as "our" Self, this divine Self is the Self of all.

Self-realization: Insightful, accurate knowledge along with direct experience of our essential nature or Self; spiritual awakening to the truth of our being.

Shakti: Divine life force, the Divine Mother. A latent potential power in human beings known as *kundalini*, which when awakened vitalizes the body and facilitates spiritual awakening.

shaucha: Purity, cleanliness; the first of the five *niyamas* or observances of the eight limbs of yoga practice.

Shiva: Ultimate Reality; Lord of yoga.

shraddha: faith, trust, reverence, belief in divine revelation, or "what is placed in the heart."

shreyas: What is good and truly beneficial, better, or superior; in harmony with spiritual virtues.

sthira: Steady, firm, still.

sukham: Easy, pleasing, comfortable, agreeable.

superconscious meditation: *samadhi*; when, during meditation, attention and awareness flows unimpeded to the unbounded, unchanging field of pure existence or being.

superconsciousness: Heightened level of awareness, above or beyond ordinary waking, subconscious, or unconscious states; the unchanging ground of being that supports the arising of various states of consciousness.

Supreme Consciousness: The divine Self; pure essence of Absolute Reality.

sutra: A terse aphorism; literally, "thread." A concise, condensed statement that carries the depth of the philosophy being taught; a basic text for a philosophical system, such as the Yoga Sutras.

svadharma: One's own natural duty or divine destiny; subset of *dharma*.

svadhyaya: Study of the nature of consciousness, Self-inquiry or Self-study, study of scripture. One of the five *niyamas* or observances of the eight limbs of yoga; the second of the three practices of Kriya Yoga designated in Patanjali's Yoga Sutras.

tamas: Inertia, darkness, resistance, stability; one of the three *gunas* or qualities of nature.

tapas: Austerity, self-discipline; literally, "to burn or to give off heat." One of the five *niyamas* or observances of the eight limbs of yoga; the first of the three disciplines of Kriya Yoga designated in Patanjali's Yoga Sutras.

Ultimate Reality: Supreme Consciousness, Spirit, God, Brahman.

Upanishads: The last portion of the Vedas; source teachings for the philosophy of Vedanta; dialogues between guru and disciple regarding the nature of Ultimate Reality and how to realize it.

Vedas: Knowledge, wisdom, revealed truth or scripture; the most ancient sacred scriptures of the Hindu tradition or Sanatana Dharma (the eternal way or religion); the source of yoga philosophy.

vijnanamaya kosha: Wisdom or intelligence sheath; the fourth of five *koshas* or coverings surrounding the soul.

Vishnu: God as the nurturer and preserver of all life; the protector of *dharma*, universal order.

yama: The first limb of the eight limbs of yoga found in Patanjali's Yoga Sutras, which includes the five spiritually based ethical guidelines for fulfilled living: nonharming (*ahimsa*), truthfulness (*satya*), nonstealing (*asteya*), right use of vital force (*brahmacharya*), and nonattachment (*aparigraha*).

yoga: Literally, to "yoke" or "bind back." A method of physical, mental, and spiritual discipline leading to harmonious integration of body, mind, and spirit, or conscious union with Ultimate Reality. The science of Self-realization; one of the six orthodox systems of Indian philosophy.

yogacharya: A title of respect given to a teacher of yoga.

Yoga Sutras: The primary text for yoga philosophy and practice; compiled from Vedic teachings by the sage Patanjali around the first to second centuries CE.

Endnotes

Introduction: Thrive for the Sake of Your Soul

1. The comprehensive approach to the four universal goals in life called *purushartha* are found in the Hindu Dharma Shastras and the epics Ramayana and Mahabharata. See Alf Hiltebeitel, "Hinduism," in *The Religious Traditions of Asia: Religion, History and Culture*, ed. J. M. Kitagawa (1987; repr., Abingdon, UK: Routledge, 2002). *Purushartha* is generally translated as "the four goals or aims of human life." The word itself — combining *purusha*, which means soul or spirit, and *artha*, which means aim, purpose, or wealth — gives us the insight that these universal goals are "for the purpose of the soul." See also Rod Stryker, *The Four Desires: Creating a Life of Purpose, Happiness, Prosperity, and Freedom* (New York: Delacorte Press, 2011).

2. This is a familiar saying by Roy Eugene Davis, which changed over the years; see *Truth Journal*, August-September 2017, 17.

3. Paramahansa Yogananda, in Roy Eugene Davis, *Living in God: 366 Themes for Daily Meditative Contemplation and Spiritual Enlightenment Through the Year* (Delhi: Motilal Banarsidass, 1988), 11.

Chapter 1: *Artha*: The Prosperity Imperative

Epigraph: Rumi, "Knowledge Is Life-Giving," in *The Rumi Daybook: 365 Poems and Teachings from the Beloved Sufi Master*, trans. Kabir Helminski and Camille Helminski (Boulder, CO: Shambhala, 2012), 31.

1. Mahabharata, "Varna-parva," 33:48, 49, in *The Mahabharata: An Inquiry in*

the Human Condition, trans. Chaturvedi Badrinath (2006; repr., Hyderabad, India: Orient Black Swan, 2013), 275.

2.   Paramahamsa Prajnanananda, *Lahiri Mahasaya: Fountainhead of Kriya Yoga* (1999; repr., Vienna: Prajna Publication, 2009), 110.

3.   Badrinath, *Mahabharata*, 275.

4.   Ibid., 285.

Chapter 2: True Wealth

Epigraph: Yoga Sutra 2:37, author's translation.

1.   Roy Eugene Davis, conversation with author, October 10, 2017.

2.   Swami Prabhavananda and Christopher Isherwood, *How to Know God: The Yoga Aphorisms of Patanjali* (1953; repr., Hollywood, CA: Vedanta Press, 1981), 149.

3.   Retelling of a traditional tale, in Noor Inayat Khan, *Twenty Jataka Tales* (Philadelphia: David McCoy, 1939), 79–80.

4.   Baba Hari Dass, trans., *The Yoga Sutras of Patanjali: A Study Guide for Book II: Sadhana Pada* (Santa Cruz: Sri Rama Publishing, 2008), 143.

5.   Roy Eugene Davis, *The Spiritual Basis of Real Prosperity: How to Have a Constant Flow of Material Resources, Timely Events, and Ideal Relationships for Your Highest Good* (Lakemont, GA: CSA Press, 2012), loc. 225 of 1450, Kindle.

6.   John Grimes, *A Concise Dictionary of Indian Philosophy: Sanskrit Terms Defined in English* (Albany: State University of New York Press, 1996), 96.

Chapter 3: Imagine Enlightenment

Epigraph: Rumi, in Helminski and Helminski, *Rumi Daybook*, 31.

1.   The story is from chapter 11 in the Brihadaranyaka Upanishad. See Eknath Easwaran, trans., *The Upanishads* (1987; repr., Tomales, CA: Nilgiri, 2007), 99, and S. Radhakrishnan, *The Principal Upanishads* (New Delhi: Indus, 1994), 281.

2.   Easwaran, *Upanishads*, 100.

3.   Roy Eugene Davis, *Truth Journal*, August/September 2014, 21.

4.   Sally Kempton, "Seeing Is Believing," *Yoga Journal*, July/August 2005, 46.

5.   Bhagavad Gita 2:55, in Winthrop Sargeant, trans., *The Bhagavad Gita* (1984; repr., Albany: State University of New York Press, 2009), 140. Here is the passage: "The Blessed Lord spoke: / When he leaves behind all

desires / Emerging from the mind, Arjuna, / And is contented in the Self by the Self, / Then he is said to be one whose wisdom is steady."

6. Mahabharata, "Shanti-parva," 241:14, in Chaturvedi Badrinath, trans., *The Mahabharata: An Inquiry in the Human Condition* (2006; repr., Hyderabad, India: Orient Black Swan, 2013), 573.

7. Lynne Twist, "The Currency of the Future: Each Other," Alexsa Consulting (blog), June 13, 2014, http://alexsaconsulting.com/blog/the-currency -of-the-future-each-other-2.

8. Bhagavad Gita 4:7–8, in Eknath Easwaran, trans., *The Bhagavad Gita* (1985; repr., Tomales, CA: Nilgiri Press, 2007), 117.

9. "Thich Nhat Hanh's Statement on Climate Change for the United Nations," July 2, 2015, http://plumvillage.org/letters-from-thay/thich-nhat -hanhs-statement-on-climate-change-for-unfccc.

Chapter 4: Be Willing to Thrive

Epigraph: Howard Thurman, from a conversation with Gil Bailie, in *A Sourcebook About Sunday*, ed. Paul Ford (Chicago: Liturgy Training Publications, 2005), 24.

1. Taittiriya Upanishad 2:6.1.

2. Grimes, *Concise Dictionary of Indian Philosophy*, 269, 270.

3. Swami Bodhananda Saraswati, *Self-Unfoldment: In an Interactive World* (Kalamazoo, MI: Sambodh Society, 2001), 27–28.

4. Meister Eckhart, in *The Enlightened Mind: An Anthology of Sacred Prose*, ed. and trans. Stephen Mitchell (New York: HarperCollins, 1991), 114.

5. Anne Lamott, *Bird by Bird: Some Instructions on Writing and Life* (New York: Random House, 1995), 121.

6. Easwaran, *Bhagavad Gita*, 93.

Chapter 5: Bring Forth Your Divine Potential

Epigraph: Yoga Sutra 1.1, author's translation.

1. Mahabharata, "Anushsana-parva," in Badrinath, *Mahabharata*, 489.

2. Swami Vivekananda, in *Wisdom for the Soul: Five Millennia of Prescriptions for Spiritual Healing*, ed. Larry Chang (Washington, DC: Gnosophia Publishers, 2006), 5309.

3. Roy Eugene Davis, *How You Can Use the Technique of Creative Imagination* (Lakemont, GA: CSA Press, 1988), 104.

Chapter 6: Realize Your Essentially Abundant Nature

Epigraph: Swami Sri Yukteswar, *The Holy Science* (1990; repr., Los Angeles: Self-Realization Fellowship, 2013), 51.

1. Paramahansa Yogananda, "Social Arts: Righteousness in the Character, Harmony in the Home, Order in the Nation, Peace in the World, How-to-Live Skills, Part III," *Self-Realization* (Fall 2017), 12.

2. Rumi, in *The Pocket Rumi*, ed. Kabir Helminski (2001; repr., Boston: Shambhala Publications, 2008), 234.

3. Joseph Campbell, *A Joseph Campbell Companion*, ed. Diane K. Osbon (New York: HarperCollins: 1991), 25.

4. Eckhart Tolle, *The Power of Now: A Guide to Spiritual Enlightenment* (Novato, CA: New World Library, 1999), 82.

5. Mahatma Gandhi, in *Mohan-Mala: A Gandhian Rosary: Being a Thought for Each Day of the Year Gleaned from the Writings and Speeches of Mahatma Gandhi*, comp. R. K. Prabhu (Ahmedabad, India: Navajivan Publishing House, 1949, 1977), 34.

6. Mark Nepo, "How to Return to Your Center," Oprah.com, February 12, 2013, www.oprah.com/spirit/how-to-return-to-your-center/all#ixzz4x-QAozwOl.

7. Grimes, *Concise Dictionary of Indian Philosophy*, 306.

8. Ellen Grace O'Brian, *Living the Eternal Way: Spiritual Meaning and Practice for Daily Life* (1998; repr., San Jose, CA: CSE Press, 2009), 13.

Chapter 7: The Streams of Happiness and the Ocean of Bliss

Epigraph: Paramahansa Yogananda, "Secrets of Lasting Happiness: The Inner Conditions of Happiness," Self-Realization Fellowship, accessed January 8, 2018, www.yogananda-srf.org/HowtoLive/Secrets_of_Lasting _Happiness.aspx#.WlZ-d6inHD4.

1. Paramahansa Yogananda, *The Science of Religion*, 3rd ed. (Los Angeles: Self-Realization Fellowship, 1994)

2. Rig Veda, Samhita 1:164.46.

3. Thomas Byrom, trans., *Dhammapada: The Sayings of the Buddha* (New York: Vintage, 1976), 66.

4. Ibid., 111.

5. Yogananda, "Secrets of Lasting Happiness."

Chapter 8: Embrace Your Divine Destiny

Epigraph: Campbell, *Joseph Campbell Companion*, 290.

1. Sri Aurobindo, *Essays on the Gita* (Twin Lakes, WI: Lotus Press, 2005), chap. 24, ebook.
2. Ralph Waldo Emerson, *Selected Writings of Ralph Waldo Emerson*, ed. Brooks Atkinson (1940; repr., New York: Random House, 1968), 146.
3. Swami Muktananda, trans., *Lalleshwari* (South Fallsberg, NY: SYDA Foundation, 1981), 70.
4. Bhagavad Gita 2:48.
5. For more information on the "Season for Nonviolence" program and the Association for Global New Thought, visit www.agnt.org.
6. Dolores Huerta, in Glenn Swain, "La Adelita: The Life of Dolores Huerta," *Science of Mind*, September 2007, 18.
7. President Barack Obama, "Remarks by the President at Presidential Medal of Freedom Ceremony," Office of the Press Secretary, the White House, press release, May 29, 2012, http://obamawhitehouse.archives.gov/the -press-office/2012/05/29/remarks-president-presidential-medal-freedom -ceremony.

Chapter 9: What We Really Want

Epigraph: Neil Douglas-Klotz, *The Sufi Book of Life: 99 Pathways of the Heart for the Modern Dervish* (New York: Penguin Compass, 2005), 267. This quote is from the first verse of the Quran.

1. Radhakrishnan, *Upanishads*, 308.

Chapter 10: Meditate and Experience Wholeness

Epigraph: Swami Adiswarananda, *Meditation & Its Practices: A Definitive Guide to Techniques and Traditions of Meditation in Yoga and Vedanta* (Woodstock, VT: Skylight Paths Publishing, 2003), 5.

1. Brihadaranyaka Upanishad 1:4.10, in *All Love Flows to the Self: Eternal Stories from the Upanishads*, trans. Kumuda Reddy, Thomas Egenes, and Linda Egenes (Schenectady, NY: Samhita Productions, 1999), 113.
2. Swami Vivekananda, *The Complete Works of Swami Vivekananda* (Kolkata, India: Advaita Ashrama, 1989), loc. 32958, Kindle.

3.   Baba Hari Dass, trans., *The Yoga Sutras of Patanjali: A Study Guide for Book I: Samadhi Pada* (Santa Cruz: Sri Rama Publishing, 1999), 57.

4.   Mirabai Starr, *The Showings of Julian Norwich: A New Translation* (Charlottesville, VA: Hampton Roads, 2013), xiv.

5.   Roy Eugene Davis, "Become More Creatively Functional," Center for Spiritual Awareness (blog), July 7, 2013, http://csa-davis.org/sites/?q=node/180.

6.   Shunryu Suzuki, *Zen Mind, Beginner's Mind: Informal Talks on Zen Meditation and Practice* (1970; repr., New York: Weatherhill, 1979), 47.

7.   Shunryu Suzuki, "Just Sitting: Sesshin Lecture No. 1," San Francisco Zen Center (blog), June 5, 1971, http://suzukiroshi.sfzc.org/dharma-talks/tag/just-sitting.

Chapter 11: How to Meditate

Epigraph: Yoga-Vasishtha 3:22.33, in *The Teachings of Yoga*, trans. and ed. Georg Feuerstein (Boston: Shambhala, 1997), 68.

1.   Yoga Sutra 2:46, author's translation.

2.   Gayatri Mantra, Rig Veda 3:62.10, author's translation.

3.   Swami Vishnudevananda, *Meditation and Mantras* (1978; repr., Delhi: Motilal Banarsidass, 1999), 32.

4.   Paramahansa Yogananda, in Roy Eugene Davis, *Seven Lessons in Conscious Living: A Progressive Program of Higher Learning and Spiritual Practice in the Kriya Yoga Tradition* (Lakemont, GA: CSA Press, 2000), 99.

Chapter 12: Discipline: Do What Pleases Your Soul

Epigraph: Taittiriya Upanishad 2:7.1.

1.   Bhagavad Gita 5:5.

2.   Yoga Sutra 2:2, author's translation.

3.   Chandogya Upanishad 7:23, in Reddy, Egenes, and Egenes, *All Love Flows to the Self*, 47.

4.   Rumi, "Moving Water," in *The Soul of Rumi: A New Collection of Ecstatic Poems*, trans. Coleman Barks (New York: HarperCollins, 2001), 79.

5.   Rick Hanson, "Seven Facts about the Brain That Incline the Mind to Joy," *Positive Neuroplasticity*, accessed January 8, 2018, www.wisebrain.org/articles/neurodharma/7FactsforJoy.pdf.

6.   John 5:35, King James Version.

7. Quote from chapter 2 of Svetashvatara Upanishad, in Andrew Wilson, ed., *World Scripture: A Comparative Anthology of Sacred Texts* (1991; repr., New York: Paragon House, 1995), 603.
8. Sutra of Forty-two Sections 15, in Wilson, *World Scripture*, 153.

Chapter 13: Ten Prospering Promises

Epigraph: Deuteronomy 30:11–12, 14. This translation is from Stephen Mitchell, ed. and trans., *The Enlightened Mind: An Anthology of Sacred Prose* (New York: HarperCollins, 1991), 6.

1. Juan Mascaró, trans., *The Upanishads* (London: Penguin Books, 1965), 49.
2. Ellen Grace O'Brian, "The Key," *The Moon Reminded Me* (Pawcatuck, CT: Homebound Publications, 2017), 71.
3. Paramahansa Yogananda, in Davis, *Seven Lessons in Conscious Living*, 33.
4. Through the centuries, many commentaries on Patanjali's Yoga Sutras have been written that address and suggest practices. The primary classical commentary was written by sage Vyasa in the fifth century. References to Vyasa's commentary are included in many excellent modern commentaries, such as Baba Hari Dass, *The Yoga Sutras of Patanjali*, and Edwin F. Bryant, *The Yoga Sutras of Patanjali*.

Chapter 14: Overcome Obstacles

Epigraph: Easwaran, *Bhagavad Gita*, 93.

1. Byrom, *Dhammapada*, 97.
2. O'Brian, "The Moon Reminded Me," *Moon Reminded Me*, 9.
3. Yoga Sutra 2:3, author's translation.
4. Swami Chinmayananda, "Sri Ganapati-Vinayaka," *Chinmaya-Tej* 23, no. 5 (September/October 2012), 8, http://www.cmsj.org/wp-content/uploads/tej/Tej_2012_Vol23_5.pdf.
5. Bhagavad Gita 18:47, author's translation.
6. Paramahansa Yogananda, "Make New Determinations: Be What You Want to Be!" Self-Realization Fellowship (blog), accessed January 8, 2018, www.yogananda-srf.org/HowtoLive/Seasonal_Inspiration/Make_New_Determinations__Be_What_You_Want_to_Be!.aspx#.WjbDpN-nHD4.
7. Antonio Machado, in *Time Alone: Selected Poems of Antonio Machado*, trans. Robert Bly (Middletown, CT: Wesleyan University Press, 1983), 43.

8.   The phrase "perfectly imperfect" was coined by Pia Mellody in her model of addiction therapy; for more on her work, visit www.piamellody.com.

Chapter 15: Optimize Success

Epigraph: Samantha Page, "10 Maya Angelou Quotes That Will Inspire You to Do Better," *O* (magazine), May 2014, accessed January 8, 2018, www.oprahmag.co.za/oprah's-world/news/10-maya-angelou-quotes-that-will-inspire-you-to-do-better.

1.   Yoga Sutra 1:22, in Roy Eugene Davis, *The Science of Self-Realization: A Guide to Spiritual Practice in the Kriya Yoga Tradition* (Lakemont, GA: CSA Press, 2004), loc. 247, Kindle.

2.   Ibid.

3.   Paramahansa Yogananda, *Journey to Self-Realization: Discovering the Gifts of the Soul, Collected Talks and Essays, Volume III* (Los Angeles: Self-Realization Fellowship, 1997), 231.

4.   Yoga Sutra 2:33, in Dass, *Yoga Sutras of Patnajali: Book II*, 135.

5.   Byrom, *Dhammapada*, 13.

Chapter 16: Mine Your Inner Resources

Epigraph: G. N. Das, trans., *Couplets from Kabir (Kabir Dohe)* (1991; repr., Delhi: Motilal Banarsidass, 1997), 42.

1.   Ibid., 48.

2.   Bhagavad Gita 14:11–13, in *The Bhagavad Gita*, trans. Juan Mascaró (London: Penguin Classics, 1962), 67.

3.   Roy Eugene Davis, "Practical Guidelines for Inspired Living," Inspired Living (blog), August 12, 2012, www.csa-davis.org/inspired/Inspired _Living/Blog/Entries/2012/8/12_Use_Affirmations_Effectively.html.

5.   Paramahansa Yogananda, *Scientific Healing Affirmations* (Los Angeles: Self-Realization Fellowship, 1958/1990), 4.

6.   Campbell, *Joseph Campbell Companion*, 21.

Chapter 17: Intend, Declare, Vow

Epigraph: Sy Safransky, "I Don't Have All Night," *The Sun*, January 1999, www.thesunmagazine.org/issues/277/i-dont-have-all-night.

1.   Suzanne DeChillo, "Relaxing, Touching the Memory: Music Helps

with the Final Transition," *New York Times*, July 3, 2011, www.nytimes.
com/2011/07/04/nyregion/music-therapy-helps-the-dying.html, and
Pam Belluck, "Live Music's Charms, Soothing Premature Hearts," *New
York Times*, April 15, 2013, www.nytimes.com/2013/04/15/health
/live-music-soothes-premature-babies-a-new-study-finds.html.

2. Dr. David Frawley (Pandit Vamadeva Shastri), *Mantra Yoga and Primal
Sound: Secret of Seed (Bija) Mantras* (Twin Lakes, WI: Lotus Press, 2010), 15.

3. Thomas Ashley-Farrand, *Healing Mantras: Using Sound Affirmations for
Personal Power, Creativity, and Healing* (New York: Ballantine, 1999), 219.

4. Rainer Maria Rilke, *Selected Poems of Rainer Maria Rilke*, trans. Robert Bly
(New York: Harper & Row, 1981), 101.

Chapter 18: Radical Prosperity

Epigraph: Thomas Kelly, *A Testament of Devotion* (1941; repr., New York:
HarperCollins, 1992), 3.

1. Rumi, *The Illuminated Rumi*, trans. Coleman Barks (New York: Broadway
Books, 1997), 81.

2. Seyyed Hossein Nasr, "The Long Journey," *Leaning on the Moment: Inter-
views from Parabola* (New York: Parabola Books, 1986), 228.

3. Bhagavad Gita 18:47 and 3:35.

4. Gospel of Thomas, verse 70.

5. R. Buckminster Fuller, *Grunch of Giants* (Santa Barbara, CA: Design Science Press, 1983), xi.

6. R. Buckminster Fuller, in L. Steven Sieden, "Buckminster Fuller Bodhisat-
tva—Trimtab Using Skillful Means on Behalf of All Humanity," *Huffington
Post*, July 16, 2012, accessed on January 8, 2018, www.huffingtonpost
.com/l-steven-sieden/buckminster-fuller-bodhis_b_1666193.html.

7. Abu Yazid Al-Bistami, in *The Enlightened Mind: An Anthology of Sacred
Prose*, ed. Stephen Mitchell, trans. Reynold A. Nicholson (New York:
HarperCollins, 1991), 77.

8. Das, *Couplets from Kabir*, 44.

Chapter 19: Keep Your Soul

Epigraph: Isa Upanishad 1:1.

1. Yoga Sutras 2:16, author's translation.

2.   Ramana Maharshi, in Mitchell, *Enlightened Mind*, 194.

3.   Svetashvatara Upanishad 4.16–17, 4.3–4, author's translation.

4.   The five factors of action are addressed in the Bhagavad Gita 18:13–16.

5.   Bhagavad Gita 2:64, 2:66, in *The Eternal Way: The Inner Meaning of the Bhagavad Gita*, trans. Roy Eugene Davis (Lakemont, GA: CSA Press, 1996), 65.

6.   Katha Upanishad 2:2, in Easwaran, *Upanishads*, 75.

7.   Kabir Helminski, ed., *The Rumi Collection* (Boston: Shambhala, 1998), 20.

8.   Bhagavad Gita 18:36–39, in Easwaran, *Bhagavad Gita*, 260.

Chapter 20: A Grateful Generous Heart

Epigraph: O'Brian, "Lark Singing through the Night," *Moon Reminded Me*, 62.

1.   Kabir Helminski, *The Knowing Heart: A Sufi Path of Transformation* (Boston: Shambhala, 2000), 263.

2.   Stephen Mitchell, trans., *Tao te Ching* (New York: Harper & Row, 1988), verse 77.

3.   H. Emilie Cady, *Complete Works of H. Emilie Cady*, (Unity Village, MO: Unity House, 1995) 22.

4.   Helminski, *Knowing Heart*, 263.

5.   Author's retelling of Fyodor Dostoyevsky's fable "The Onion," which appears in *The Brothers Karamazov* (New York: Farrar, Straus & Giroux, 1990) ebook edition: April 2011, loc. 352 of 777, Kindle.

6.   Paramahansa Yogananda, *Where There Is Light: Insight and Inspiration for Meeting Life's Challenges* (Los Angeles: Self Realization Fellowship, 1988), 70.

7.   Bhagavad Gita 17:20–22, in Davis, *Eternal Way*, 253–54.

Chapter 21: Becoming Wealth

Epigraph: Rabindranath Tagore, *Show Yourself to My Soul*, trans. James Talarovic (Dhaka, Bangladesh: University Press Limited, 1983; Notre Dame, IN: Sorin Books, 2002), 35.

1.   Ramana Maharshi, *The Spiritual Teaching of Ramana Maharshi* (1972; repr., Boston: Shambhala, 1988), 61.

2.   Mundaka Upanishad 3:10, in *Upanisads*, trans. Patrick Olivelle (1996; repr., Oxford, UK: Oxford University Press, 2008), 275.

3. Abu Sa'id ibn Abi'l-Khayr, in Mitchell, *Enlightened Mind*, trans. Margaret Smith, 85.

4. Pandit Rajmani Tigunait, *The Practice of the Yoga Sutra: Sadhana Pada* (Honesdale, PA: Himalayan Institute, 2017), loc. 3025 and 3033 of 7518, Kindle.

5. Joel Goldsmith, *Living the Infinite Way* (New York: Harper & Row, 1961), 14.

6. Mundaka Upanishad 3:2.2, in *The Early Upanishads: Annotated Text and Translation*, trans. Patrick Olivelle (1996; repr., Oxford, UK: Oxford University Press, 1998), 451.

7. Jacob Needleman, *Money and the Meaning of Life* (New York: Doubleday, 1991), 154.

8. Paramahansa Yogananda, *Autobiography of a Yogi*, rev. ed. (1946; repr., Los Angeles: Self-Realization Fellowship, 1997), 548–50, 561.

9. Tigunait, *Practice of the Yoga Sutra*, loc. 3025 of 7518, Kindle.

10. Elizabeth D. Hutchison, *Dimensions of Human Behavior: The Changing Life Course*, 4th ed. (Thousand Oaks, CA: SAGE Publications, 2011). See Wikipedia, "Generativity," accessed January 9, 2018, http://en.wikipedia.org/wiki/Generativity.

11. Dan P. McAdams and Ed de St. Aubin, "A Theory of Generativity and Its Assessment through Self-Report, Behavioral Acts, and Narrative Themes in Autobiography," *Journal of Personality and Social Psychology* 62, no. 6 (June 1992), 1003–15. See Wikipedia, "Generativity."

12. Dan P. McAdams, "The Generative Adult," the Virtue Blog, accessed January 9, 2018, thevirtueblog.com/2015/10/29/the-generative-adult/#more-110.

13. Paramahansa Yogananda, in Roy Eugene Davis, *Paramahansa Yogananda as I Knew Him: Experiences, Observations, and Reflections of a Disciple* (Lakemont, GA: CSA Press, 2005), loc. 1480, Kindle.

14. Mahatma Gandhi, in Prabhu, *Mohan-Mala*, 3.

15. Ela Gandhi, conversation with author, Durban, South Africa, October 21, 2015.

16. Yogananda, *Autobiography of a Yogi*, 550–51.

17. Bhagavad Gita 18:73, in *The Bhagavad Gita*, trans. Brian Hodgkinson (Dublin: John Scottus School, 2000), 85.

18. Bhagavad Gita 18:78, adapted from Sargeant, *Bhagavad Gita*, 739.

19. Bhagavad Gita 18:76, 77, ibid.

Index

abhinivesha (clinging to life of body-mind), 169, 268

Abi'l-Khayr, Abu Sa'id ibn, 254

Absolute Reality. *See* God; Ultimate Reality

abundance, 19; as essential nature, 66–68; jewel of, 27–28, 115, 251–52, 254–56, 263–64; law of, 27–28, 156. *See also* prosperity

action: alignment with thoughts/speech, 105–6, 146, 156; as "drawing the circle" effect, 141; five factors of, 230–33; meditation vs., 151–54; skill in, 99

activity, 193, 194–95, 237, 238–39

Adiswarananda, Swami, 113

affirmations: changes as result of, 199–201; discernment and, 202; mind changed through, 195–97; obstacles and, 176; of prosperity, 213; regular use of, 201; as spiritual tool, 195–97, 198–99; staying the course with, 197–98

Aham Brahmasmi ("I am totality"), 115, 268

ahimsa (nonharming), 25, 268. *See also* nonharming

ananda (soul's bliss), 4, 67, 268. *See also* joy

anandamaya kosha (bliss sheath), 107, 111, 268

Angelou, Maya, 179

anger, 87

annamaya kosha (physical sheath), 106, 107, 268

anti-apartheid movement, 261–62

aparigraha (nonattachment), 25, 268. *See also* nonattachment

Arabic language, 207, 208

artha (prosperity): as aim of life, 3, 10; author's interpretation of, xiv–xv; defined, xiv, 3, 268; interconnection of, xv, 4, 10, 11, 95–96; Western knowledge of, xiv. *See also* prosperity

asana (posture), 118, 119, 268

asceticism, 82, 135, 227–28

Ashley-Farrand, Thomas, 209

asmita (I-am-ness), 169, 268

287

thoughts/speech/action alignment,
    105–6, 146, 156
thriving. *See* prosperity
throat *chakra*, 36, 37
Thurman, Howard, 42
Tigunait, Pandit Rajmani, 255
Tolle, Eckhart, 70
toxic environments, 108
transcendence vs. immanence, 151–54
truth, insight into, 22
truthfulness, 25–27, 154, 155, 156, 159,
    160
Twist, Lynne, 37

Ultimate Reality: author's confidence
    in, 196–97; conditions and, 166;
    connection to, during medi-
    tation, 128; defined, 269, 273;
    dharma and, 155; discovery of, as
    prosperity, 28; enlightenment as
    knowledge of, 29, 32; existence
    of, 76; generous nature of, 47;
    grace and, 61; gratitude and,
    240–41; humans as expressions
    of, 49, 76, 200; Kriya Yoga and,
    28; obstacles and, 177; Self-re-
    alization and, 3, 80–81; soul as
    expression of, 67. *See also* God;
    Supreme Consciousness
unhappiness, 85–87
UNICEF, 63
United Nations, 41, 63
United States, 15
Upanishads: defined, 273; on enlight-
    enment, 30–31; on happiness
    quest, 152–53; "I am That" state-
    ment in, 114–15; on joy, 135, 138,
    234; on prosperity, 253, 256–57;
    on renunciation and enjoyment,
    227, 234; on spiritual discipline,

147; on Supreme Consciousness,
    43; on thoughts/speech/action
    alignment, 105–6; on true Self,
    229–30; on wholeness, 59

Vedanta, 45, 114–15
Vedas, 273–74
Vedic knowledge/wisdom, xiii–xiv, 2,
    43, 60, 272
Vedic texts, 14, 40, 80, 152, 230–31. *See
    also* Bhagavad Gita; Rig Veda;
    Upanishads; Yoga Sutras (Pa-
    tanjali)
vijnanamaya kosha (wisdom/intelli-
    gence sheath), 107, 111, 274
Vishnu (Hindu deity), 11, 274
Vishnudevananda, Swami, 130
vital force (*prana*): defined, 128, 271;
    "destinations" for, 109–10; heal-
    ing with, 110–11; mantras and,
    205–6; most important, 105–6;
    nourishing, 108–9; *panchakosha*
    model, 106–8; prosperity and,
    111–12; right use of, 25, 26, 154,
    156, 159, 269
vitality, 145
Vivekananda, Swami, 62, 116
vows, 203–4, 205, 213

war, 10, 39
wealth: befriending, 11–14; as cor-
    rupting, 15; defined, 17; material,
    14–15, 151; measure of, 17–18;
    nonstealing as basic law of,
    18–19, 25–27; prosperity vs., 3;
    spirituality and, 14–15
wholeness, 30, 31–32, 68–70; affirma-
    tion and, 198; experiencing of,
    114, 115, 120; as innate, 182–83,
    198; life purpose and, 96; in now

About the Author

Yogacharya Ellen Grace O'Brian, MA, is a meditation teacher, a writer, and the spiritual director of the Center for Spiritual Enlightenment (CSE, www.CSEcenter.org) with headquarters in San Jose, California. CSE is a Kriya Yoga meditation center serving people from all backgrounds who are seeking Self-realization. Yogacharya O'Brian was ordained to teach in 1982 by Roy Eugene Davis, a direct disciple of Paramahansa Yogananda, who brought Kriya Yoga from India to the West. She has taught yoga philosophy and meditation practices for spiritually conscious living at retreats, spiritual centers, and conferences throughout the United States and internationally for over three decades.

Yogacharya O'Brian is the author of several books on spiritual practice, including *Living the Eternal Way: Spiritual Meaning and Practice in Daily Life* and *A Single Blade of Grass: Finding the Sacred in Everyday Life*, as well as three volumes of poetry, including the award-winning Homebound Publications book *The Moon Reminded Me*. She writes regularly for *Truth Journal* magazine and is the founding editor of *Enlightenment Journal*, a quarterly yoga magazine, and host of *The Yoga Hour*, a weekly radio podcast with Unity Online Radio.

Yogacharya O'Brian is the founder and president of Meru Institute, offering certification programs, leadership training, and education in yoga, Ayurveda, and community ministry since 1996; and of Carry the Vision, a community-education nonprofit organization teaching principles and practices of nonviolence to all sectors of society. She served as the vice chair of the board of trustees of the Parliament of the World's Religions and is a recipient of several community service awards, including the prestigious 2015 Mahatma Gandhi Award for the Advancement of Religious Pluralism from the Hindu American Foundation.

Yogacharya O'Brian lives near the beach in Santa Cruz, California, with her husband, Michael Amarnath Scott. They count among their blessings three fabulous grown children and their amazing spouses, and two precocious grandchildren.

www.ellengraceobrian.com